ABANDONED PERTH

Memories and Photos of the Lost and Found

DELPHINE JAMET

AUSTRALIA THROUGH TIME

Australia Through Time
is an imprint jointly owned by

Woodslane Press Pty Ltd, 10 Apollo Street, Warriewood, NSW 2102, Australia
Email: info@woodslane.com.au
Tel: 02 8445 2300 Website: www.woodslane.com.au

and

Fonthill Media, Millview, Toadsmoor Road, Stroud, GL5 2TB, United Kingdom
Tel: 01453 886959 Website: www.fonthill.media

First published in Australia in 2021 by Fonthill Media and Woodslane Press

ISBN 978-1-925868-73-9

NATIONAL LIBRARY OF AUSTRALIA

A catalogue record for this book is available from the National Library of Australia

Printed in England

WOODSLANE PRESS

FONTHILL

CONTENTS

INTRODUCTION

The mysteriousness of life intensifies with atmospheric dark scenes. Echoes of footsteps, punctured with walking on broken glass. Creaks from ageing timber, worn out like an old man in his numbered days and almost always, clichéd sound effects from a drip nearby.

Yet overall, there is an undisturbed silence and fascinating loneliness that can be found in abandoned places, which does wonders for the mental health. Equivalent to calming waves of lavender, rolling to the tunes of Enya.

Life, contaminated with oppressive toxic negatives, debilitating personal dramas, and emotional burdens, which relentlessly attracts to us like a magnet. With little time to recover in a fast-paced world full of endless international crises, we become worn down to the ground like scattered ashes. Prematurely for some, as a result of no lifesaving self-care or outlet of distraction.

It never ceases to amaze me, how many depressed and suicidal people come to places like this to find some peace. Although I am yet to hear of anyone self-harming or attempting suicide there.

Mirroring that of a chemical addiction controlling one's life, exploring an 'abando' can be considered similar in many aspects. Abandos as buildings, homes, schools, warehouses, hospitals, and farms, to name just a few. Seismic disruptions to the brain, endlessly interrupting thoughts. The attractions and cravings for a desire to explore feels so difficult to explain and understand. It is easier to lump it with the psychology of the subconscious and unconscious minds, hidden below the surface like an iceberg.

Urban exploration shares traits of danger and unpredictability. Not knowing what is around the next corner can provoke sensations of adrenaline, making you feel so alive, although for others, it is a paralysing anxiety making them feel so munted.

The alluring fascination increases with observing the way in which people lived. What were their stories, their struggles, and their triumphs? What tragedies took place here, who died and how many?

The architecture and decor left behind offers an intriguing glimpse into the past. Trends, resembling a foreign language to the newer generations, in forms of colours, textures, and an overall conscious style of living.

At times, evidence of squatters have come and gone, although more often than not, the evidence is a sight ideally unseen, if you know what I mean.

Abandos are home to artists of the street, like a playground is to a child exploring, developing, and having fun. Walls once bare are turned into canvases displaying creativity and imagination. Snapshots into the minds of an artist, with incredible murals and, at times, barely legible, yet vibrant graffiti pieces. For some, it is how they start before they progress to extremely high-paid artists.

An urbexer's dedication to preserving and photographing history feels like a strong sense of purpose—as if it gives our depressing existence some form of meaning. Recording history, someone's history, before demolition destroys all the evidence.

Mirroring life, it is about looking for beauty in anything and everything. It could be a discarded shoe with light projecting through a broken window above. Dust fairies dancing in the beam, contrasting the dark corridor waiting to engulf us with its undiscovered secrets.

I first became intrigued with abandoned buildings when my friends and I saw them as squats, representing safe havens. Particularly years after my own personal experiences of homelessness, I continued to associate with street-present friends who certainly opened my eyes to abandos.

I feel deep emotional regret for not taking more photos back in the day. Almost every place I saw has since been demolished, with only a handful restored. Memories that could have been preserved, now limited to nothing more than fragments of a broken mirror in my head.

In early January 2020, something rekindled my interests and I began photographing abandoned houses and buildings. For the first half of the year, I was mostly going alone—something which contravenes the international urbex code. Thankfully by August, I had found someone to go with me.

The top three rules most commonly promoted in urbexing:

1. Never explore alone. Safety should always be at the fore of your mind. Buildings may be dilapidated, collapsing, or full of trip hazards and holes; doors may lock and trap you in forgotten rooms, you might not find the exit, your torch could die, you may be invading a squatter or drug user's turf, and if anything goes wrong, you are on your own with no guarantee of phone reception or a sufficient phone battery. Even sudden panic attacks, spider and snake bites, a swarm of bees, or an unknown health condition that puts your life at risk.
2. Take and touch nothing. Leave everything the way you found it so that others can enjoy the same experience. Some abandoned locations make you feel like you are the first person to have visited in such a long time, so respect the history and integrity of the building.
3. Never break or damage anything in order to enter. If you cannot find an entry, do not enter. Only use pre-existing entrances. Trespassing is a contentious legal issue. Breaking or damaging anything exacerbates the crime to the level of burglary or worse. On many occasions, I have been granted permission to access locations either from the owner, security guard, or a contractor. While most people you ask may say no, you will not know until you ask.

While on the subject of safety, it is important to take into account that most abandoned sites will put you at risk of being exposed to asbestos. An ordinary dust mask is not effective to prevent you from inhaling asbestos fibres and dust. A respirator with a P2 Filter can stop 94 per cent of airborne particles including micro-organisms (as well as bacteria, fungi, and algae).

A good pair of gloves can help protect you against exposed wires, broken glass, nails, and many sharp objects. Some people also choose to wear safety glasses.

Lastly, wearing long-sleeved clothing and boots or solid shoes is important. I also recommend carrying a small lightweight bag with a torch, spare battery, portable charger, first-aid kit, bottle of water, identification, and a snack, in case you are in there for longer than you planned and your energy begins to wane.

Returning to the first year of my urbex passion, by October, I had helped create the most amazing, fun-filled, and exciting crew. Never could I have imagined such positive energy and excitement coming from like-minded friends. Our love and passion for photography and exploring what few get to see makes us feel so much alive, especially on weekends. Our troubles and depression eased by spurring each other to keep on going. Despite the broad mix of ages, it became a great way to support and mentor each other, at the same time as encouraging us to grow. All as a by-product of urbexing.

As the years continue to fly past, something my parents used to always say when I was a child at school and never believed to be true, I still chase dreams of one day obtaining a brilliant DSLR with all the fancy lens and whatnot. For the moment, as well as the past decades that progressed well into the history of time, I am still taking photos on my phone, which includes every photo in this book.

I must admit though, technology these days make mobile phones on par with a good DSLR. They are small enough to fit in your pocket, quick to pull out, and can take high-quality photos, especially at night with the incredible night mode.

And reiterating the motivation of many urbexers, exploring abandos is about photographing and preserving history, someone's history. My phone camera does just that, meaning I can share with you a different thought-provoking view of the world. My world here in Perth, Western Australia.

AKERINGA FIRE UNITS

Someone had posted photos on Facebook of a boarded-up, double-storey apartment complex. This one was close to home, so I went to check it out the very next day.

The site consisted of two apartment blocks: one was still being lived in, while the other was mostly boarded up. They were both managed by the one caretaker. He was watering the garden.

We had a brief chat. Briefest of brief, but after letting him know my intentions, which were naturally best as always, he told me to be quick taking photos. Not that I look like trouble, especially being a female but because there were potential dangers in 'there'.

I nodded profusely, more focused on shooting anything I could in what little time he had given me. Not that he gave me a specific time limit, which certainly suited me.

As I approached the abandoned complex, it became quite clear to me that there had been a fire. Initially, it appeared to be limited to the one unit on the top floor and certainly not serious enough to warrant the eviction of all tenants.

Most of the units remained boarded up, so I photographed the few that were accessible. It was easy to assume the ones boarded up were replicate units, all devoid of both human presence and possessions.

It did not take long to reach the blackened door on the second floor, barely hanging on its hinges. The clear balustrade panel in front of it had peeled back like melted plastic. I slowly open the door, as if any creaking would awaken a demon or perhaps a spirit of someone who had met their fate. At the time of my visit, I had no idea what had taken place.

With barely a crunch emitting from under my feet, the strong smell of smoke was evident, despite a few openings in various parts of the unit. My mask gave little comfort.

The walls were near pitch-black, contrasting orange and light-coloured retaining surfaces. Pink ceiling insulation drooped from damaged rafters, looking more like a theatre stage ready for a show. Many personal possessions remained behind, burnt and melted, particularly in the bathroom.

I felt overwhelmed with emotion, largely as a result of the energy radiating in everything I saw. I could feel the fear and hear the screams. Silent but vivid.

With no information on the cause of the event, nor the resulting survival rate, the atmosphere felt as intense as a compression bandage wrapped around my head.

Thankfully, I was soon finished and I later found out that no one had died.

A fifty-year-old man had lit a fire on the balcony of a unit, at approximately 7:50 a.m., on a Monday morning. It quickly engulfed the man's unit, where two others were sleeping and severely damaged one other unit. There were no reports of anyone requiring medical assistance, and firefighters were able to contain the blaze within twenty minutes. The man was charged with one count of criminal damage by fire but I have not been able to find any more information or updates, other than noticing the complex has since been demolished (in early 2021).

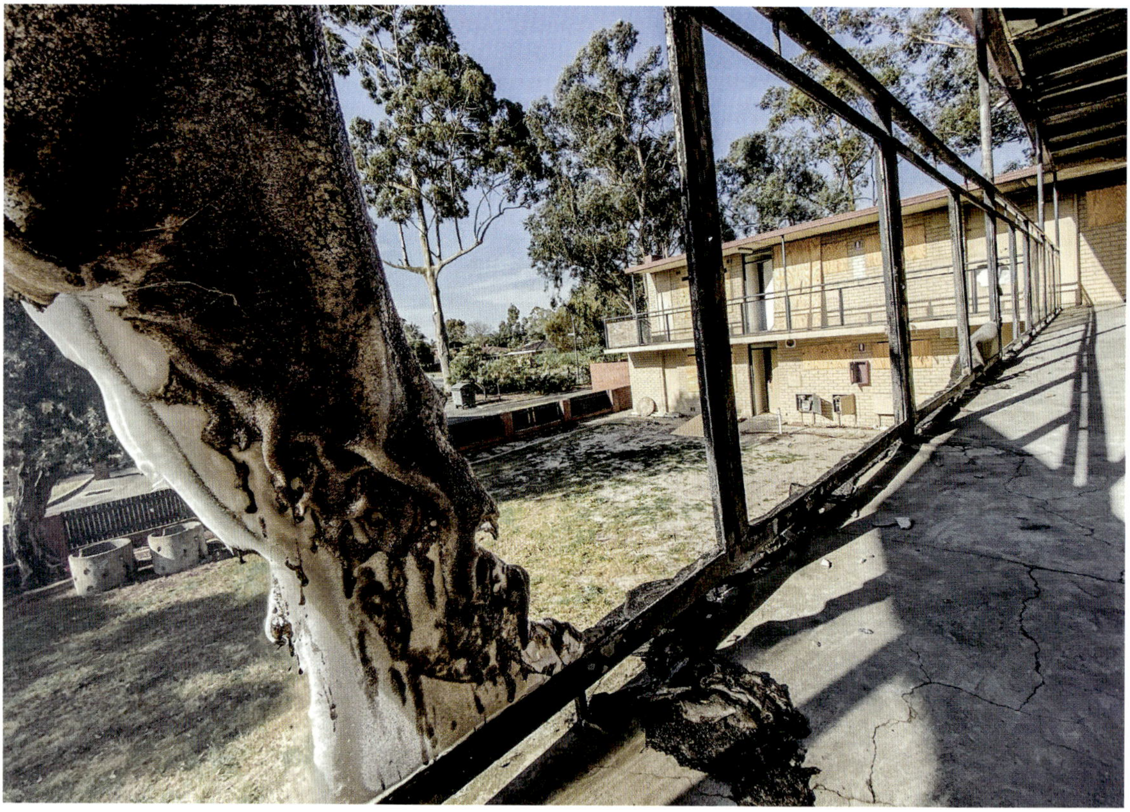

The melted remains of a Perspex panel, taken directly opposite the apartment fire.

OPPOSITE PAGE:
A close-up photo blended with a long shot, taken through the hole of a door handle. *Below:* Smashed shards of glass litter the floor, reflecting what remains of the window.

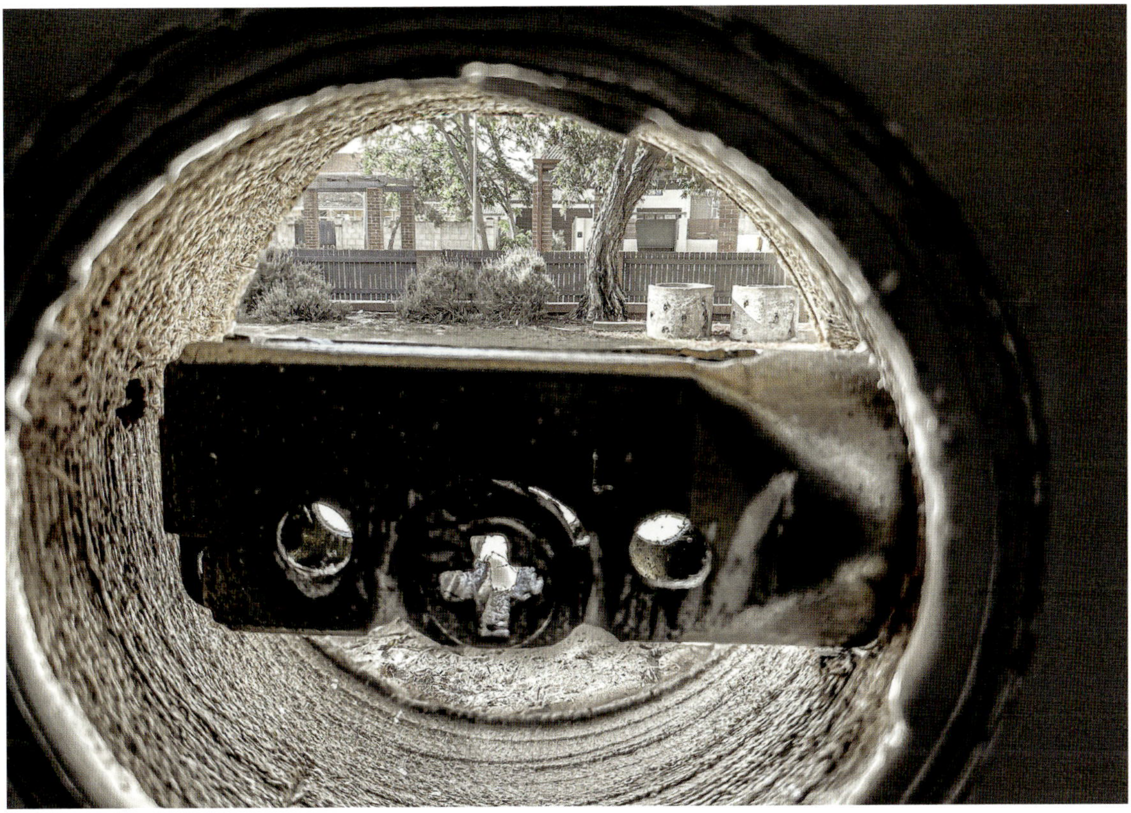

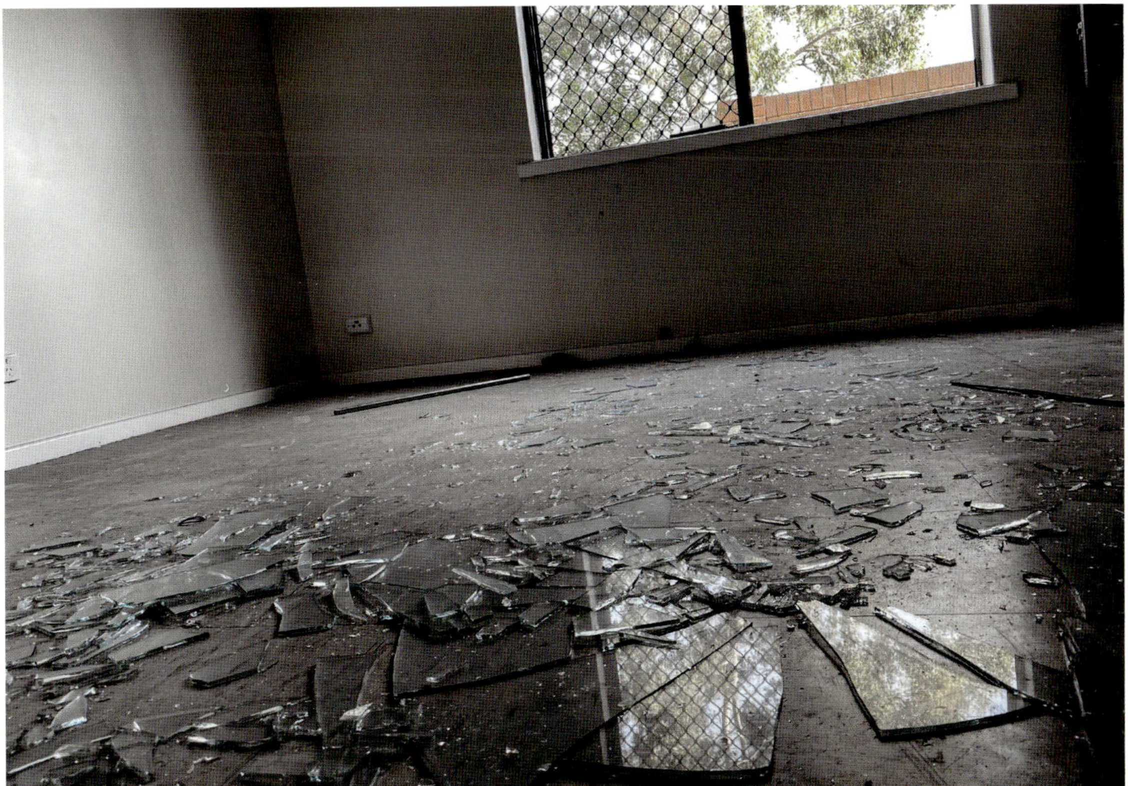

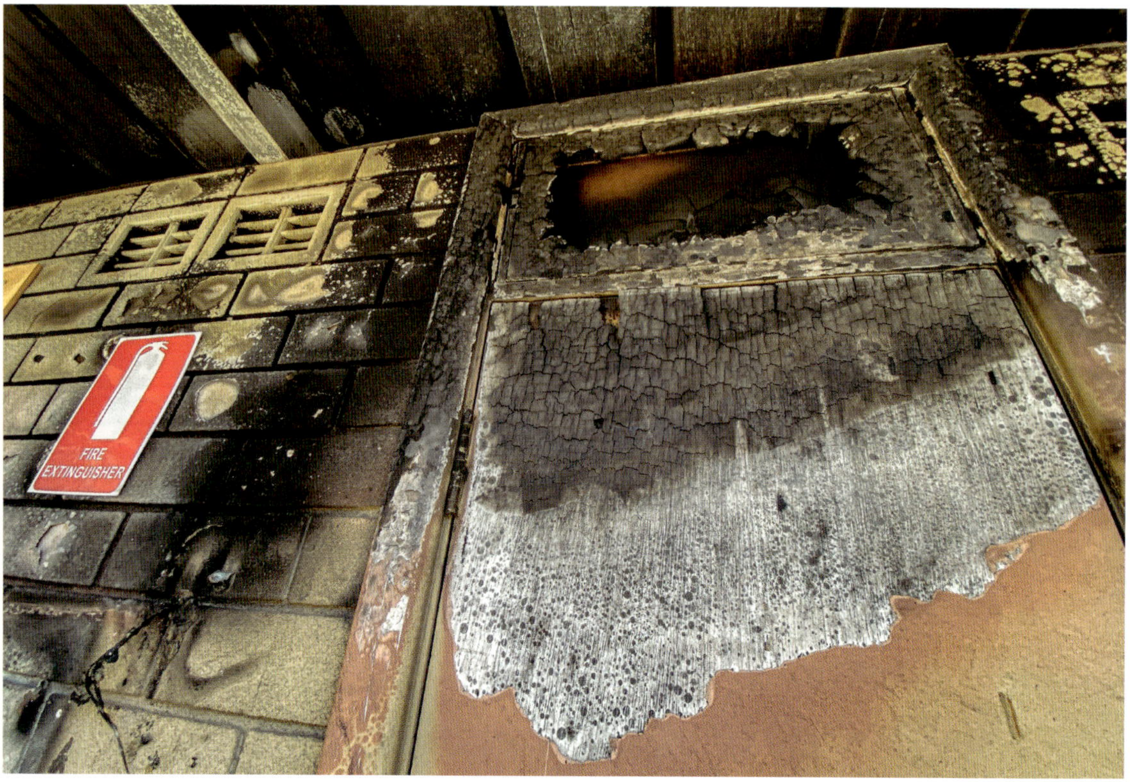

A fire extinguisher sign displays where an extinguisher was once located, in close proximity to the apartment fire.

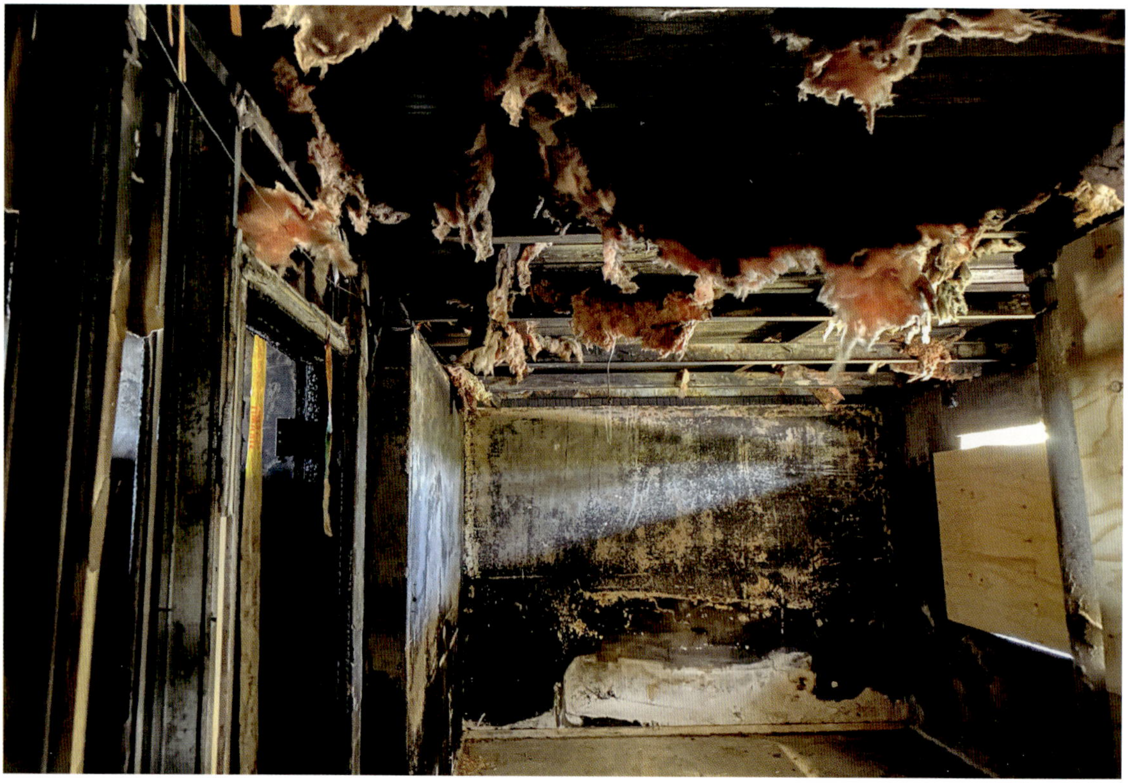

Roof insulation drapes from damaged rafters, contrasting with background colours created by the fire.

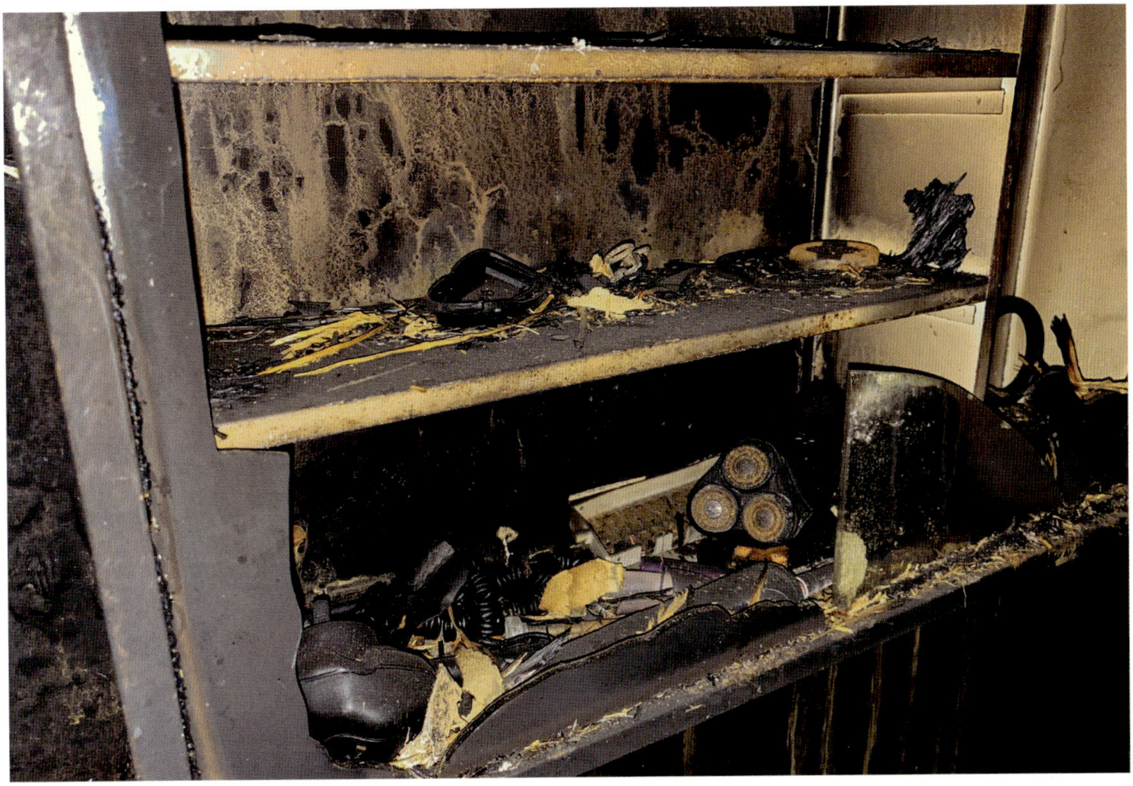

Surviving possessions left behind in a burnt-out shell of a bathroom cabinet.

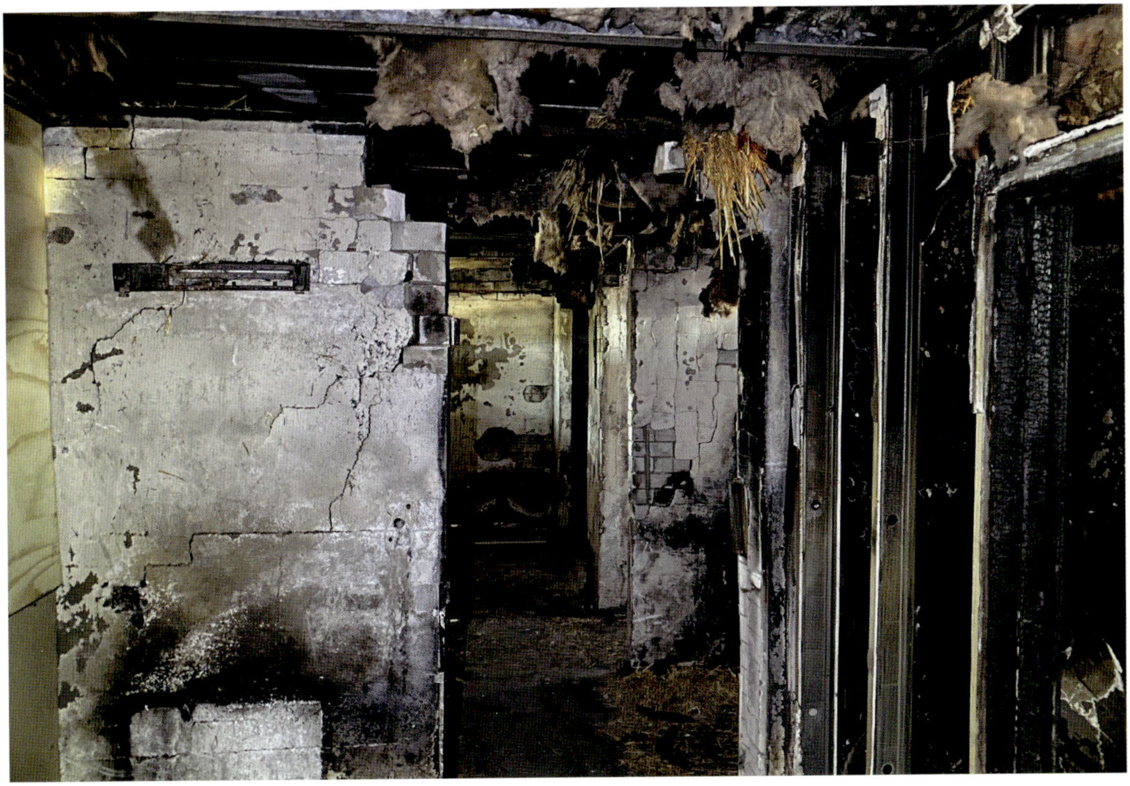

The apartment where the fire was lit, now resembles more of a derelict horse stable.

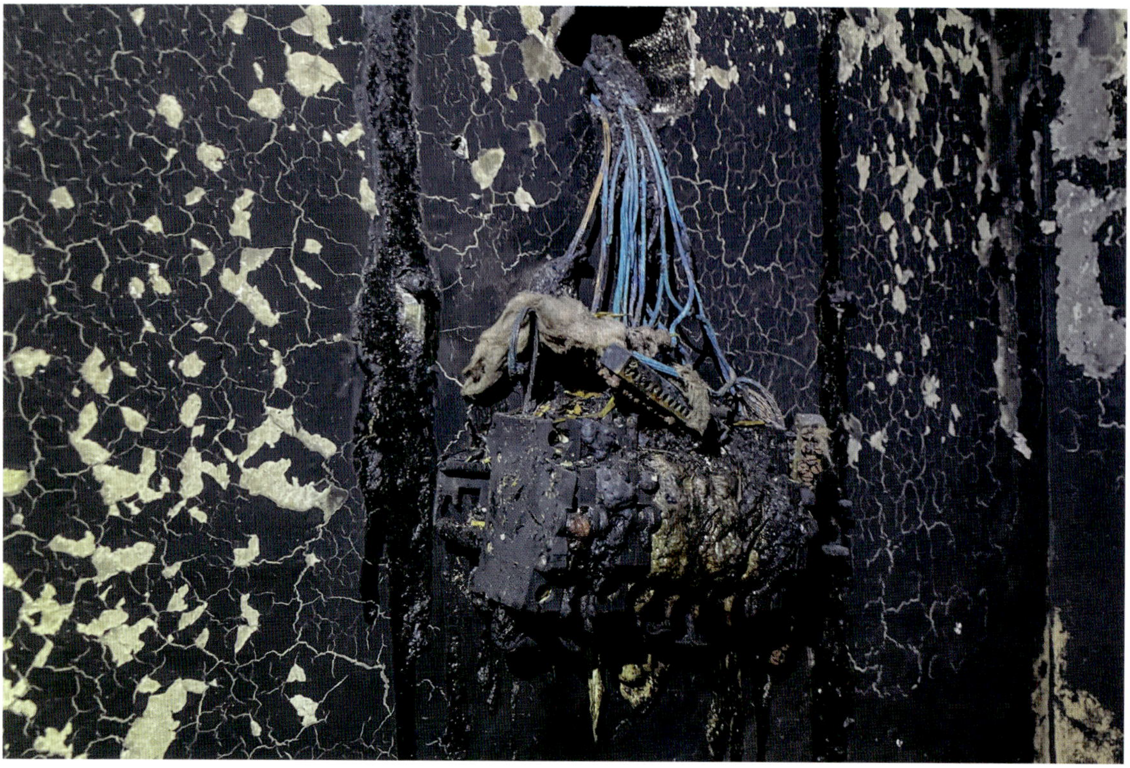

The remains of a circuit breaker.

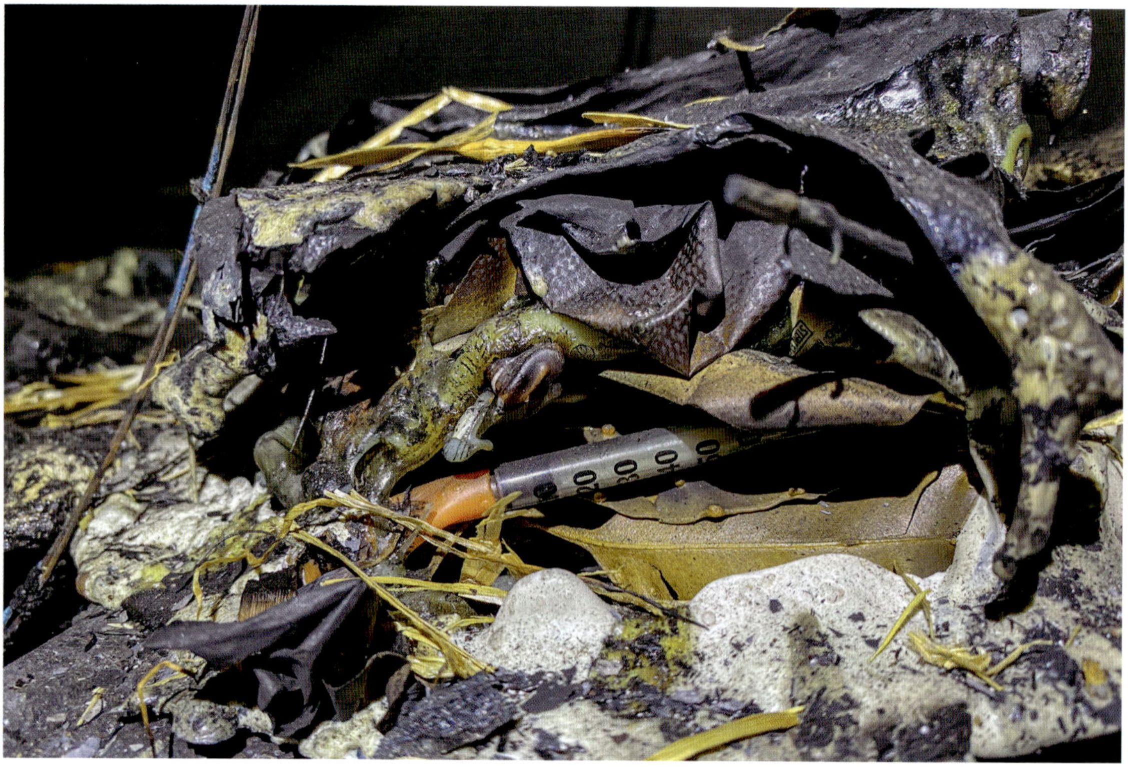

Syringes in a toiletry bag: something that tends to attract a negative stereotype, particularly in circumstances where the fire was a result of arson.

BELMONT DECEASED ESTATE

My first companion, who had been a passionate urbexer for quite some time, took me to a small house in Belmont. It certainly appeared to be abandoned and uncared for, what with its tall grass almost waist high, the remains of a dead tree cut short of any branches and a few fence panels strewn about.

It was a beautiful October morning. The sun was out in force and the perfect azure blue sky contrasted well against the colours of the backyard. A boat that had seen better days, waited for someone to free it into the sparkling blue, coastal waters. Trashy graffiti marred the hull and an object had broken a triangular shape in the windshield. A definite lack of respect for someone's property.

We headed to the porch, where a number of interesting possessions were in full view of ourselves and the elements of weather. A vintage suitcase, just like what the actors carried in the olden day movies from when my parents were young. A ripped cardboard box nearby spilled audio cassettes, some appearing to contain home recordings.

The kitchen was a place of fascination. Aside from a large inventory of standard kitchenware and belongings that no doubt had been viewed and rummaged through by many before us, some were older than myself. An Education Department of WA exercise book on the counter, a sheet of newspaper dated May 11, 1983 on the floor, a retro thermos that brought a smile to my face, with decor I believed to date back from the 1970s and so much more.

Back in the days when possessions were cared for, rather than materialistic items that could easily be tossed and replaced, someone obviously had respect and pride to keep them in such good nick for so long. Yet now, it was easy to presume that little remained in comparison of what was. Anything of value was sure to have been removed from the property a long time ago, by thieving muppets.

My initial thoughts were that the surviving family were not too bothered with the possessions left behind by the elderly man, who had since passed away. A lifetime of history and many documents showed me a snapshot into what was his life. There were a number of horse racing carnival posters and result sheets, dating from as far back as the 1970s. Perhaps this gentleman had some financial stakes in a horse that ran.

For someone like myself, a few generations more recent than the man in question, it was interesting to see possessions that were, at times, most alien to me. Like a very real insight into history, that just was not the same seeing it on the internet. A few items were vaguely familiar, like a WA Gold Polyunsaturated Table Margarine container, which my Maman used to keep to store knick-knacks to organise the cupboards.

I found it interesting to say the least, the amount of relics I saw at the cost of modernisation. So many of the possessions left behind had not been traded in for newer ones.

There were a few eyebrow-raising moments, such as seeing a bommy-knocker made out of what appeared to be a mallet handle and a doll's head. Although I did not check to see if the mallet was actually wedged inside the dolls head. Perhaps it was a weapon of choice for a squatter, who did not necessary want to embed an obvious yet brutal shape into someone's forehead.

While later researching the history of this location, I could not find any information about a female residing in this house. Yet there were many feminine items that did not necessary identify with what I would have expected a man to possess for himself. Vintage fabrics and belongings, perhaps they were keepsakes which had helped comfort him with the memories of the past he had once shared with a loved one. Most likely the mother to his surviving children. Colours and textures, designs and items that could be traced back to long before my time. A few items of clothing were stored in a cupboard, with the bulk strewn around the room like party streamers. Sadness penetrated my emotions. Items discarded carelessly and yet, would continue to be a regular scene in places I later visited.

Of course, like anything, what is left behind never has the same meaning for the person who once owned them. Memories are not always passed on and the materialistic collection is too much for the bereaved, who have their own belongings and memories that accumulate over time.

With floorboards creaking, we headed from room to room, taking photos of all that remained. One bedroom, which contained two single beds, appeared to have once been home to a squatter. Judging from what was left behind including supermarket receipts, it was not recent.

A yellow hairbrush and blue razor sat on a weathered windowsill, slightly open to the cold winter temperatures and occasional rains. When had they last been used? Was it on the last day of this man's life or did he fail to wake up one morning?

Being the highly inquisitive person I am (insert the eye-rolling of my fellow explorers), I like to look in every hole in the wall, under the floorboards, and in the attic. The floorboards in one room had been popped open in two areas. I climbed down into the thick dust and debris, spider webs weaved into many corners of the crawl space. This house was certainly one of a kind and crawling through it, turned up some incredible vintage treasures.

It was like finding more pieces to the puzzle. From building materials to a few toys, to a big collection of shells, including some conch specimens. More importantly, as my astonishment nearly wiped the air out of my lungs upon sight, I saw antiques I could only imagine in old books and movies. A wooden high chair, pieces of a dismantled pram, kitchenware from the 1970s, a record player, and television. It was like going back in time. Instead of seeing these relics on public display, I was viewing them privately in a perfect, atmospheric setting. It was fascinating! A museum of forgotten treasures, items that once had value in someone's family.

Even the house and adjoining VCR repair shop were of little worth, compared to the land that was rich enough to free the surviving families of any debt and mortgages. Come demolition day, it seemed very likely that the remaining possessions would be scooped up by an excavator, once the walls were sent toppling to the ground.

In its place would be a grand hotel comprising of 147 rooms and forty serviced apartments. Assets clearly more important to future generations and members of the public on an extensive scale.

Truth be told, it was time to move on. Memories associated with possessions rarely seem to be passed on, and if they were, it would not hold the same meaning for other people. Either way, they would surely soon be forgotten with time.

A fire broke out in the house in April 2021, severely damaging the roof. I have not been able to locate any news reports or find any more information. At the time of my third visit with friends some months prior, we disturbed squatters who were living there, but I do not know if they had a role in the cause of the fire. The boat had also since been stolen.

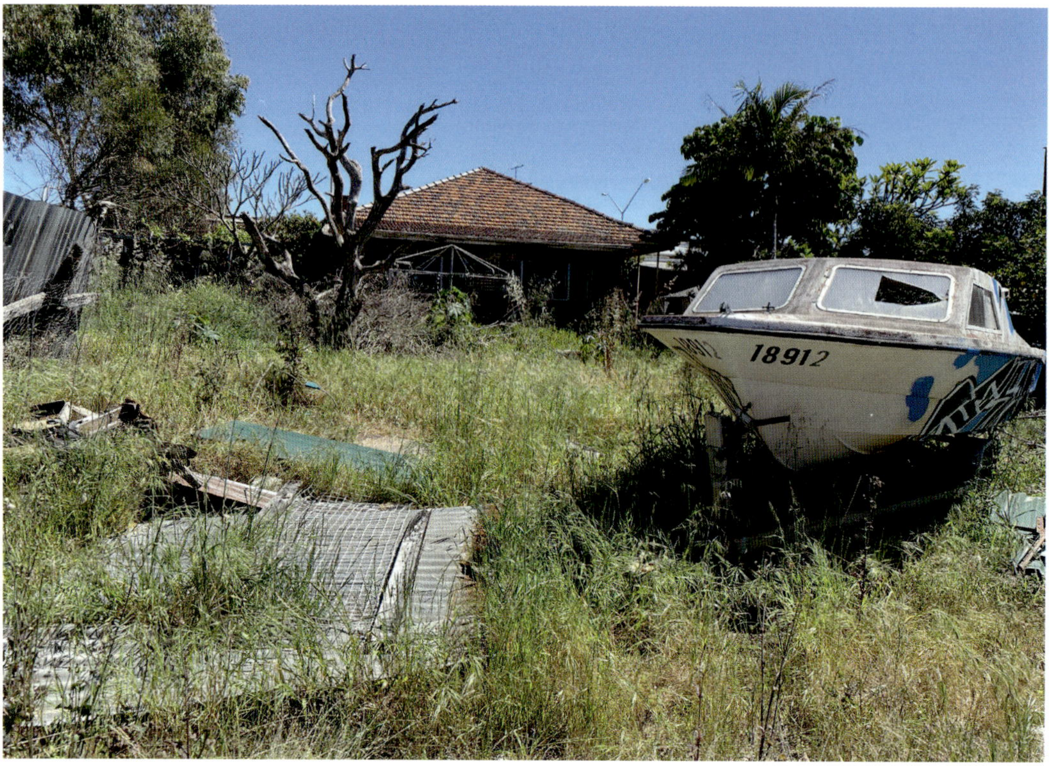

View of the backyard from what should have been the fence line.

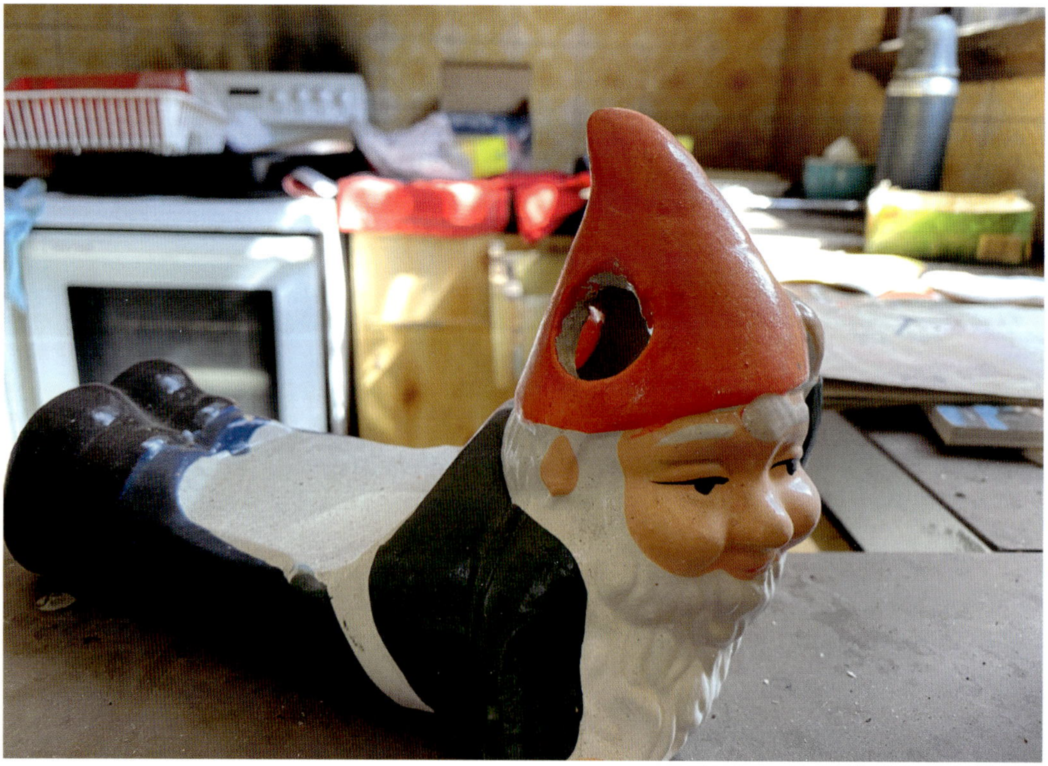

A gnome ornament, possibly to hold cooking utensils.

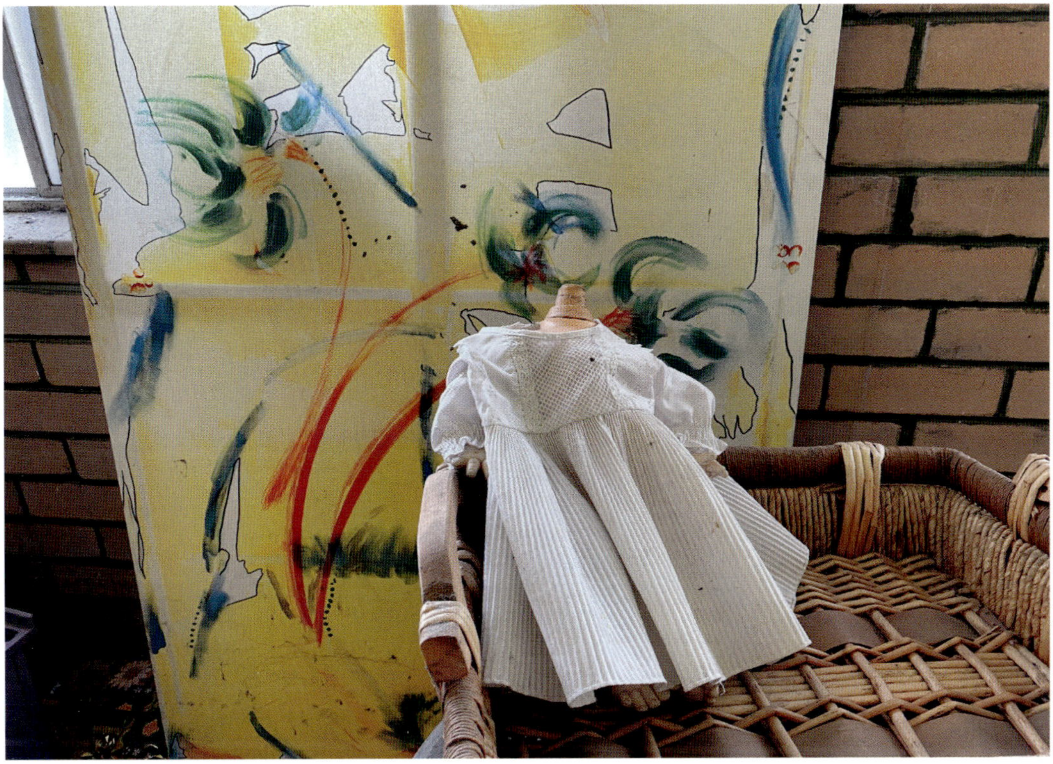

Despite the sight of a headless doll (which for some, may feel rather disturbing), a contrast of colours and textures captures my attention.

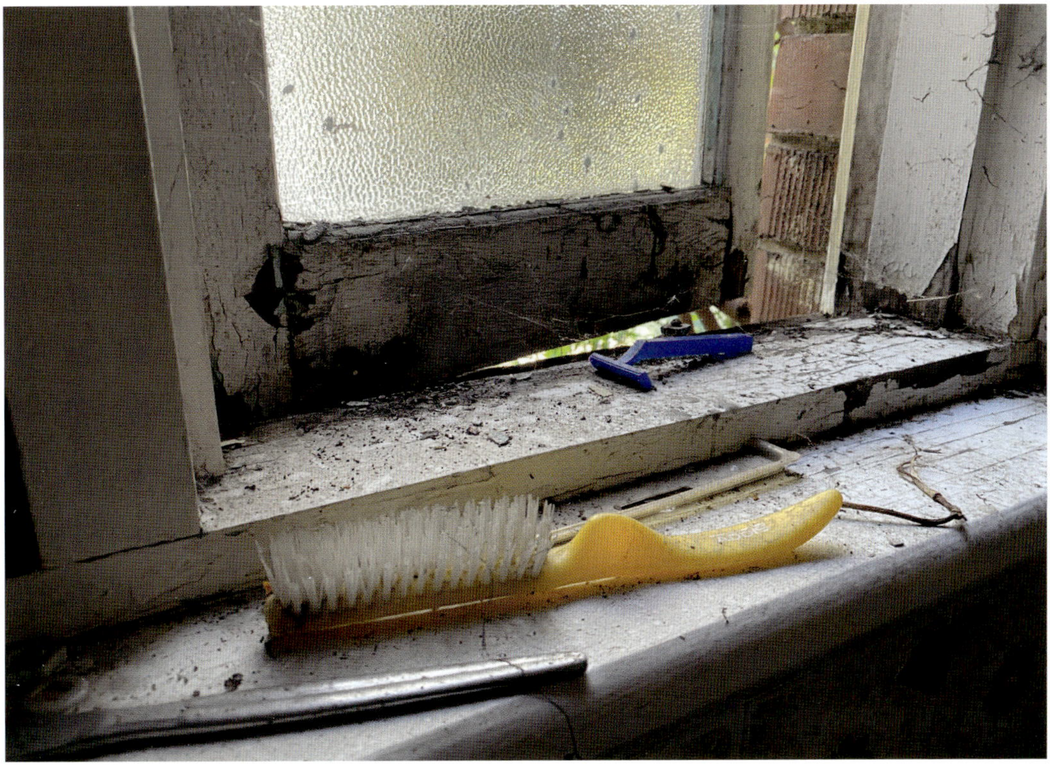

A razor and brush gathers dust and dirt from weather conditions peeking through the window's gap.

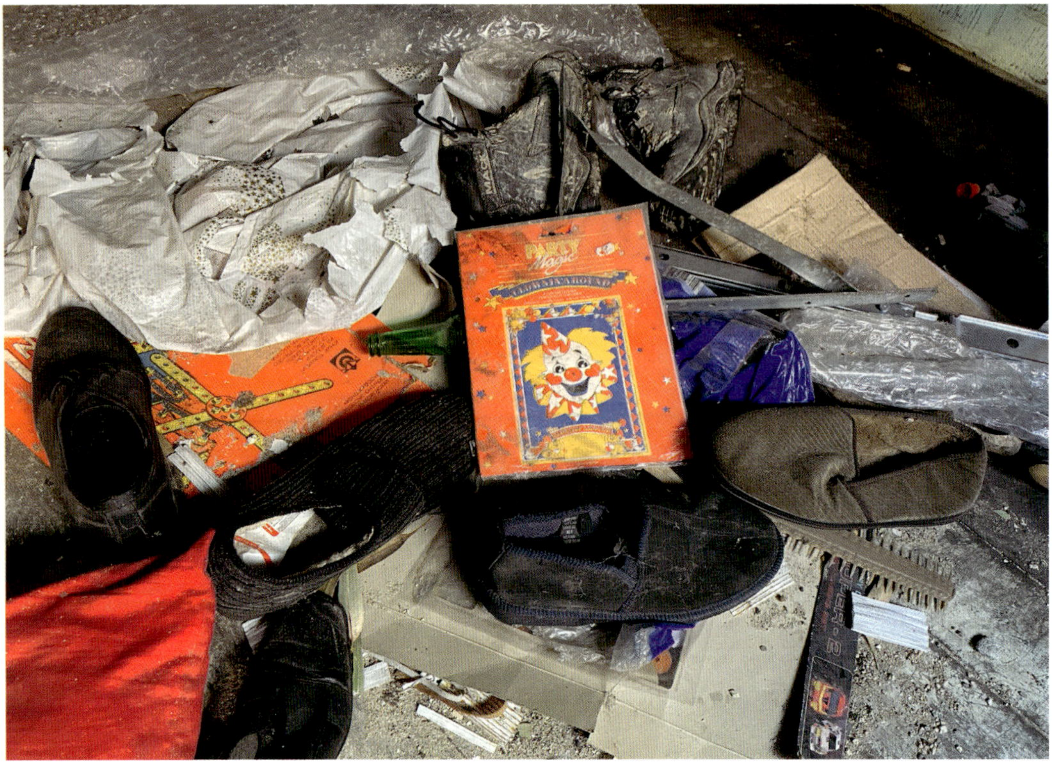

Five mismatching shoes and slippers with a pair of Mack work boots, seemingly out of place with an unopened party game and old Christmas wrapping paper.

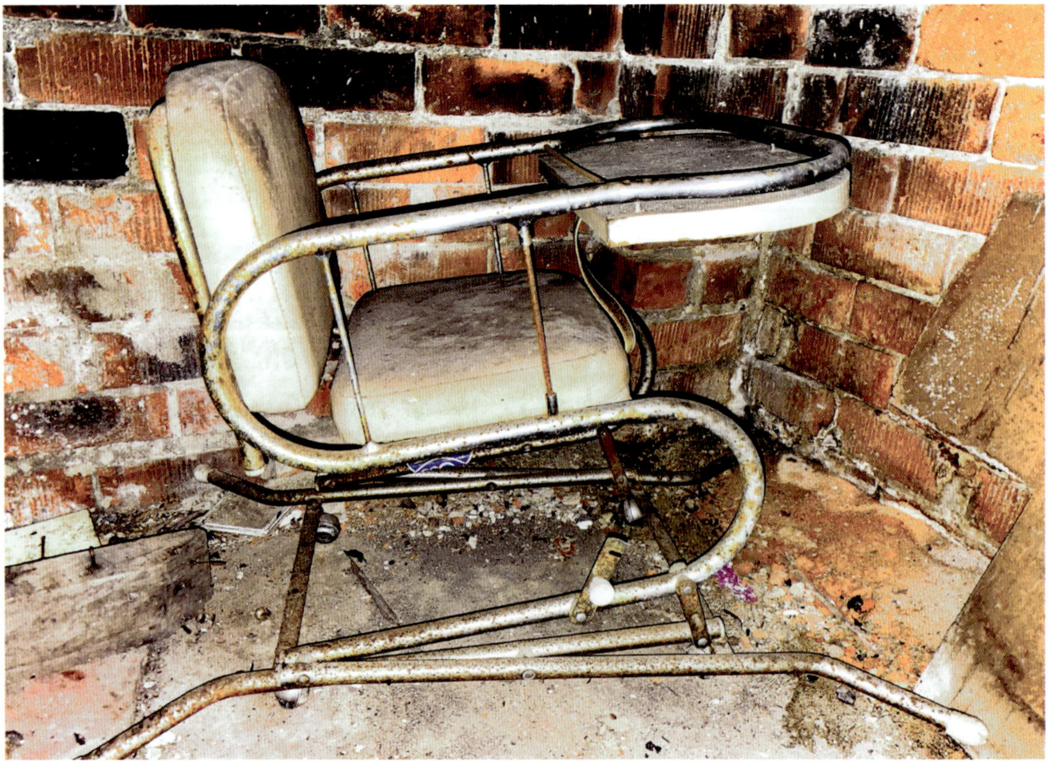

An old-fashioned baby chair rusts away, forgotten with time, under the floorboards of the house.

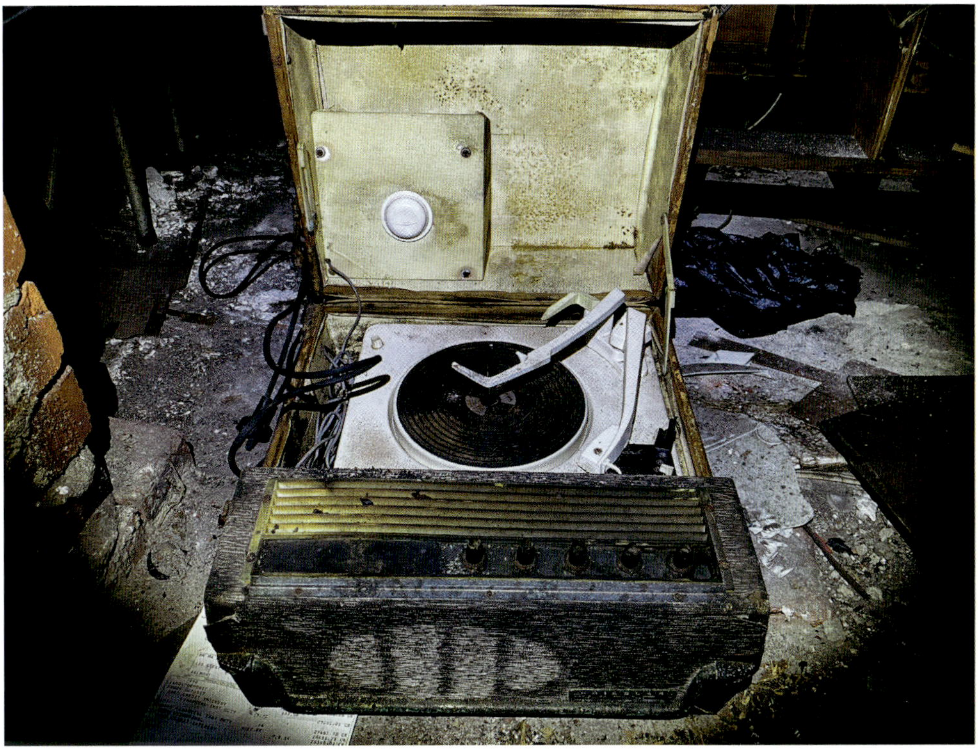

A Kreisler portable record player from the 1950–60s. The Kreisler Radio Company was founded in 1928 by brothers Alec, Leo, and Rae Weingott in Sydney.

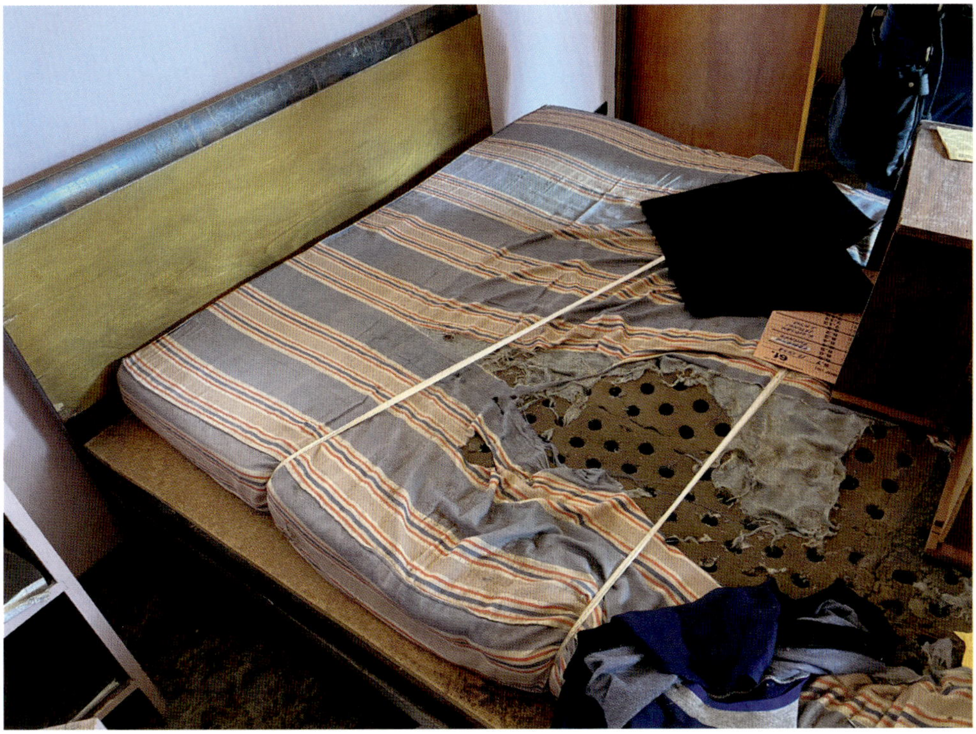

A mattress that appears to have been made from synthetic foam is so shabby, it is easy to mistake what remains of its cover as frayed bedsheets.

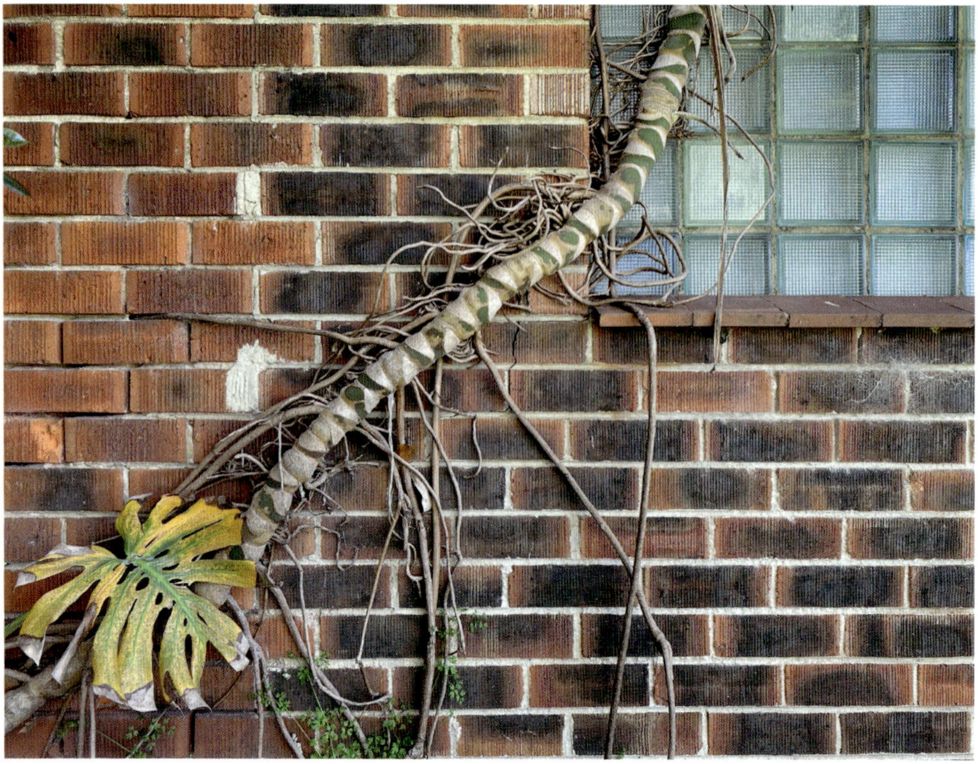

Nature takes back control with many of the backyard plants and trees growing wild, climbing up the walls and even into holes of the foundations.

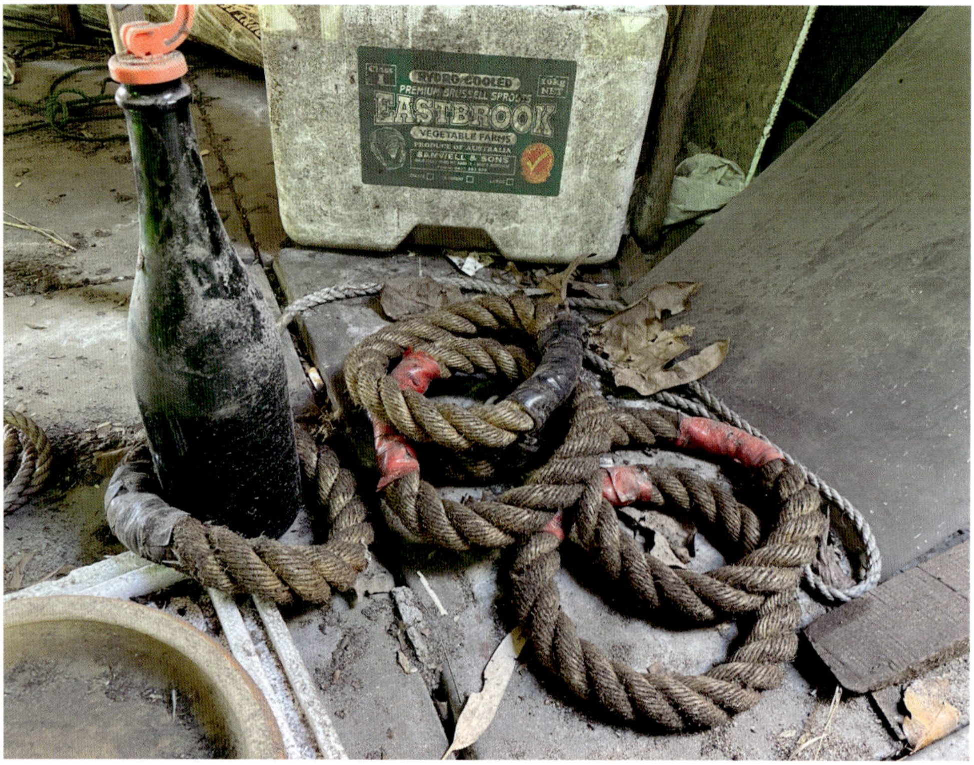

A homemade game of quoits on the floor of the shed.

COMO HOUSE

It was a simple dark-peach-coloured brick house, sitting on a fairly big block of land. The frontyard resembled a wheat field, what with its pervasive crop of wild oat weeds. The colours contrasted quite nicely, with a cloudy light-blue coloured sky and a low-lying whitish brick wall, which had seen better days.

All the windows and doors were wide open, giving a whole new meaning to an open home. It felt symbolic of an empty house that no longer had any warmth, love, or memories to share, nor any secrets to bare. It was a skeleton of the past, remnants limited to the physical structure.

Interestingly, the colour scheme of the front of the house and throughout its interior helped maintain its rather quaint characteristic. It seemed to me that just about every house these days preferred modest colours that were more conforming. Perhaps it had something to do with the council, but it would certainly make sense that houses were not allowed to stand out or, at least, attract more attention than the one next to it. Then again, most houses were happy to remain the colour of the bricks they were given birth with rather than a slip slop slap coat of paint.

Particularly with the image of a yellow towel dropped on the floor, the scene feels so perfectly presented, like artwork on display.

The interior design looks so basic, it is as if the owner had better things to do than fuss around with the latest whatnots of home decorating. Like time forgotten and we have just stumbled into the mid-'80s. Without taking into consideration the personal living contents of a house, what we see now both inside and out would probably be no different to what it looked like some thirty years ago.

In a sense, it is comforting, as if it represents a lack of materialistic greed and wealth. 'Let's keep this house simple, so we can focus on the more important things in life'. The opposite creed we live by today, with materialistic distractions in a world full of endless woes and dramas which seem to dictate our life in every way.

Upon noticing the Mother's Day card on a painted yellow floor, I wondered whether there had ever been any carpet laid. The basic maintenance of a simple house would be just to sweep the floors, with a vacuum every once in a while.

Forgotten bundles of letters, postcards, and photos makes me question where they emerged from. Was the house not previously emptied out by the bereaving family? Were they located in the attic or under the floorboards, where a few panels were missing in the front room? Did they not mean anything to the family or did they already have enough memories from their mother?

Every year, millions of people complain how quickly the year has gone and state their disbelief how fast the next one is approaching. Naturally, I am as guilty as sin, as I am one of them. In one of the letters from the late mother, she writes about how she is finding it difficult to believe that 1984 is approaching fast. Reading someone's thoughts about what life is like for them gives an important insight into their experience—their story. I have always been fascinated with other people's stories, views, and experiences. The few postcards and letters left behind are the only glimpse I have into the life of the person who once lived here.

This house was sold in May 2021.

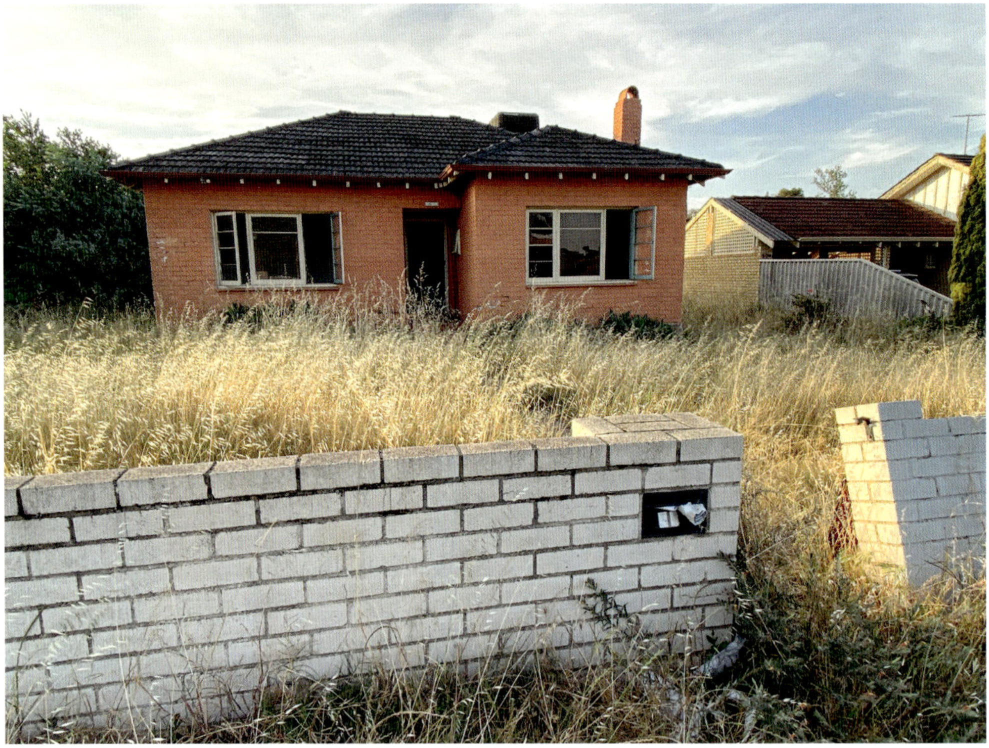

Dark peach-coloured paint makes the old house stand out from the standard conservative white or light-coloured houses.

OPPOSITE PAGE:
A colourful contrast of colours in the rear rooms of the house that did not even need an editing touch to stand out like a piece of artwork. *Below:* A queen-sized mattress now home in the middle of the kitchen.

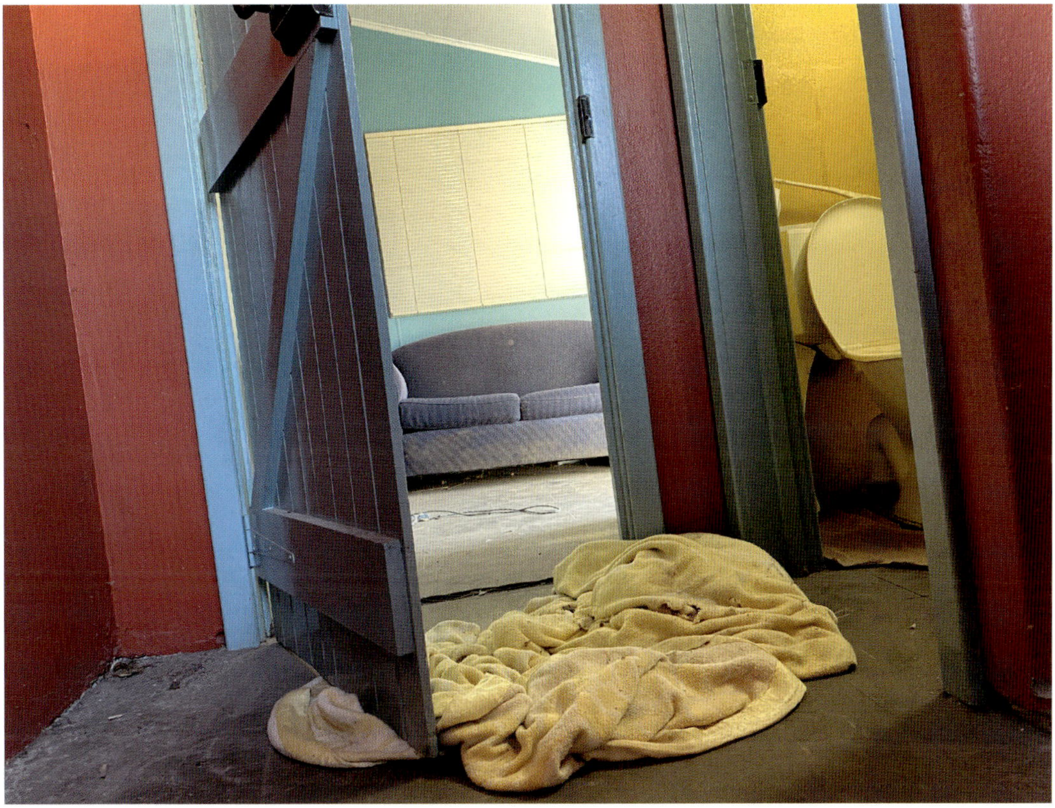

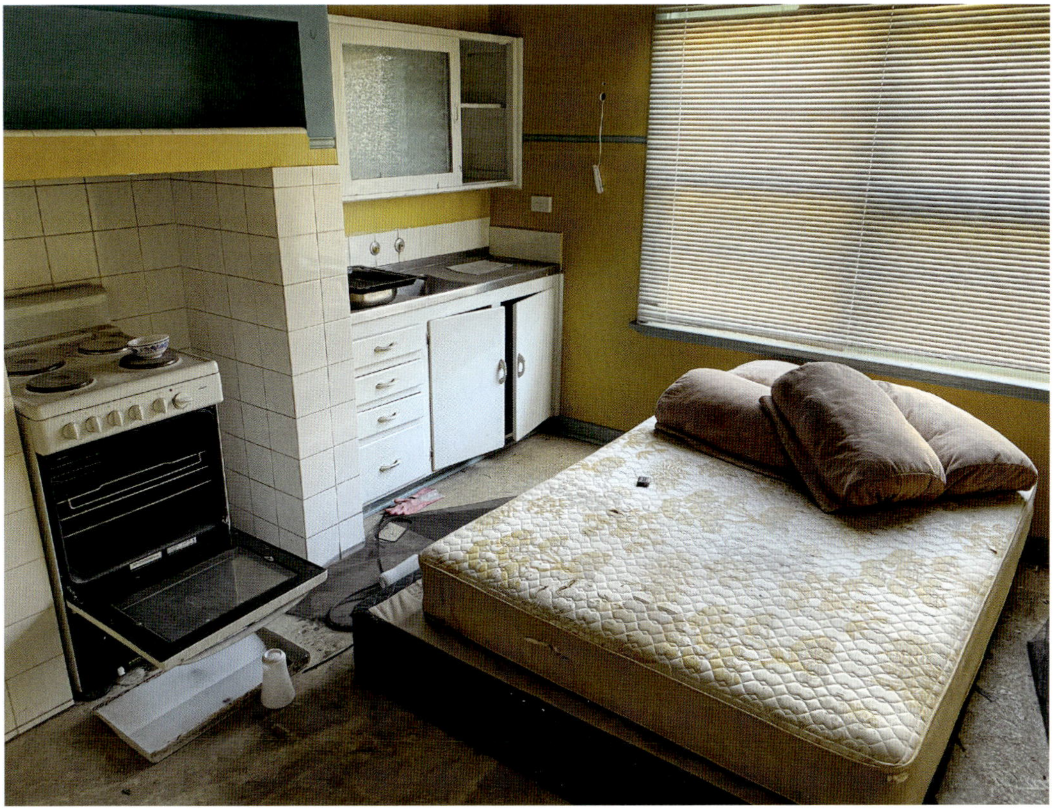

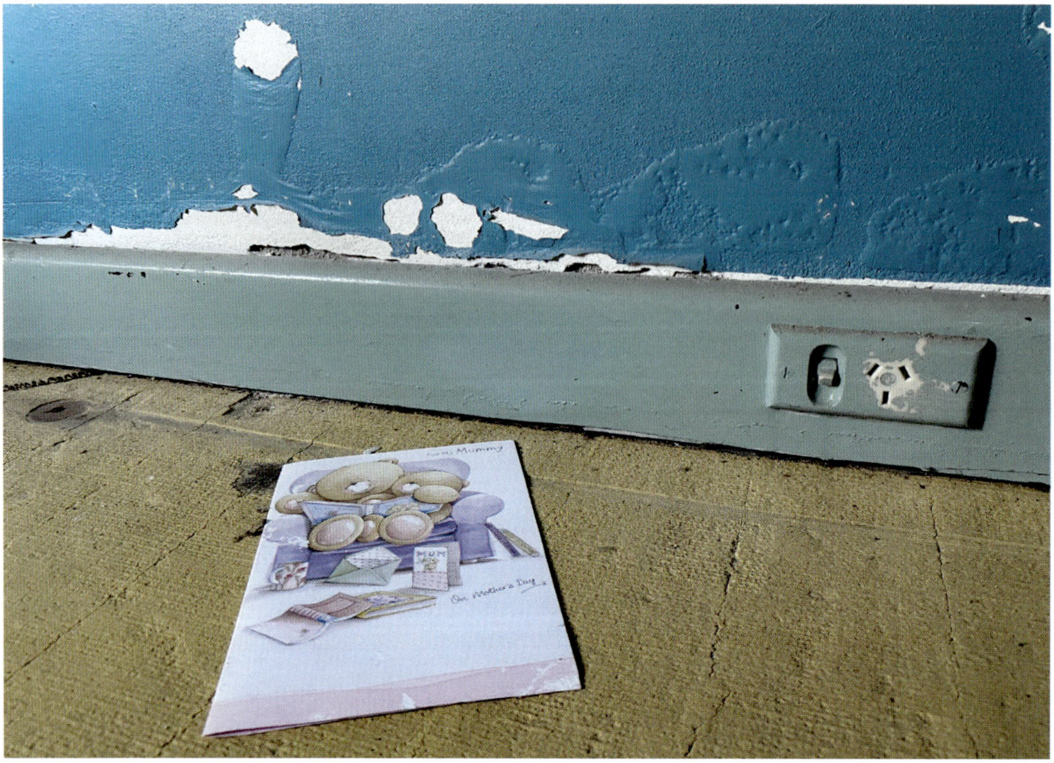

A discarded Mother's Day card that once had so much more value and meaning, when the cherished mother was still present to enjoy the company of her children.

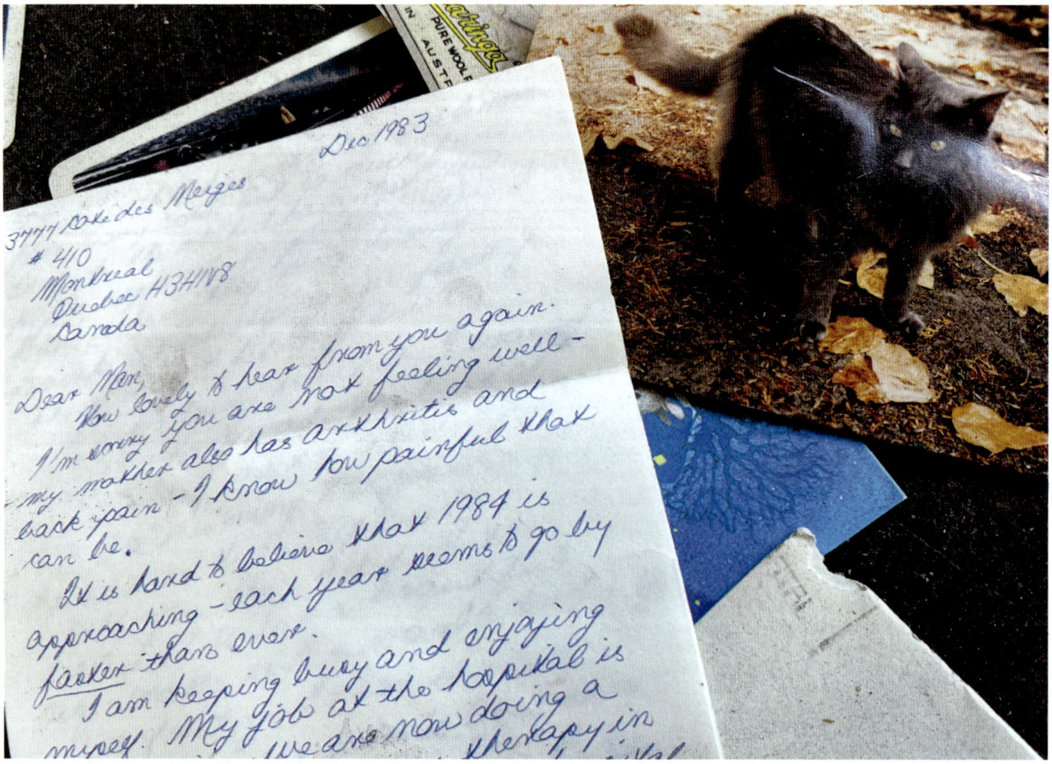

A letter dated December 1983 mentions how the writer cannot believe how fast 1984 is approaching.

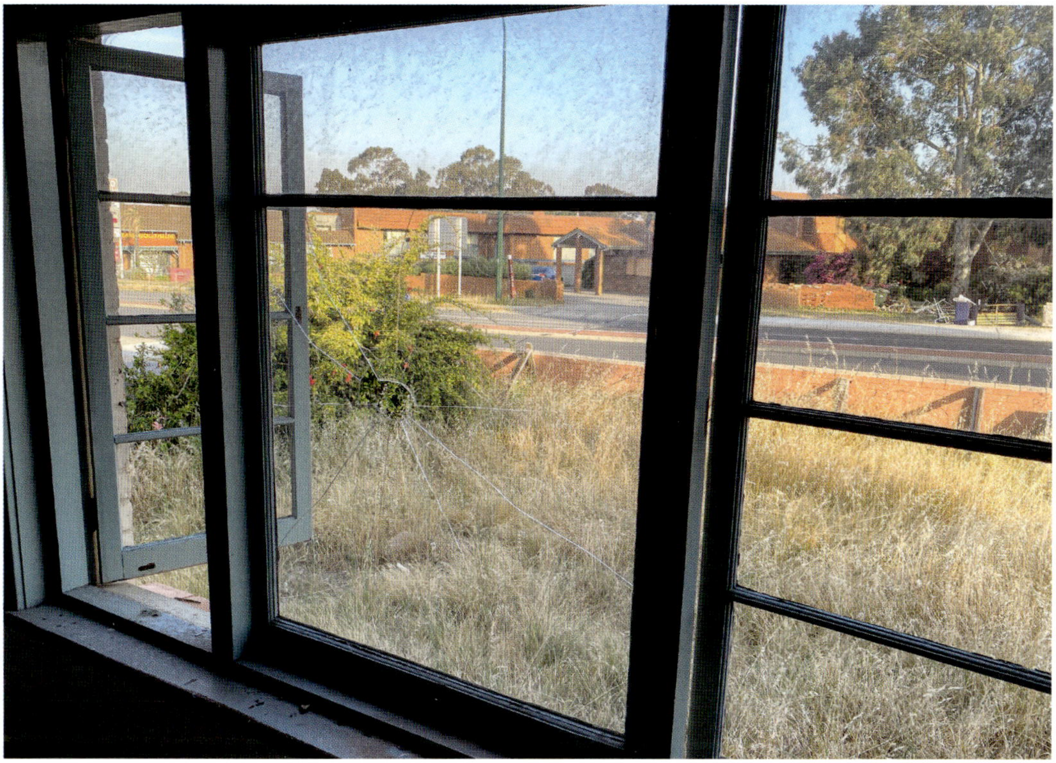

A broken window looks out onto the busy highway, where thousands of cars a day speed past, oblivious to the existence of this quaint little house.

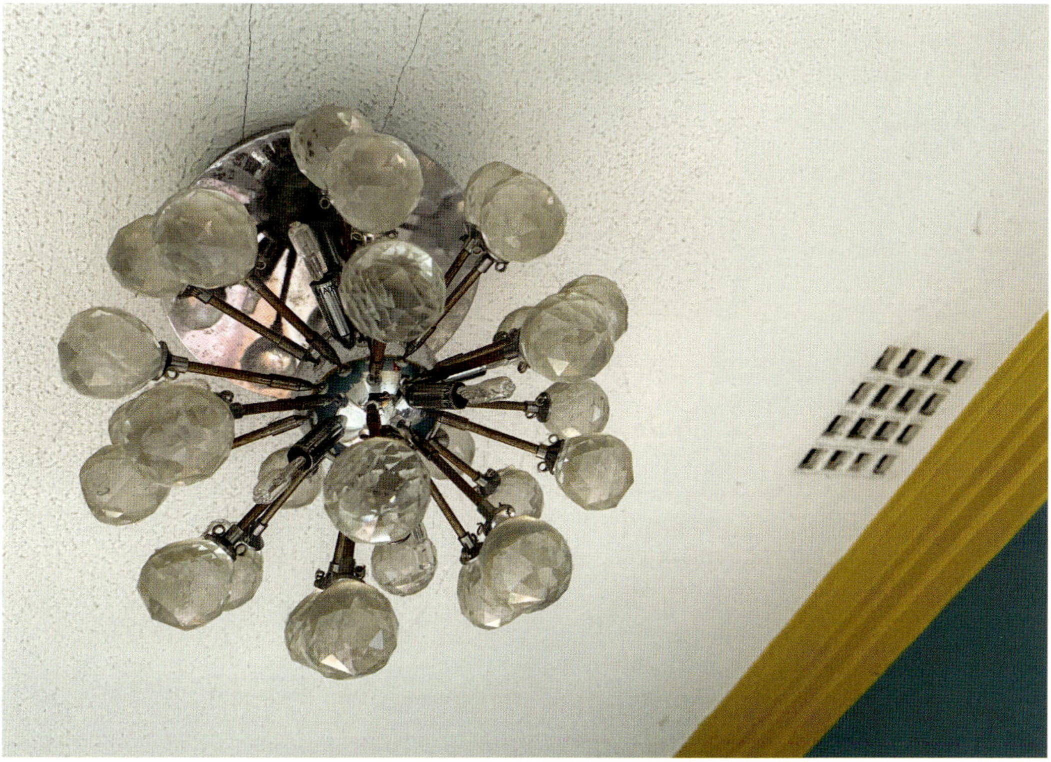

Small globes sets the mood of the foyer, giving the house an unusual feel.

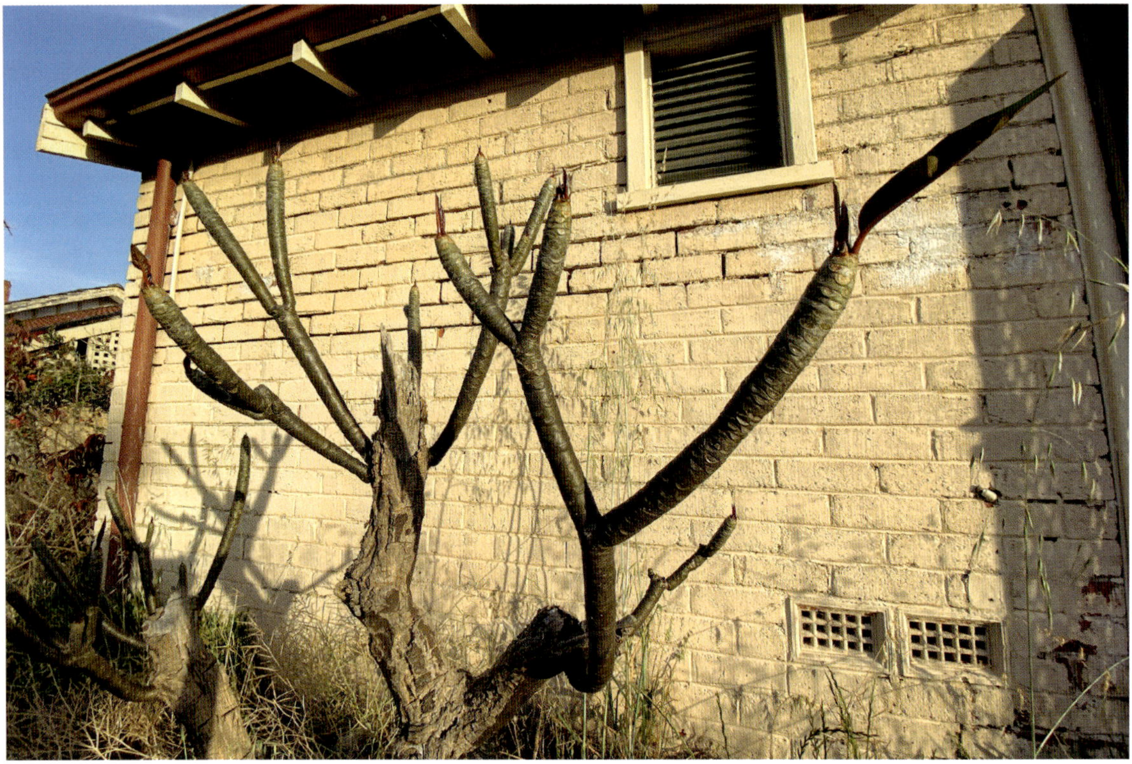

Frangipani shoots begin to emerge from branches, which look like they are coming out of an old tree.

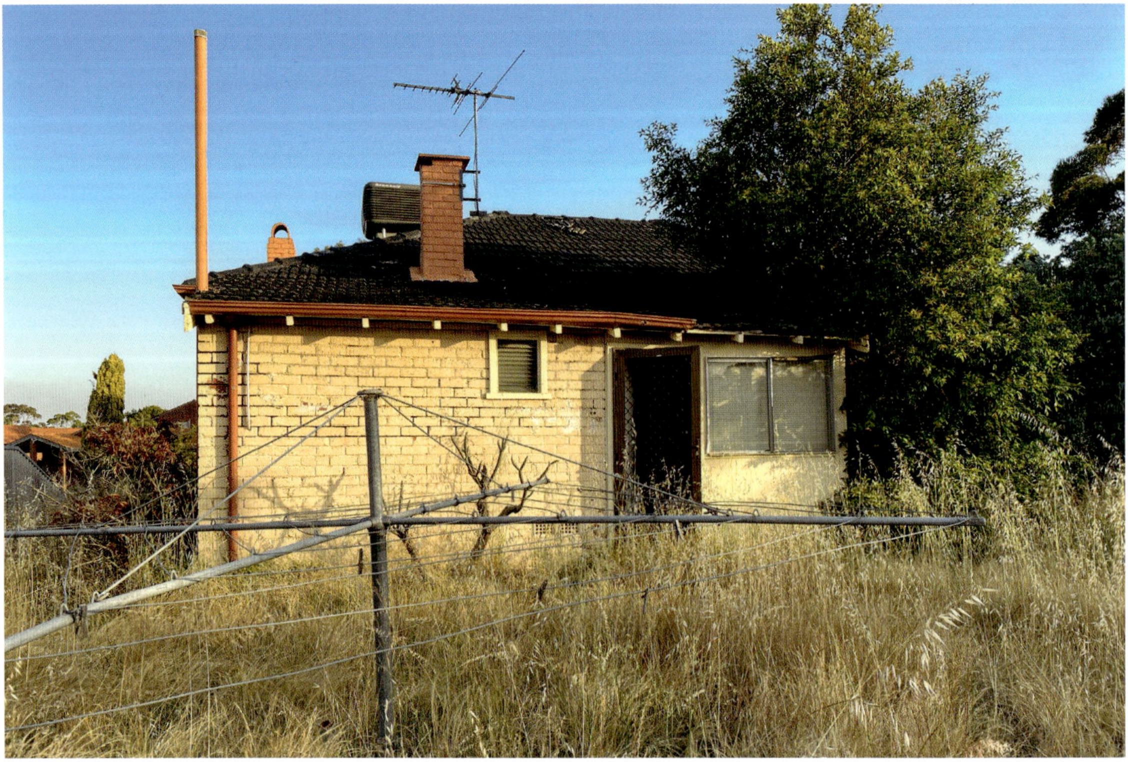

A view of the backyard with an old Hills Hoist that may have sank with time or purposefully been lowered for the elderly lady to reach.

FREMANTLE BEACH HOSTEL

I was fortunate enough to meet a young man in his mid-forties, wandering around a Fremantle carpark one sunny afternoon. It was clear he had lost his way in life, but at the same time, he turned out to be a local with the answers to my questions.

The Fremantle Beach Hostel, an interesting limestone and red-bricked building facing the Fremantle Port. Despite its unusual appearance, which tends to be common with Freo's unique architecture, it seemingly blends in well with its frontage.

Cutting the story short, the man was previously a lodger in the hostel before it closed down, and yes, he still had access to the building. The front gate was dummy locked with a thick chain, which he removed to let me in. The man of few words then headed back across the road, giving me the freedom to explore on my own.

I entered a strange world, which at times, resembled a scene from *Alice in Wonderland*. Stairs ran like a maze; two separate sets of stairs located in close proximity of each other led to two different locations, while other staircases nearby also ran in different directions, without ever once connecting.

It was rather difficult to confirm how many storeys this hostel actually was, but I believe it was three. Small concrete rooms faced the walkways, their single windows were either all boarded up or covered with a towel. Only the rooms facing the street enjoyed fresh air and natural light.

Very few rooms had any light fixtures, let alone power points. The rooms were already stifling hot. I imagined lodgers would have had to invest in good-quality batteries for torches and lamps. Candles would certainly be a cheaper option, at the cost of further heating up the rooms. Using a fan at the same time would only serve to blow out the flame. What a horrible place to live in, but on second thoughts, back in the olden days, they did not have power or cooling systems and they survived.

The pitch black of the night continued once lodgers stepped out on to the walkways, where there were no fixed lights on the landings or the stairs. In fact, there were no lights anywhere! No fire hydrants, smoke detectors, or emergency lighting, and the only exit out of the building were two steel gates that were padlocked at night.[1]

I later found a few renovated rooms that had a light fixture, as well as a smoke detector. Particularly with the stylish rendering of the internal walls and the luxury of furniture and seating, I suspected they were either communal rooms or reserved for the use of the owner.

There was only one toilet to service all the lodgers and it was located on the top floor. The downstairs one has been smashed to pieces.[2] I could imagine how stressful it would have been if someone urgently had to go. Even worse if it was occupied by someone giving birth, had the runs, or were in the process of extracting their nightly bender. With what appeared to have been minimal air circulation, if any at all, it serves no point to delve any further into detail.

A perimeter of scaffolding tubes surrounding the centre of the building either held up the roof or was once enabling renovations to take place. Old building materials, rubbish, furniture, and appliances filled the centre of it.

On 19 June 2015, the Fremantle council issued an emergency eviction notice to all lodgers on the grounds that 'the property is unsafe as it does not meet basic fire, safety and health requirements for the occupation of the buildings'.[3]

Lodgers were given four days to pack up and go. For some, all their worldly possessions were contained in their small concrete cells. Too much to carry, particularly if they did not have a car. The only assistance given to them by authorities was in the form of a piece of paper listing crisis accommodation centres in the area. Being winter at the time, it was unlikely there were any vacancies.

Much of the property was illegally built, and throughout the years, owner Jack Fazio had been prosecuted on a number of occasions. In fact, he was even listed on the Western Australian Attorney General's website as the second-biggest fine defaulter, owing a whopping $248,490.[4]

For many residents, despite the horrible state of the property and living conditions, they felt no choice but to live there.[5] At least they were safe with a roof over their head.

Interestingly, Mr Fazio's company Able Lott Holdings Pty Ltd, was appointed a liquidation status on 1 August 2013.[6] So regardless, this hostel was a ticking time bomb.

---

1. D. Bell, 'Evictions in Beach Street' (*Fremantle Herald Interactive*, 2015).
2. D. Bell, 'Freo moves on skid row' (*Fremantle Herald Interactive*, 2015).
3. *Ibid.*
4. *Ibid.*
5. *Ibid.*
6. ASIC. Notice of Meeting of Creditors (2016).

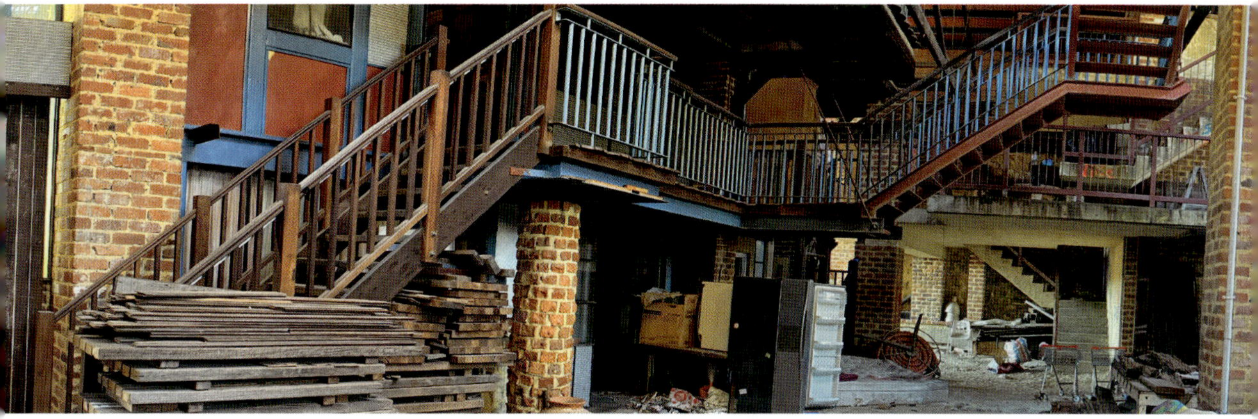

A panoramic view of the hostel's ground floor that was said to be just as full of rubbish as when the lodgers resided here.

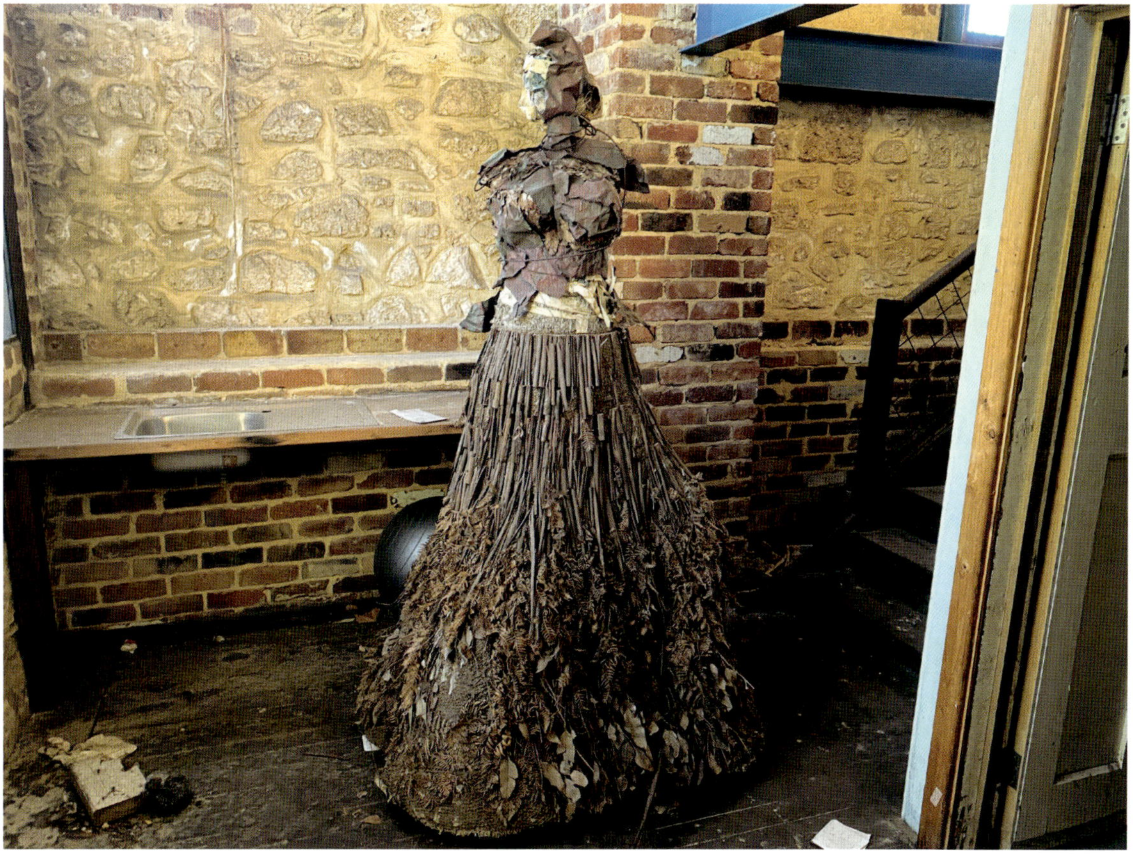

A statue of a lady made from a variety of natural resources. The day makes it an interesting piece, but at night your imagination flows with its dark silhouette hijacking your mind for the worst.

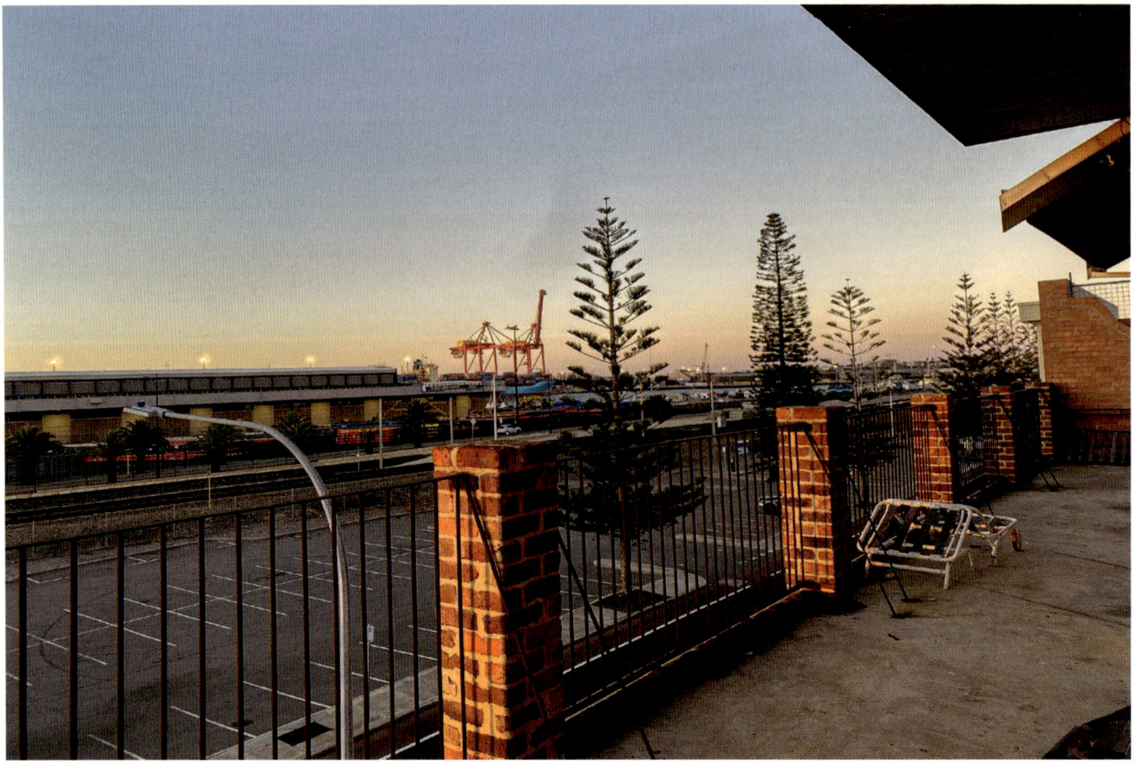

A picturesque view from the terrace overlooking the busy Fremantle port, as the sun begins to set. An impressive ZPMC quayside container crane can be seen on the other side of the port.

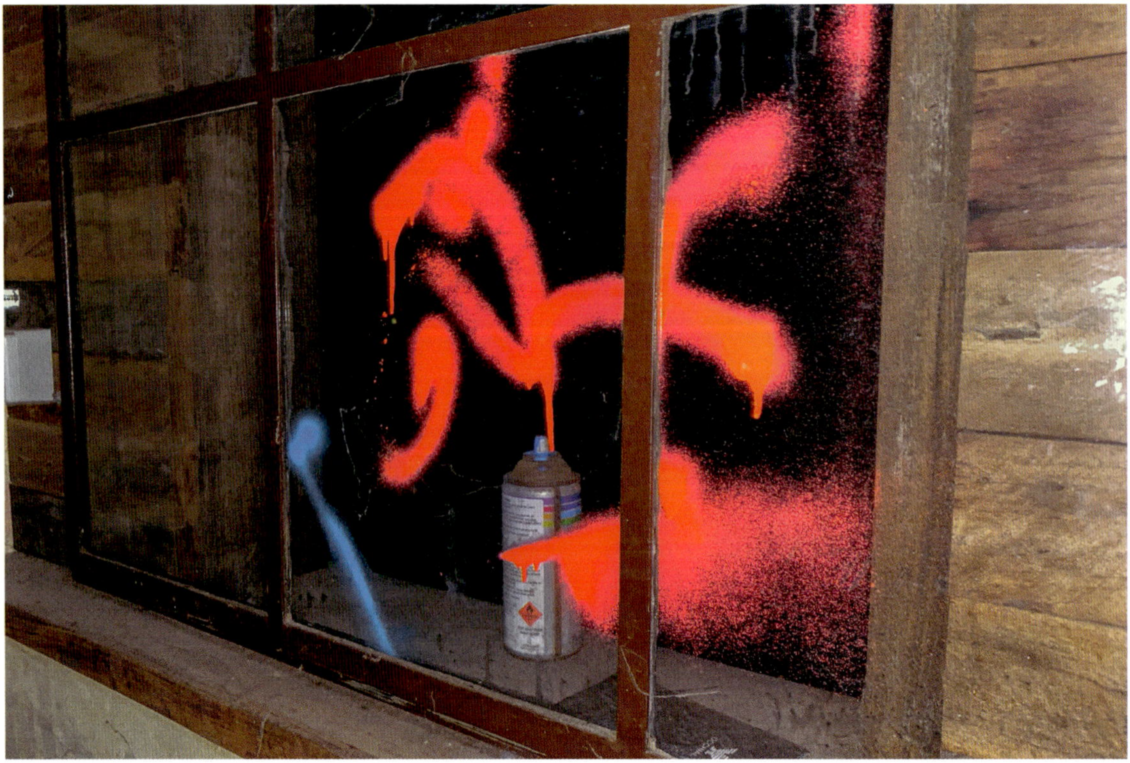

A can of blue spray paint sits on the windowsill of a small unit, overlooking the internal walkways of the hostel.

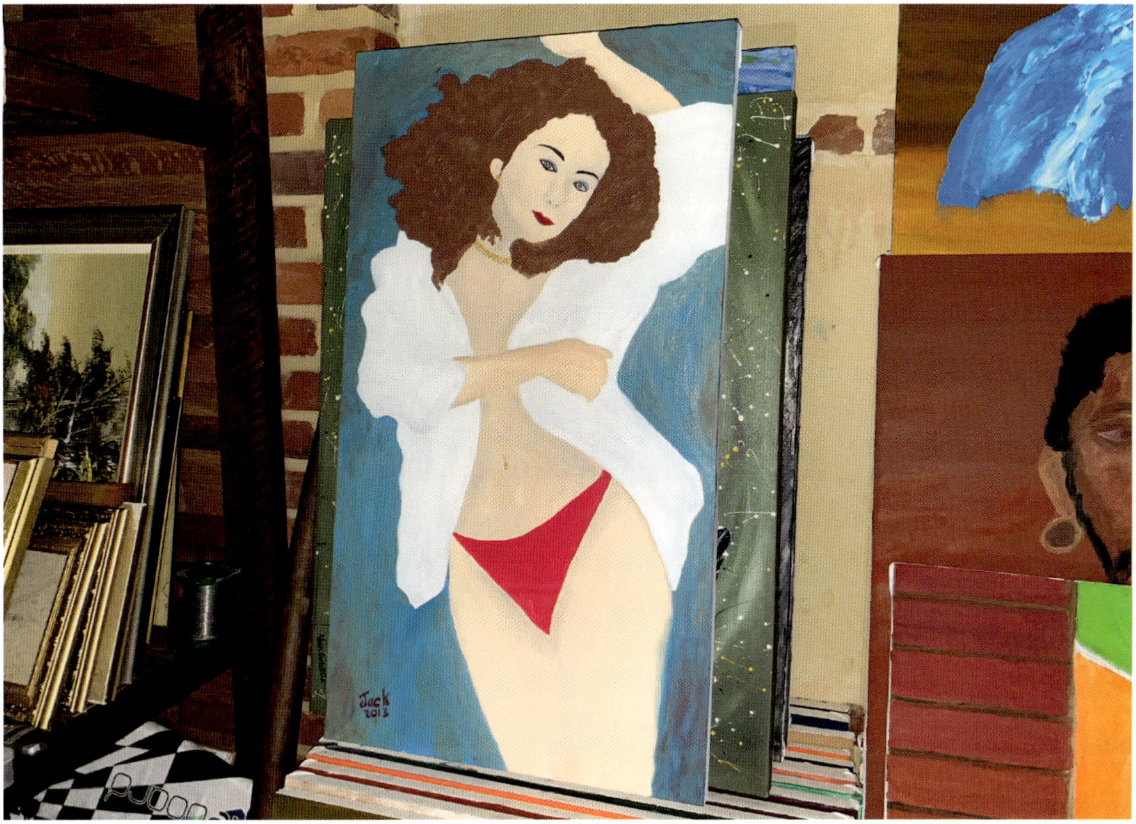

A small room is filled with artwork from the previous owner and most likely headed for landfill, once the new owners eventually come around to do something with the hostel.

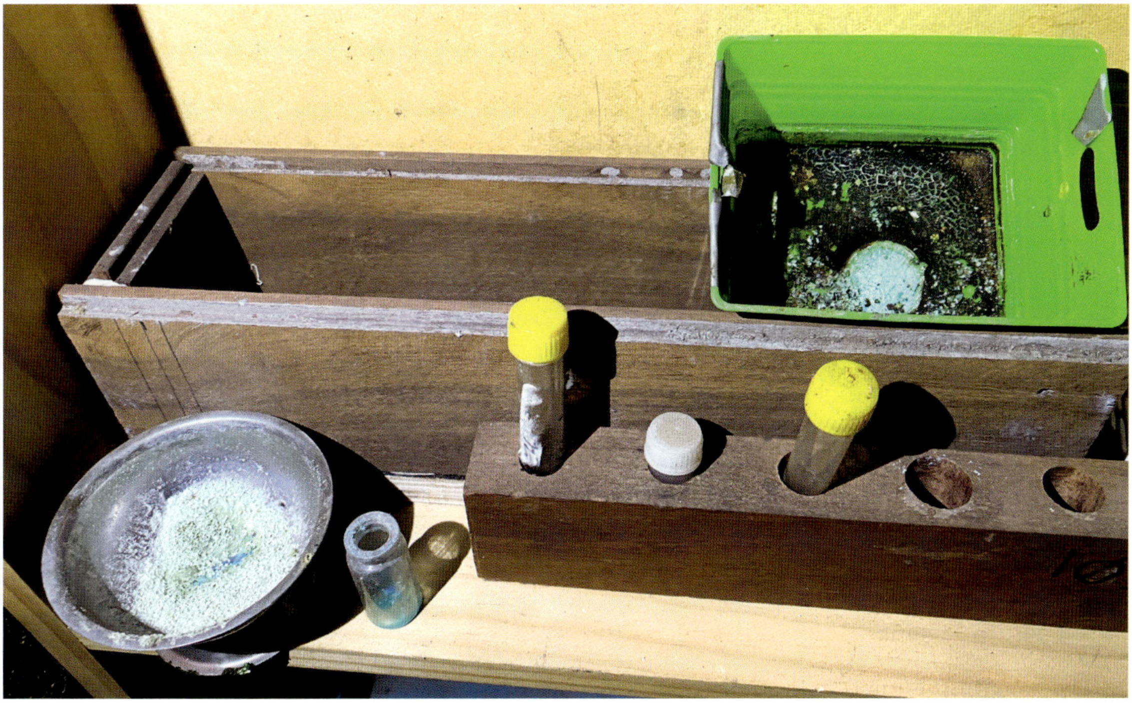

Implements said to have been used to manufacture methamphetamine.

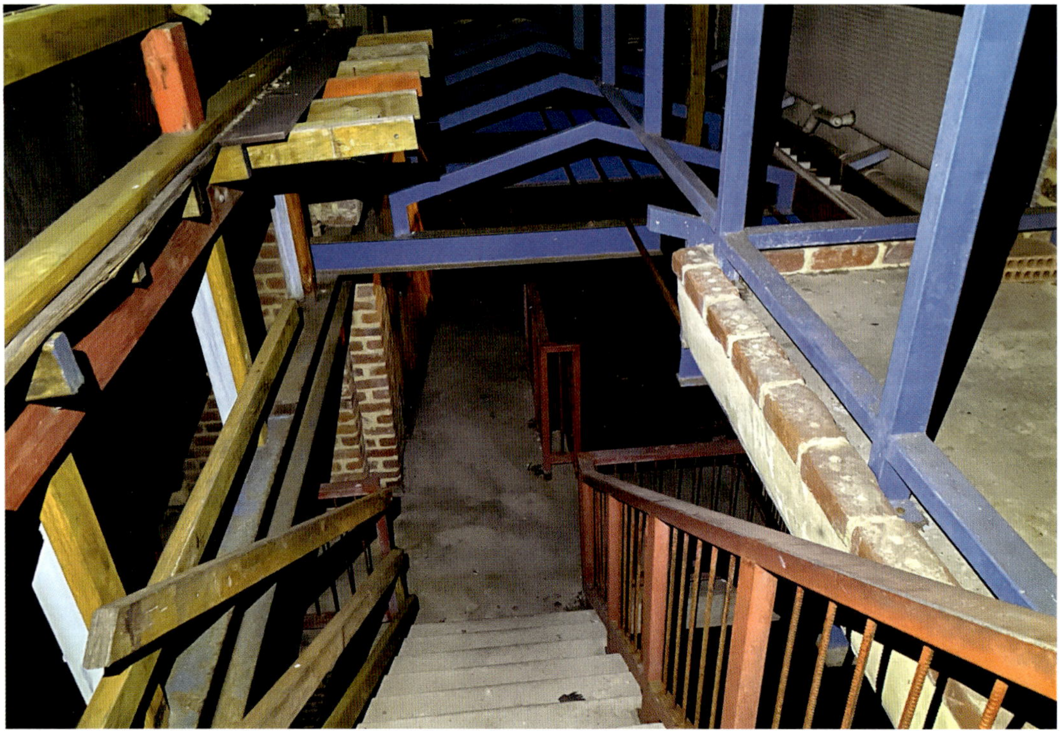

Stairs connecting the second floor to the third, while a number of other staircases on these floors take people to different areas of the hostel without ever connecting.

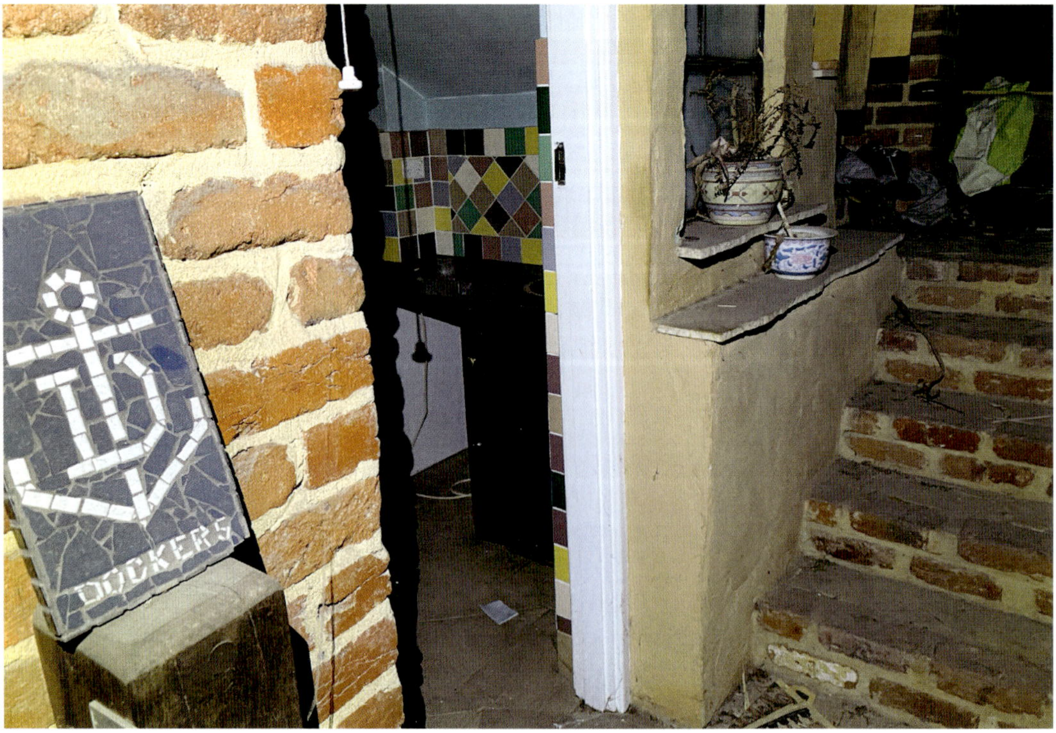

One of the very few rooms that are actually appealing, with multi-coloured tiles and wooden built-in furniture. A Dockers mosaic unfortunately tarnishes any aesthetic appreciation one could have for this scene, despite the football team claiming Fremantle as their territory.

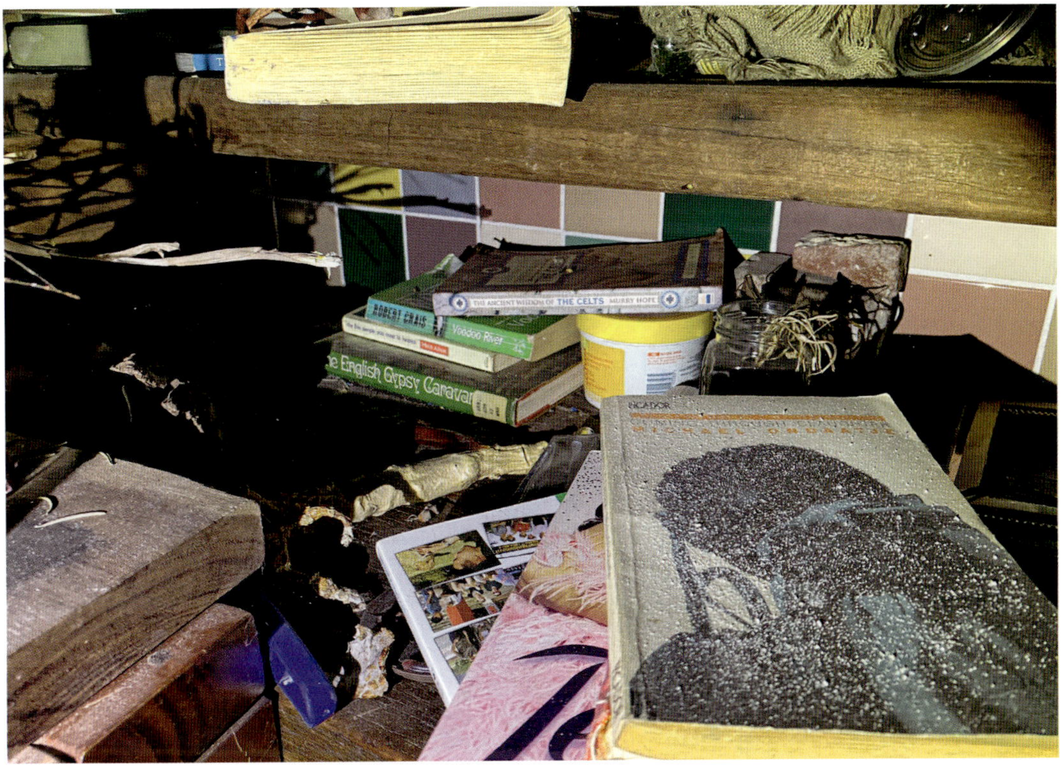

An interesting range of books await the return of its owner among bits and pieces of apparent witchcraft-related items.

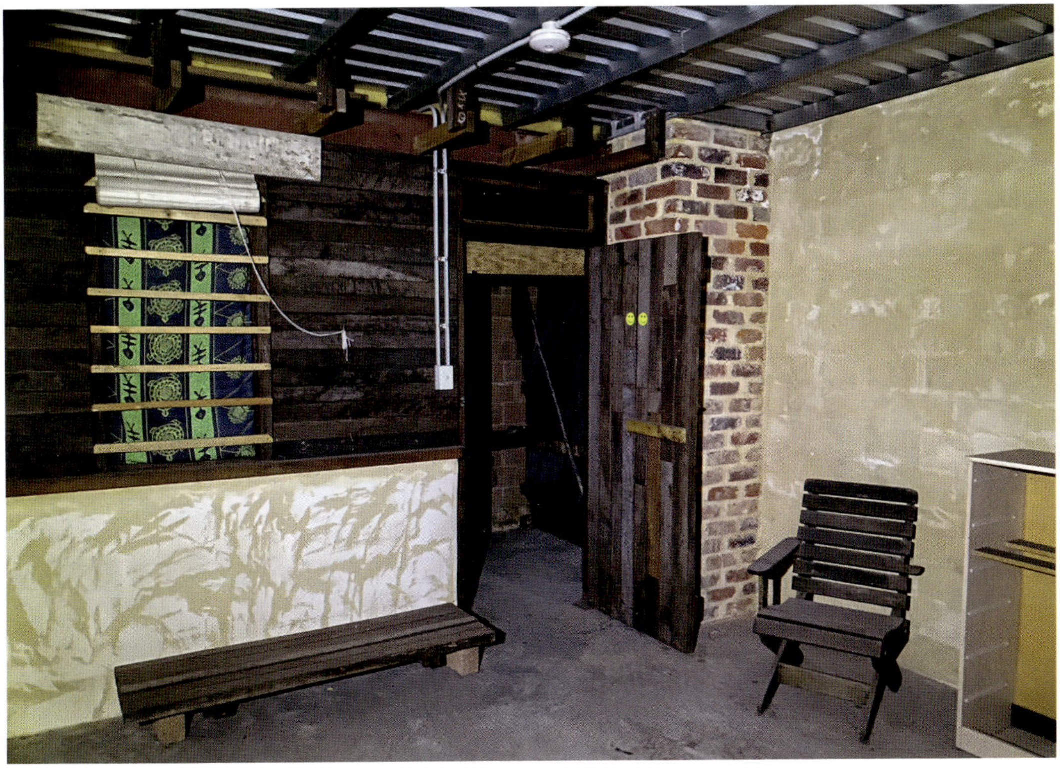

One of the nicer units, although this may have been a communal room. The only window here is covered by a towel. Privacy at the cost of air circulation, if that was even possible at all.

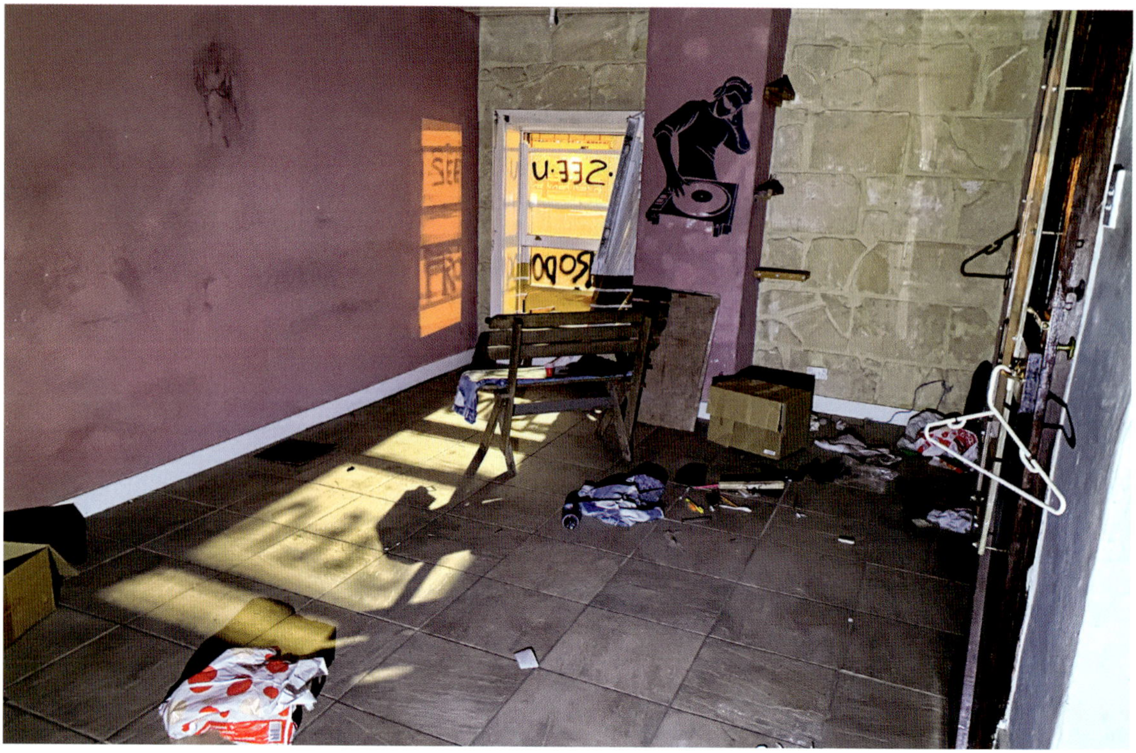

A stencil of a DJ gives the room a cool look, as streetlights shine bright through the small window. Facing the port, this is one of the very few units to enjoy a breeze.

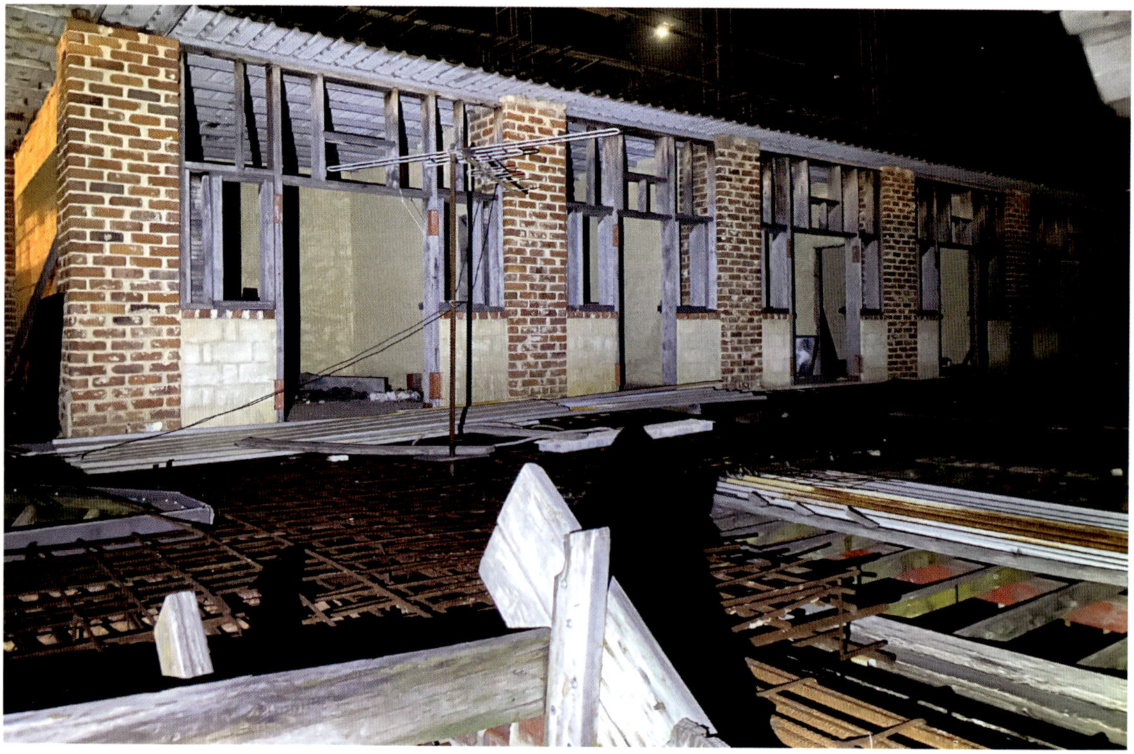

Unfinished single-room units line both sides of the top floor. Access to them could be considered on par with an obstacle course, although safeguards appear to be non-existent—just like many features and areas of this questionable hostel.

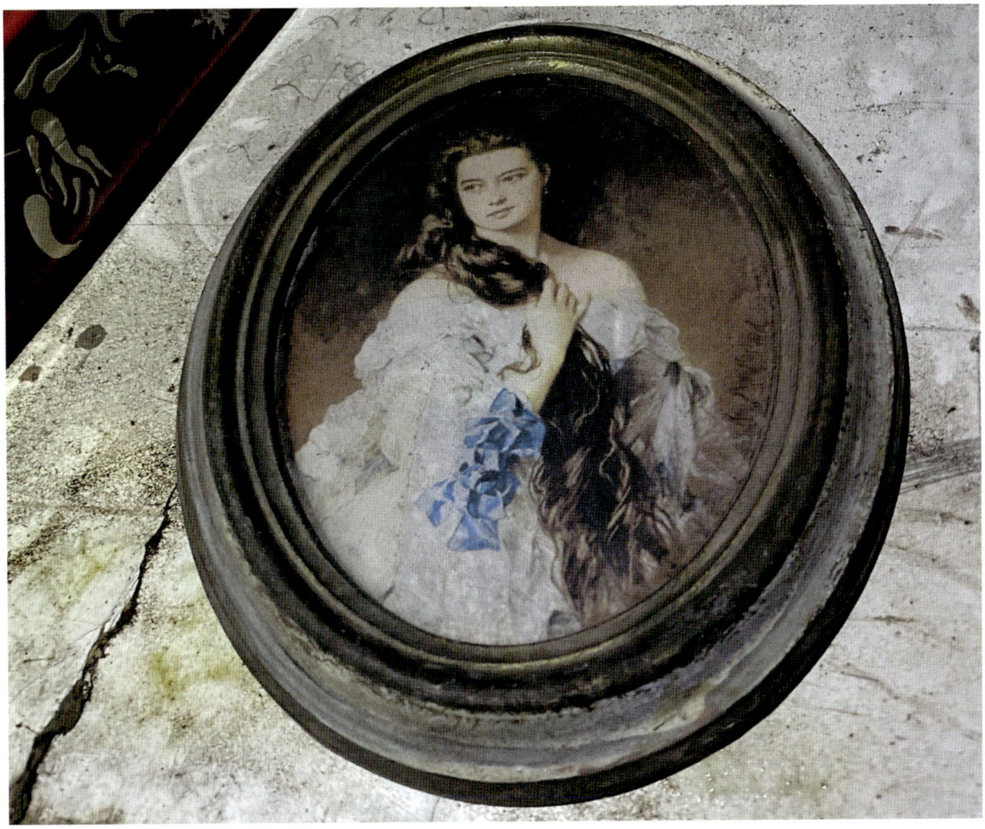

A beautiful image of a young lady from another lifetime. Perhaps the portrait depicts the mother of the previous owner.

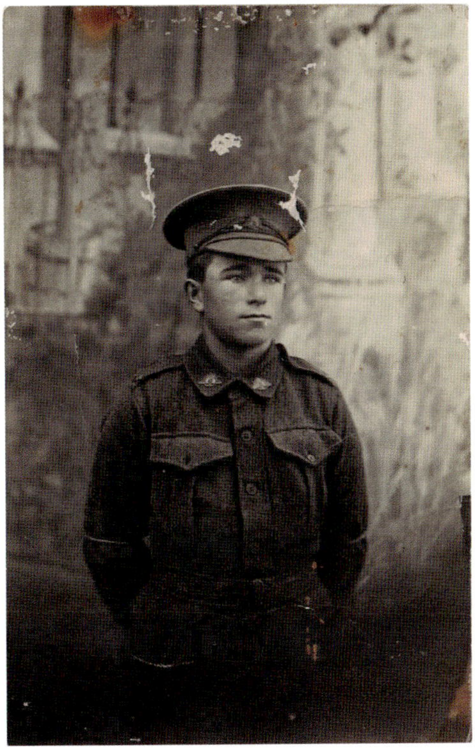

An undated photo of Eric Reynolds on the front of a Kodak postcard sent from the Blackboy Hill Training Camp. Another picture postcard found with this one bore the date of 1917.

HOSTEL MILLIGAN

Every day, thousands of people pass this old hostel in the city. Few would likely know anything about it, let alone notice it, judging from its rather bland appearance. Boarded-up windows, faded paint, and certainly nothing remarkable to see, this building stretches far back into the history of Perth.

Built from 1886 to 1930, it appears to have had a colourful history, judging from the few recorded anecdotes.[1] Originally known as Pearl Villa, it was built as a residence by pearler Joseph Clarkson, whose family were among the first few settlers in the Swan River colony.[2]

The hostel was added in 1930 and it is what we can see today, if we look up as we pass.

Lodgers were evicted in September 2019, to make way for a new $180 million mixed-use development.[3] The proposal encompasses a fifty-two-level residential tower, with 359 apartments and a thirty-seven-level hotel, containing 406 hotel rooms.[4] Seventeen months later, the site remains boarded up.

The first thing I noticed in the driveway of this property was the amount of rubbish that had accumulated over time. A big portion appeared to be possessions left behind, once all the lodgers had left. On closer inspection, I noticed some of the rubbish was more recent, judging from its condition, as well as the dates printed on the food packaging. It did not surprise me in the least it was a home to squatters and certainly a safe one at that. Particularly from authorities, judging from the access points.

Inside the hostel, the accumulation of furniture was extensive. Like the internal decor and architecture, much of it was borderline vintage, particularly items that were built into the structures. Everything felt old, and juxtaposing it with modern life certainly made me feel out of place.

It was another site that resembled my own private museum viewing that very few people in Perth would get to see had I not taken any photos to share. What an amazing privilege!

A few rooms were full of possessions, that had clearly been rummaged through, presumably by squatters.

An old meth lab was identified by one of my fellow explorers, who had previously studied clandestine drug labs. Another makeshift lab was later located in an abandoned shop, at the back of the property. It appeared to him that both had been destroyed by someone other than the authorities.

I imagined the rent to have been fairly cheap, considering its impressive views of the city, albeit limited to two storeys high. I tried to think back to when I was associated with the homeless community, in case I could recall any memory of this hostel. Strangely, nothing came to mind. The Alexandra Men's Hostel was located one street back and I was certainly familiar with that place, as it housed many of the homeless, criminals, and parolees I saw on a regular basis. Hostel Milligan certainly had the same feel to it, one that gave me the strong impression it was not exactly a desirable place to reside or feel safe in.

With the amount of clothing hanging on a makeshift clothesline, as well as a collection of potentially stolen bicycles and empty handbags on a rear pathway, we decided to make this explore a brief one. Just in case the squatters suddenly decided to come home.

A fire guttered the hostel in March 2021, although I have not been able to ascertain the extent of the damage in any of the published media articles. A few people were seen leaving the building and a woman was arrested, but it appears that no charges have been laid.

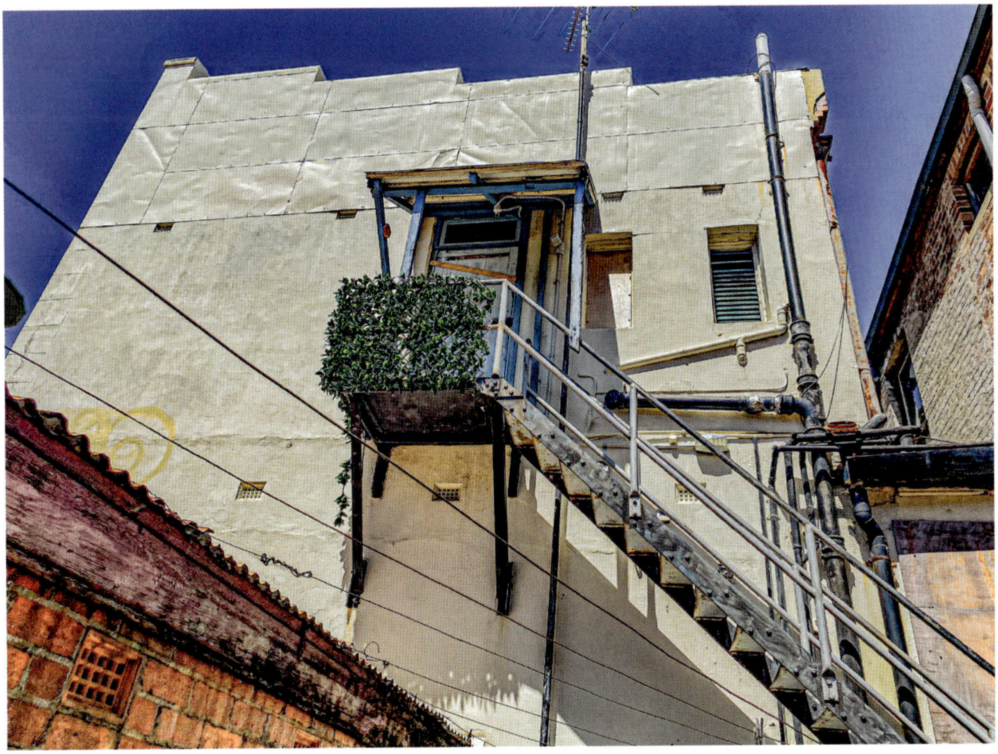

A building connected to Hostel Milligan that appears well-kept and in good condition.

---

1. Heritage Council, Hostel Milligan, Perth. Government of Western Australia (2013).
2. S. Grant & D. Bell, 'Hidden Gem' (*The Perth Voice Interactive*, 2019).
3. D. Bell, '91 and left to sleep in a shed' (*The Perth Voice Interactive*, 2019).
4. B. Lake, 'Fragrance Group propose their second Perth City development', *Off The Plan*, 2016.

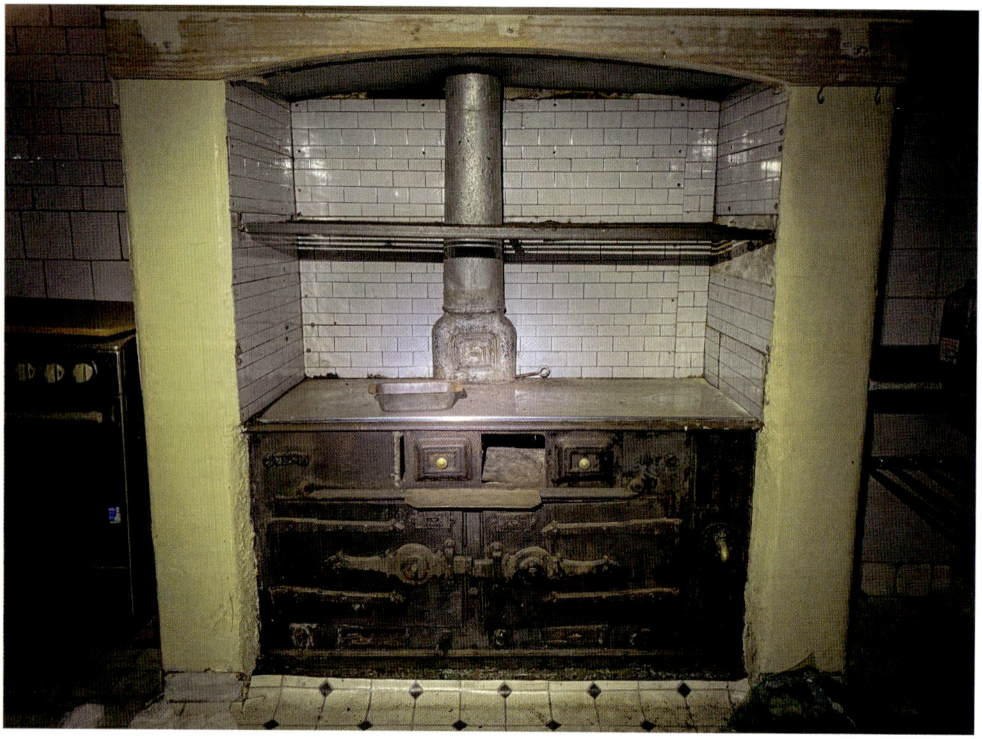

A Metters No. 5 antique cast-iron stove that may be dated from as far back as 1901. Perhaps the developers will restore and keep it to compliment the aesthetic feel of the place when they come to build their grand hotel on top of this heritage-listed site.

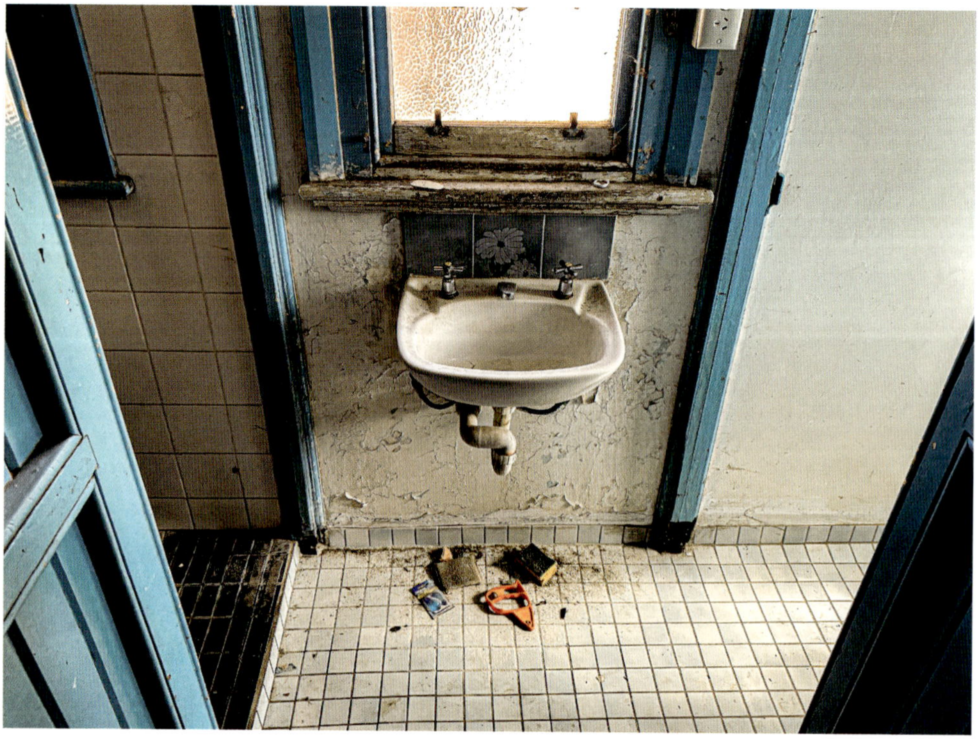

A simple basin in one of the shower rooms, used by thousands over the course of its long history.

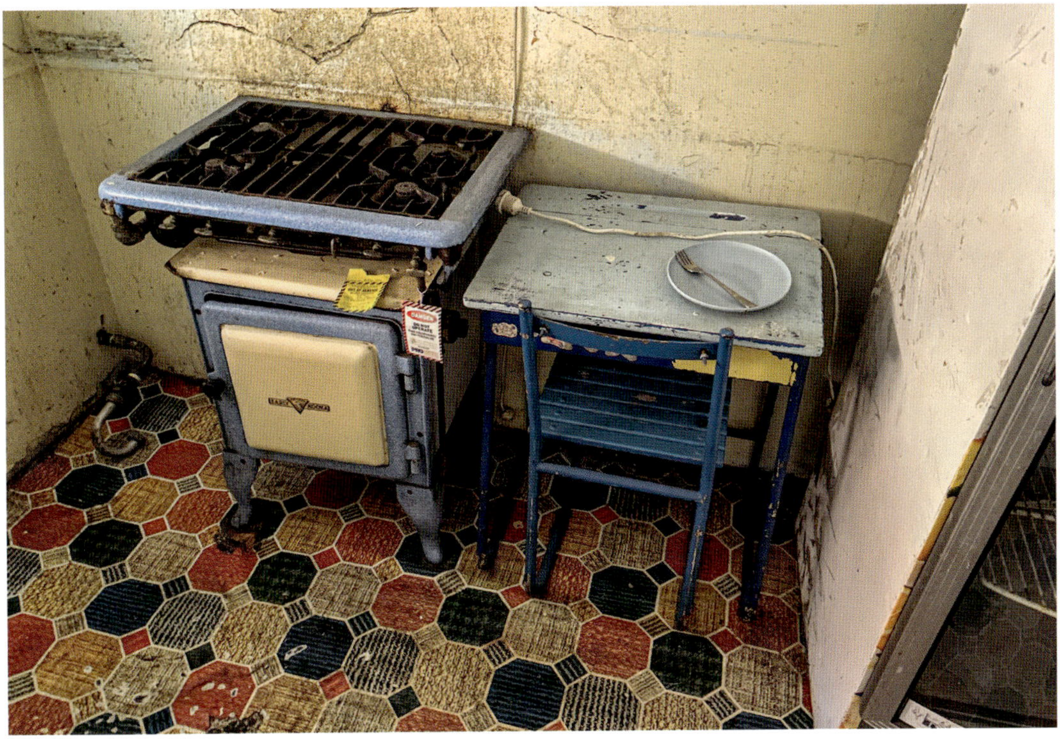

Going back in time with colours and designs that would surely make anyone smile. An old school desk still bearing stickers children would plaster on to personalise. A Metters Early Kooka No. 12 stove, possibly dating as far back as 1939, sits beside it.

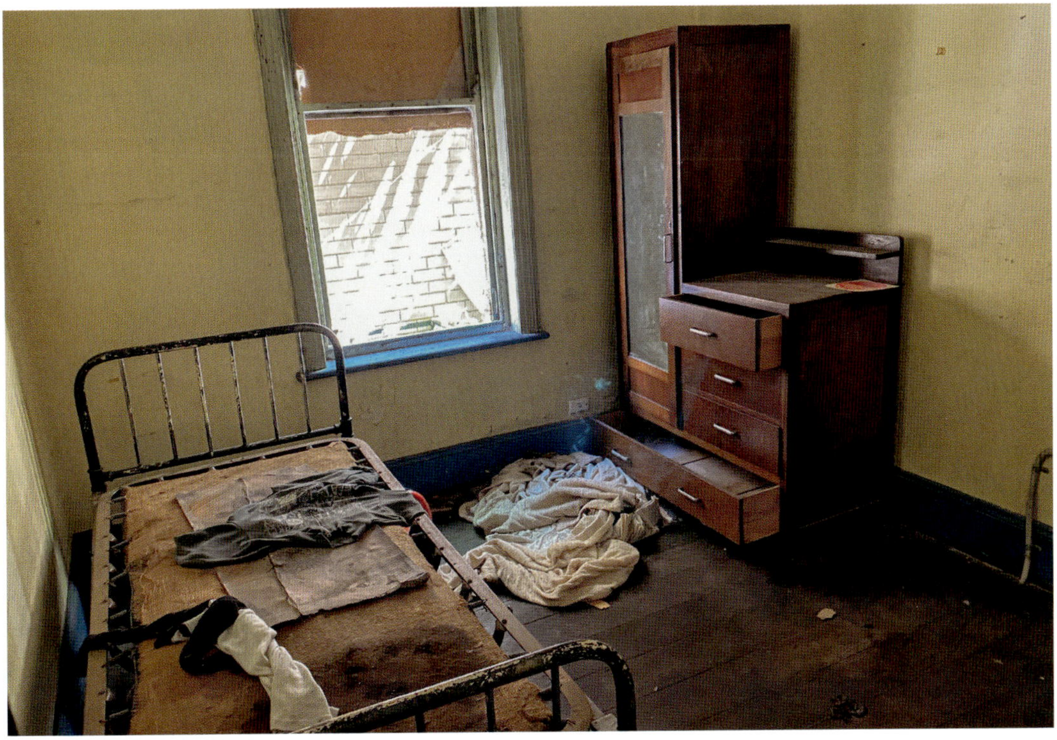

This simple room with a lovely view of a white-brick wall would have been nice enough to enjoy away from the chaotic city life outside the front door.

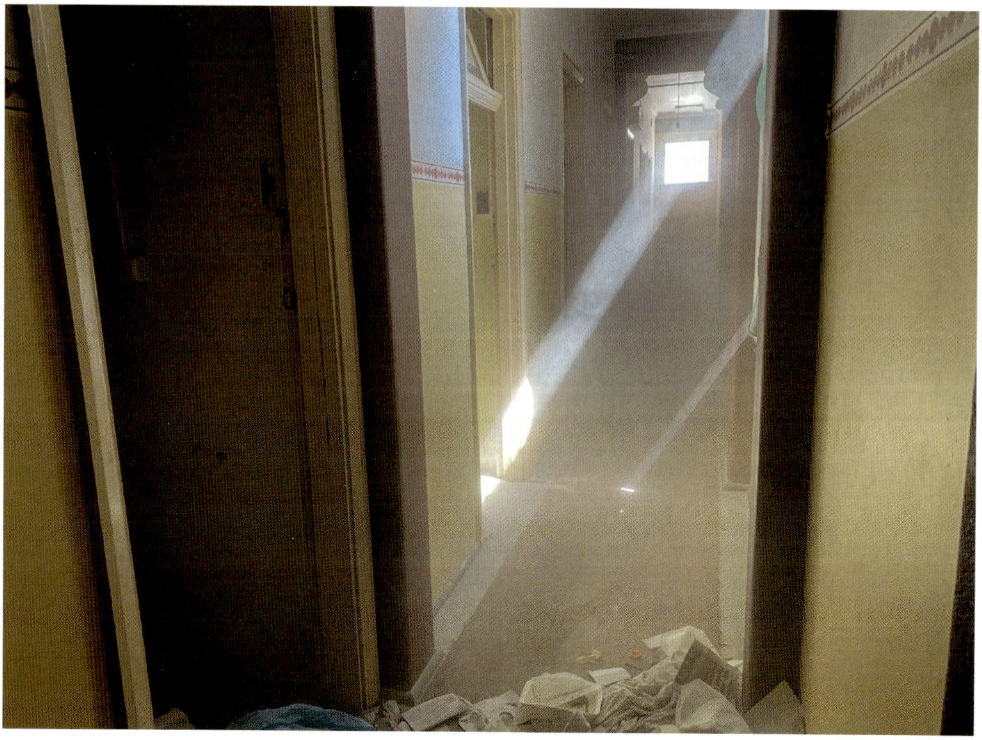

Thick dust fills the corridor with beams of light shining through holes in the wall, like a spotlight on something rather unspectacular. Piles of collected rubbish litter the walkway every 5 or so metres.

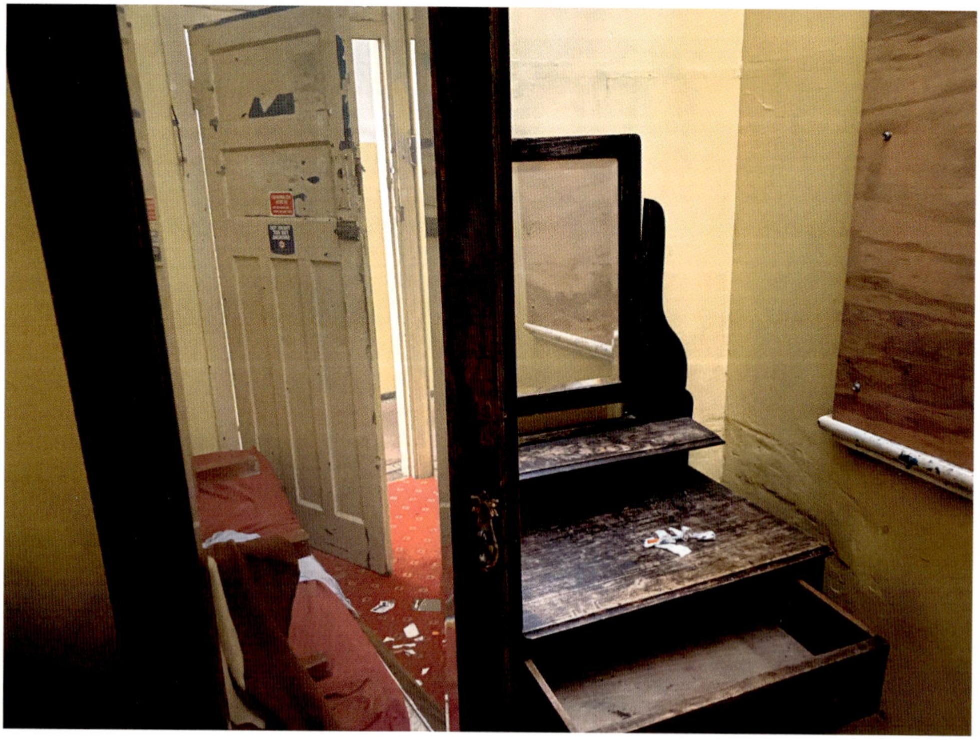

A mirror reflecting the door gives an idea how big the room is for someone whose worldly possessions were most likely stored here. A used syringe on the dresser, one of the many in this questionable place which, since its closure, has attracted a raft of drug cooks and users.

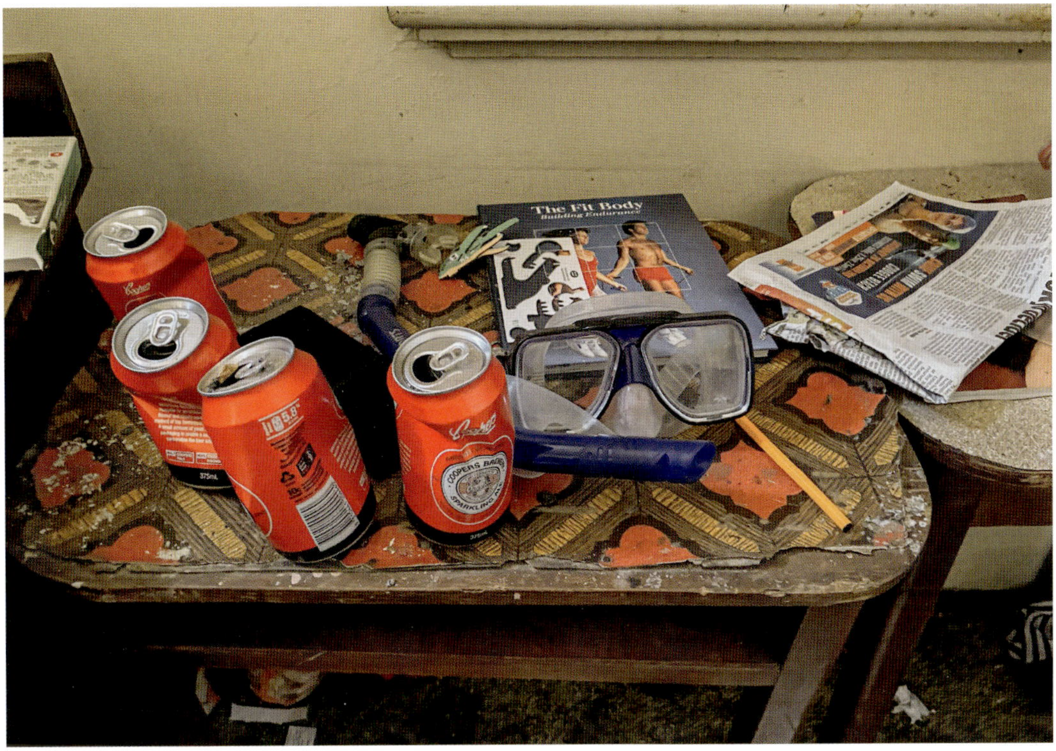

A somewhat contradictory image: empty beer cans sit on a table besides a book titled *The Fit Body* with a snorkel set next to it.

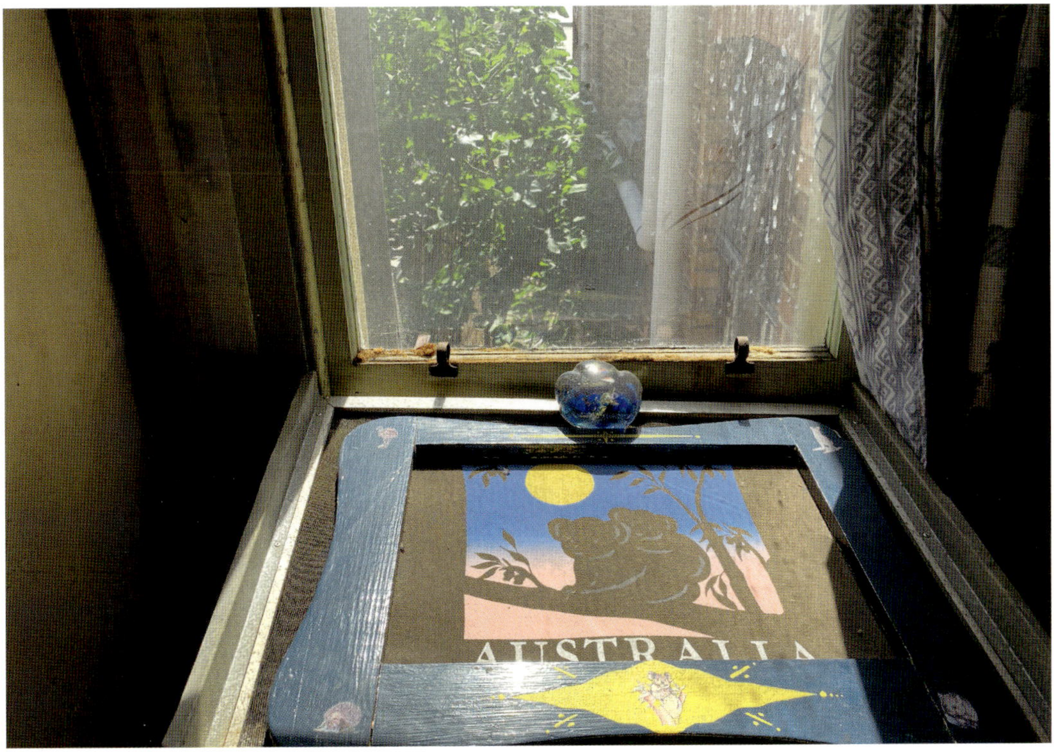

A view that could have been taken from a wildlife sanctuary. A photo frame depicting koalas sitting on a tree branch, which could simply represent a plaque of what you should be able to see outside the window.

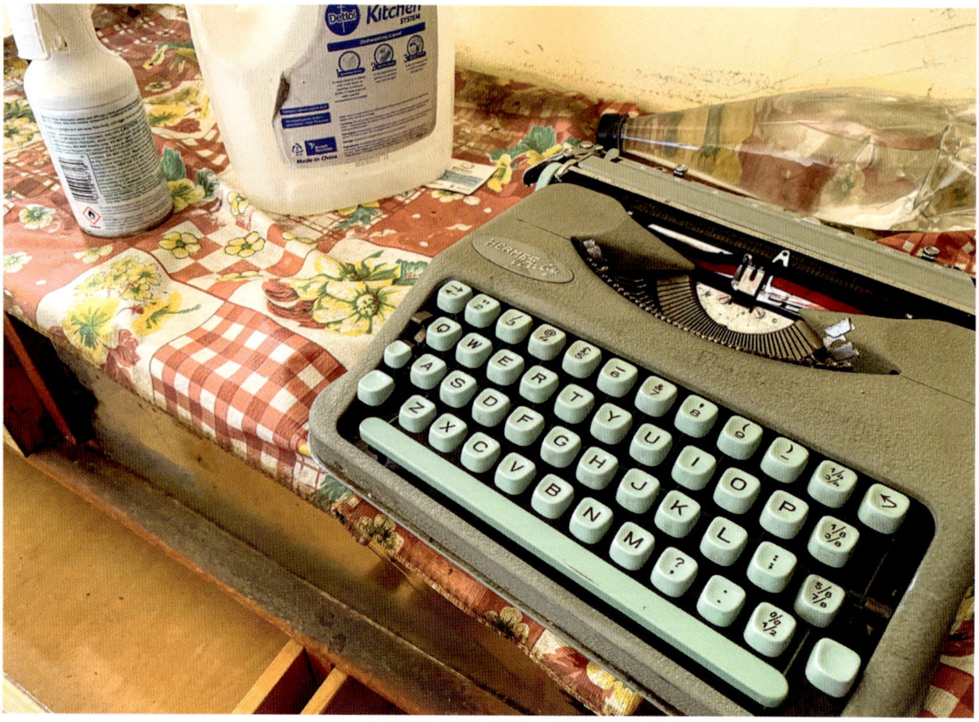

A Hermes 3000 portable typewriter that was produced between 1958 and 1966 lies forgotten on a bedroom table. Particularly as it appears in good condition, it may one day be used again to record the words that spill from someone's creativity. Or perhaps their seriousness.

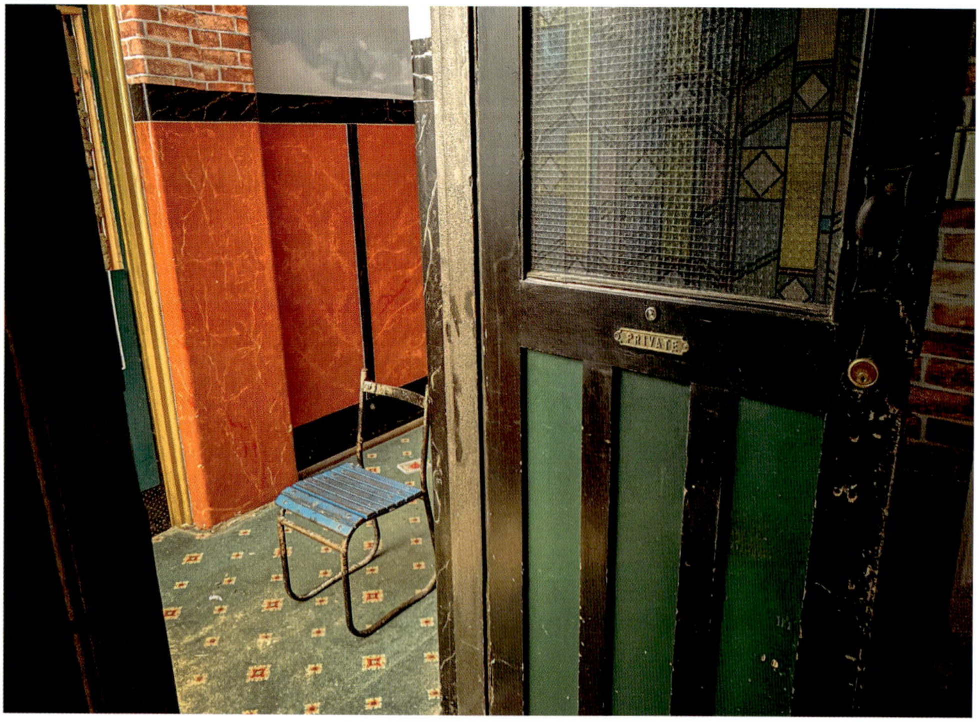

A contrast of vintage colours that appear potentially as strong as the day they were painted, unlike today's rather conservative pale colours that seemingly need a coat of love every seven or so years. The door alone is quite fascinating, with the intricately designed window and plate of privacy.

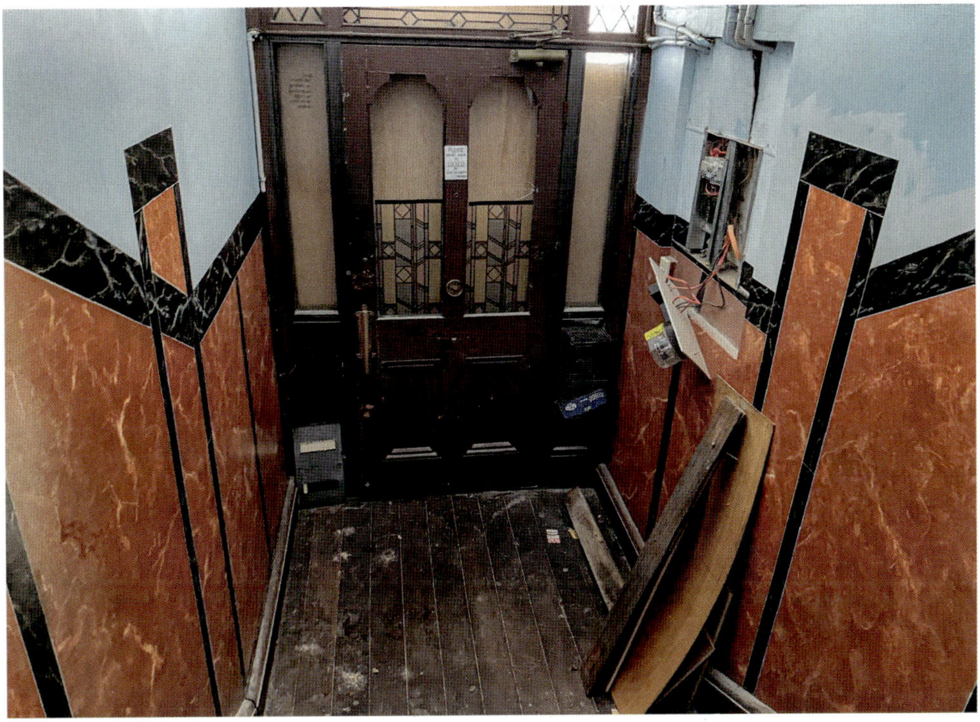

A front door that looks like it ought to belong in an old-fashioned pub. Thousands would have walked in and out of this exit over many generations, sporting different styles of clothing with a wide range of life experiences, since it first opened as the Pearl Villa around 1886.

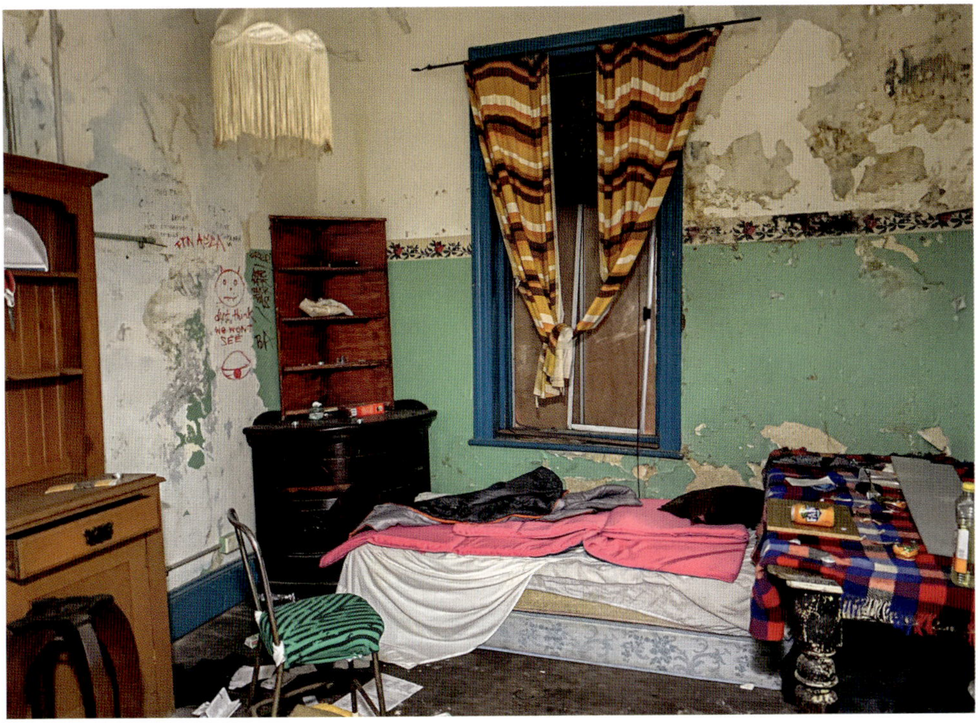

Had the colours, patterns, textures, and contrasts in this photo been legitimate, rather than shades of mould, graffiti, and potentially unhygienic matter, it just might have made one of the substandard home fashion magazines—if they even exist at all!

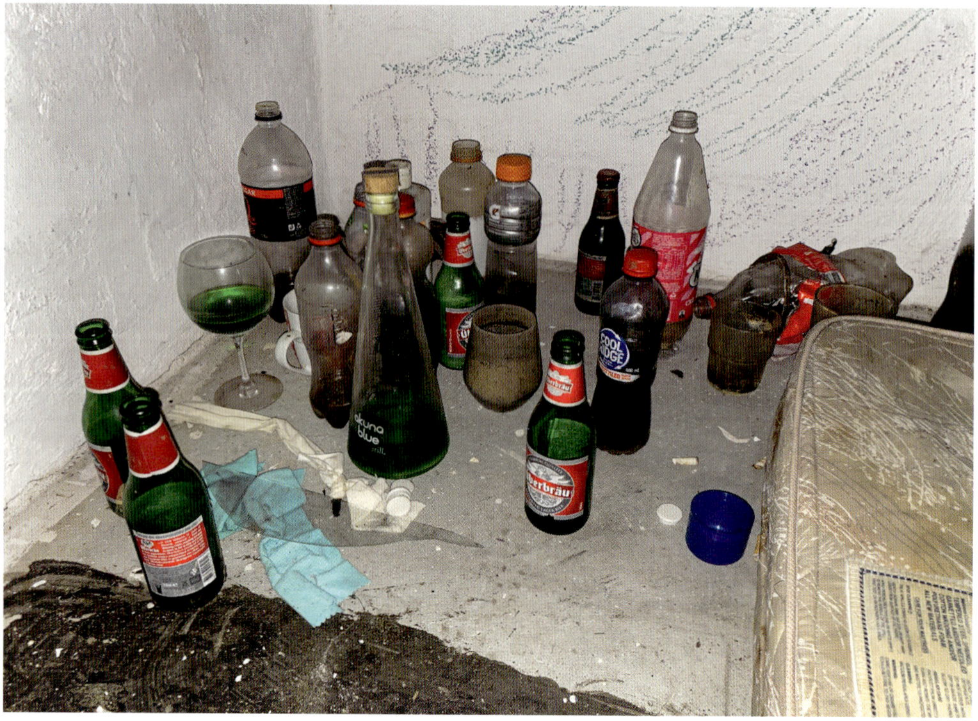

A range of plastic and glass vessels looking quite suspect with its brown and green liquids—with or without their said involvement in making brain-killing, life-distilling stimulants.

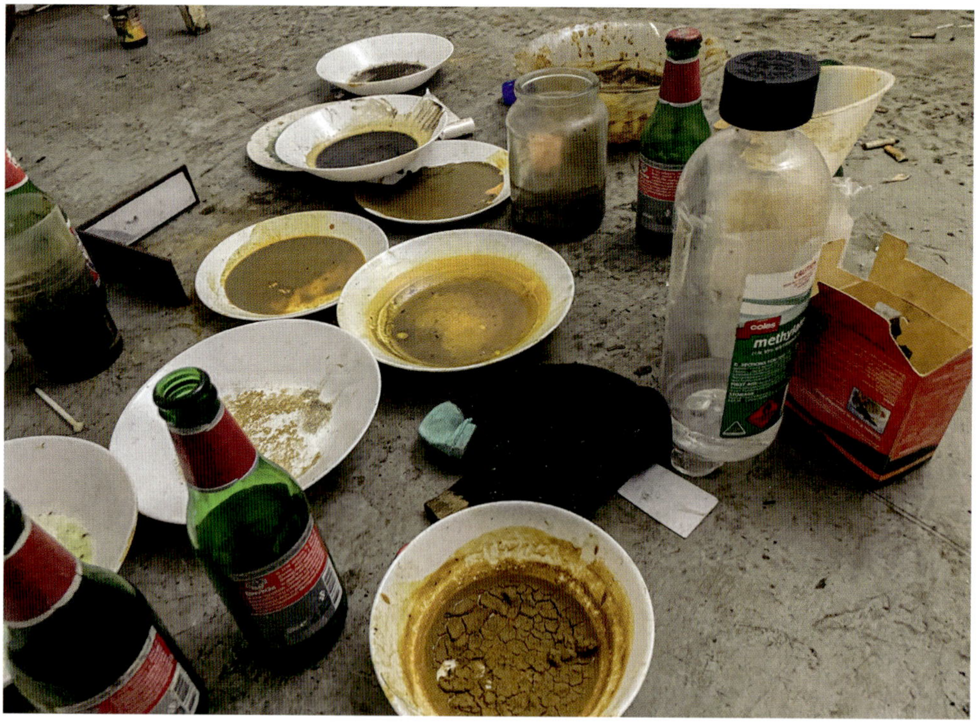

The same was said about this image, but it could honestly be something more innocent. People use mud on their faces for a range of health benefits. Perhaps babies know better than us and eat mud for some unknown nutritional benefits. Perhaps methylated spirits is being used *in lieu* of dishwashing liquid and someone was just enjoying a beer or two.

KWINANA BULK JETTY

The old jetty once owned by BHP, continues to lie derelict as it rots away. Home to scavenging seagulls and pooping pigeons, it is a popular hangout for locals, as well as an attraction for both fishers and scuba divers.

This may very well be the hardest location I have ever attempted to research. Finding information on this jetty would presumably be as easy as extracting potassium nitrate from guano (pigeon poop).

Also known as BHP Jetty Number 1 and the Bulk Jetty Dive Site, it became disused in the 1980s. That is all the information I can find.

To get to the jetty is an interesting feat. Some wise guy decided to cut out a portion of the jetty to terminate access to it (which certainly makes sense, when considering the potential dangers associated with the jetty). Some even wiser guy (or girl) installed two ropes to make it accessible. The crossing sounds rather simple, but I would certainly recommend anyone who ever decides to cross it to either work on your arm strength or pack some high energy supplements. While I have always had good arm strength from my long term BMX (bike) passion, I certainly have a long way to go before I can start doing any productive achievements with my strength.

Facing either side of the jetty, you have to slide or walk your feet along the bottom rope and guide your hands doing the same on the one above your head. I have to laugh at how easy that sounds until I recall the pain of my blood-drained arms and the beat of my heart almost deafening the silence in my head.

A word of caution, it is important to note that fun-sized people may have a predicament in reaching the top rope. Judging from the height requirements some theme parks stipulate for rides, this potential disappointment should not be taken to heart by such height-challenged people, who would presumably be accustomed to such disadvantages.

It was certainly a relief to have completed the crossing, as I tend to self-doubt most things I do in life, particularly if it is something new. Human nature no doubt, but I am not a fan of heights, the water, or sharks for a start.

Before I knew it, I had my feet firmly on the ground. A fairly dangerous substitute at this stage being the jetty, but nevertheless, safer than the rope.

Putting it simply, the jetty was dead-set munted. With gaping big holes between planks that were big enough for a shark to jump up and grab your leg—one slip and you were gone! Realistically, if you removed any thought (or physical presence) of sharks, stingrays, jellyfish, dumped deadly objects under the surface of the water, rips, and your inability of being able to swim (if that is the case), it was just a 2-metre drop into the water and a short (doggy paddle) swim to the shore.

The jetty was equipped with two observation towers. The first one trembled like a child, rust eating at the core of its stability. My mate Jake and I decided to give it a miss, which was fairly disappointing, as we like to face our fear of heights and we assumed the second one further up was in the same boat.

The wind was fairly strong, which always seems to come hand in hand with the seaside. Jake's drone struggled against the gale. It was likely to decapitate us or someone with its sharp blades had we kept on trying to fly it.

A few young fishers were chilling in a concrete pipe at the end of the jetty. The type you find in a child's playground, when you want to hide from the teacher. They were having a smoke, which was fairly brave of them if they wanted to risk not having a straight judgment navigating themselves off the dodgy jetty's surface. I was having trouble myself navigating myself away from the end of the jetty, without almost tripping over their haphazardly placed fishing rods, and I was not even a stoner!

Thankfully, the second tower was in a more suitable condition to climb, although we both had to plug in some high-energy motivating beats into our ears to garner any confidence. I sent Jake up first, in case the tower happened to topple over into the water. He made it up and just as quickly, came back down. Then it was my turn. I examined the nuts and bolts and rusted whatevers fastening what I was about to stake my life on, but my imagination was obviously running rife. The chances of anything happening to it or me would surely be slimmer than myself.

The view at the top was amazing, the water was rough as chops and the wind was packing a gale. I was sure the tower permanently moved at least a degree while I was up there, but I made it down, so I did not bother to overthink it.

After conquering our fears, we decided to head back to shore. Jake walked off ahead of me to answer a phone call and I certainly kept my distance, as I filmed him being attacked by a ruffled seagull. Perhaps her nest egg was stashed nearby. I had a good laugh but Jake was clearly far from impressed, as he tried to hide under his bucket hat. My time came to pass the territorial seagull's turf and we switched roles. Thankfully Jake was still on the phone and not in a position to film me being attacked, although he enjoyed a good laugh.

I can safely say I had the last laugh in the end. I took a few photos of him crossing the rope back and happened to Photoshop in a massive shark in the water, right behind him. It sickened him to think how close he could have been to facing an attack had he fallen into the water or if the shark had jumped up the 2 metres to grab him. It was a few months later before I told him the truth.

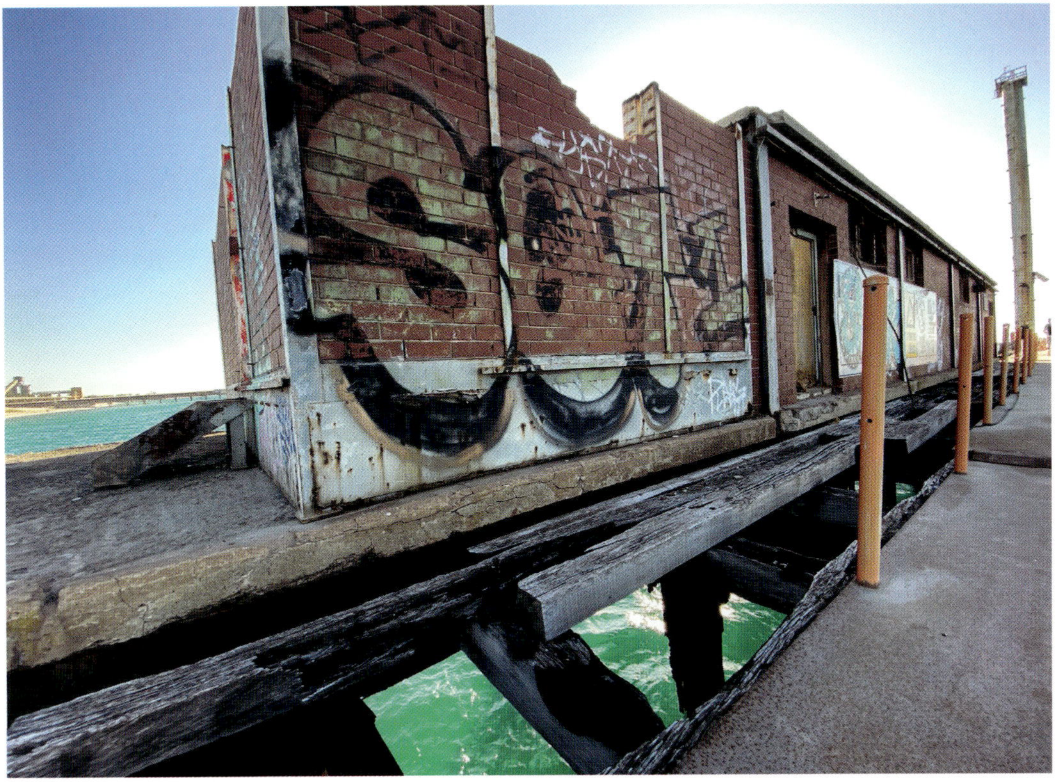

Derelict remains of a building on the BHP Jetty Number 1, also known as the Bulk Jetty Dive Site, is covered with graffiti.

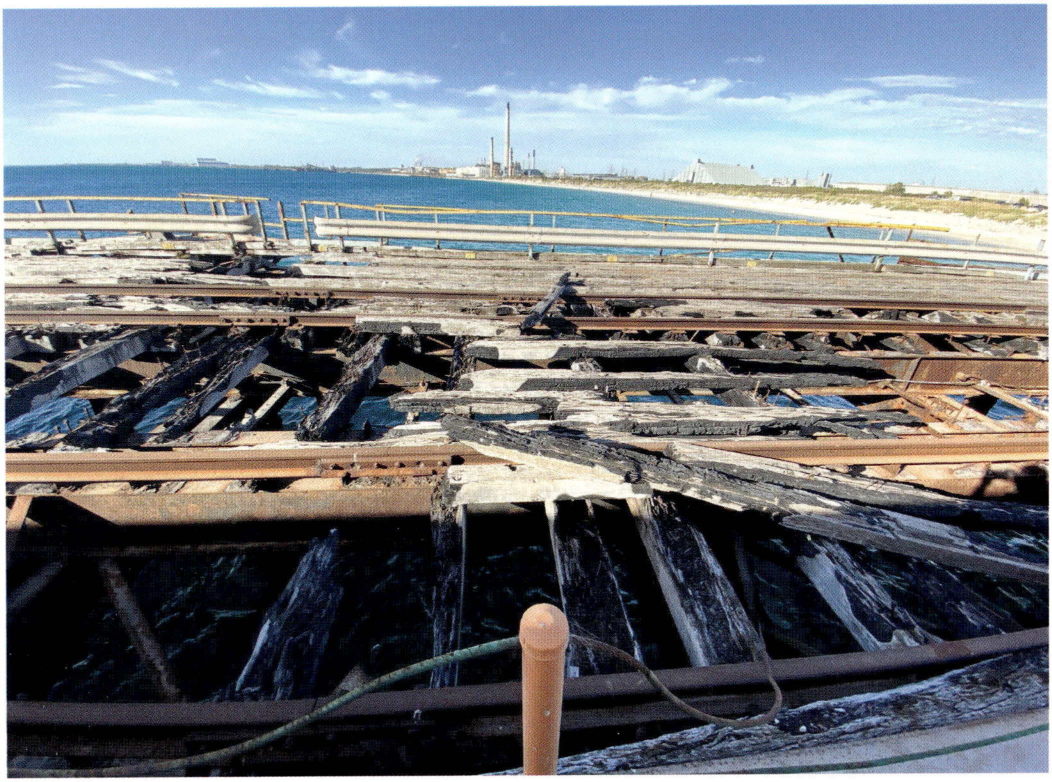

The metal beams hold the jetty's structure together, as pieces of timber continue to erode or somehow become torched.

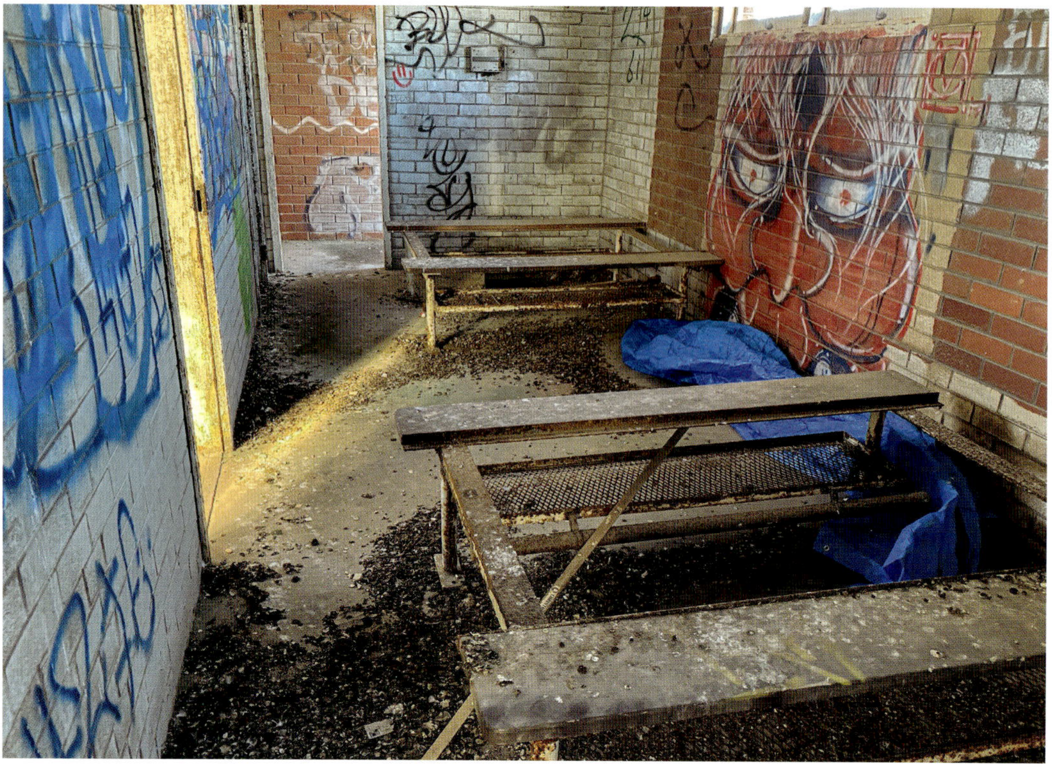

A red devil finds a home on the internal walls of the building, artwork that becomes increasingly familiar the more you visit abandoned locations in Perth.

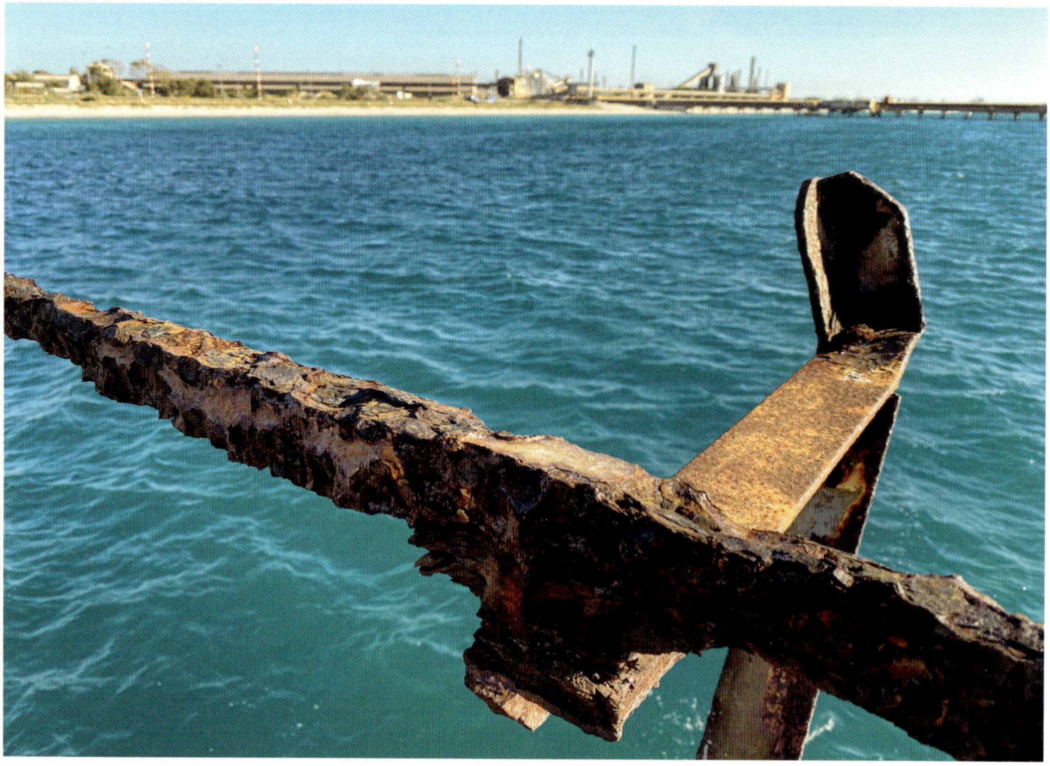

Erosion on a metal barrier looking more like a wafer biscuit but instead, comprising of fingernails or some similar texture.

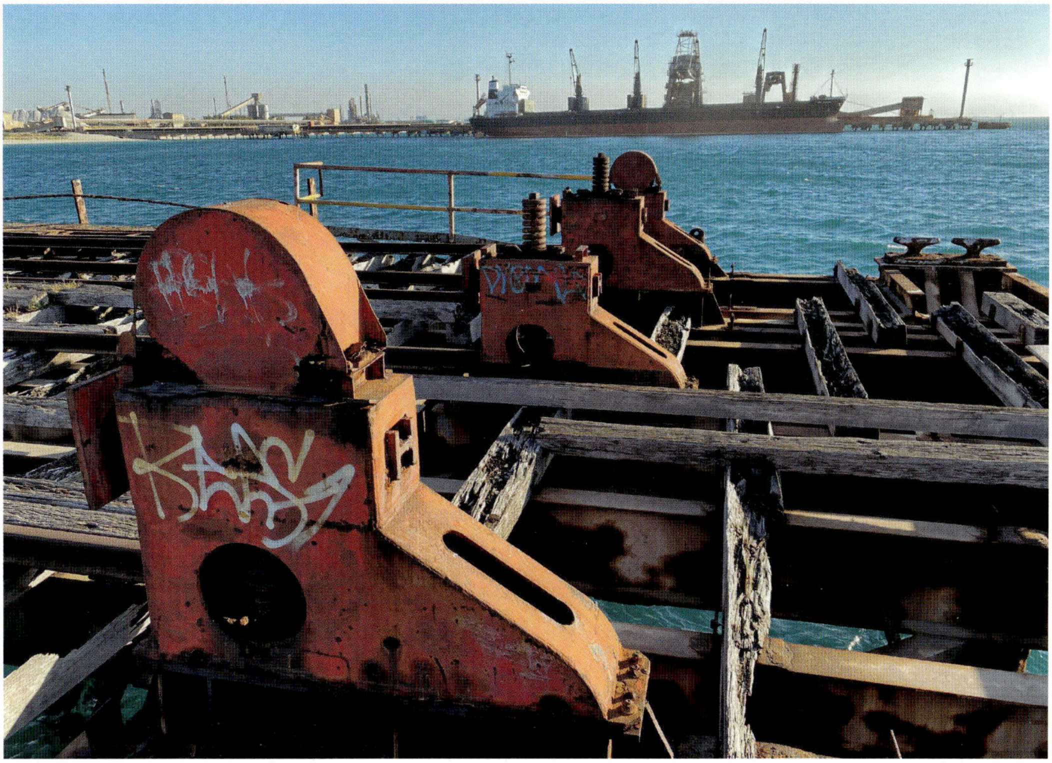

The remains of marine loading arms from back in the day when the jetty was active.

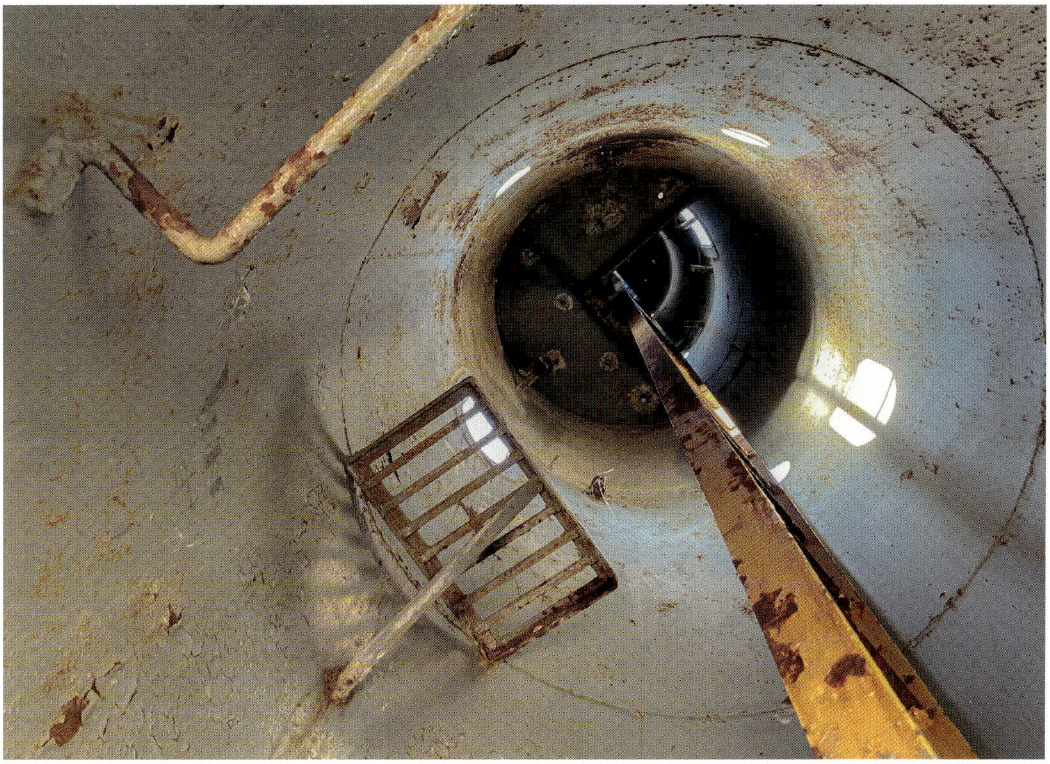

Inside one of the towers showing the ladder that leads to the top, where a viewing platform gives you amazing 360-degree views.

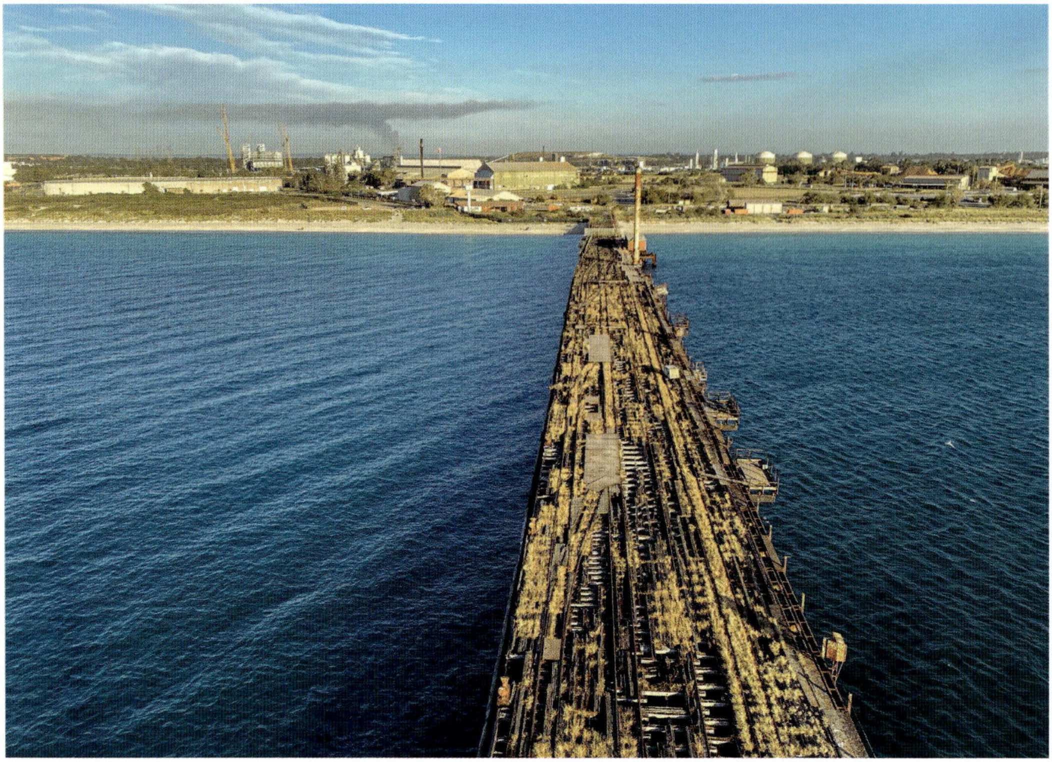

View from the tower platform looking out on to Kwinana Beach and the industrial area.

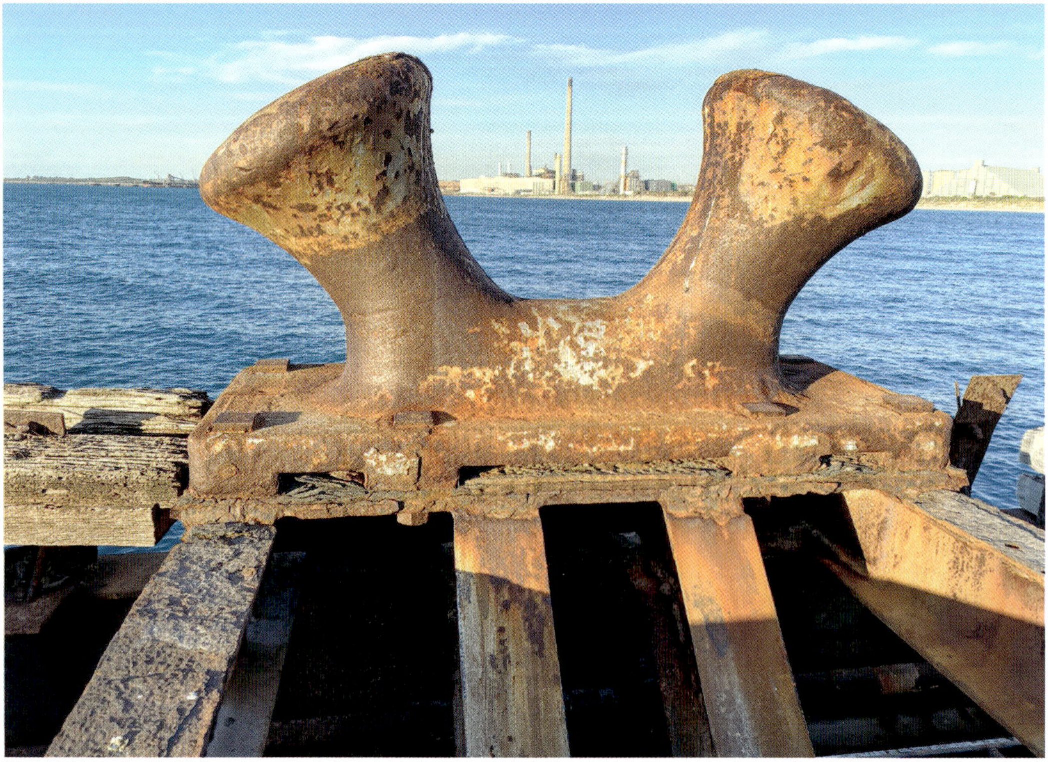

A ship anchor point still looking quite impressive, despite the build-up of rust at its base. The Kwinana Power Station, owned by Synergy, can be seen in between the two anchor points.

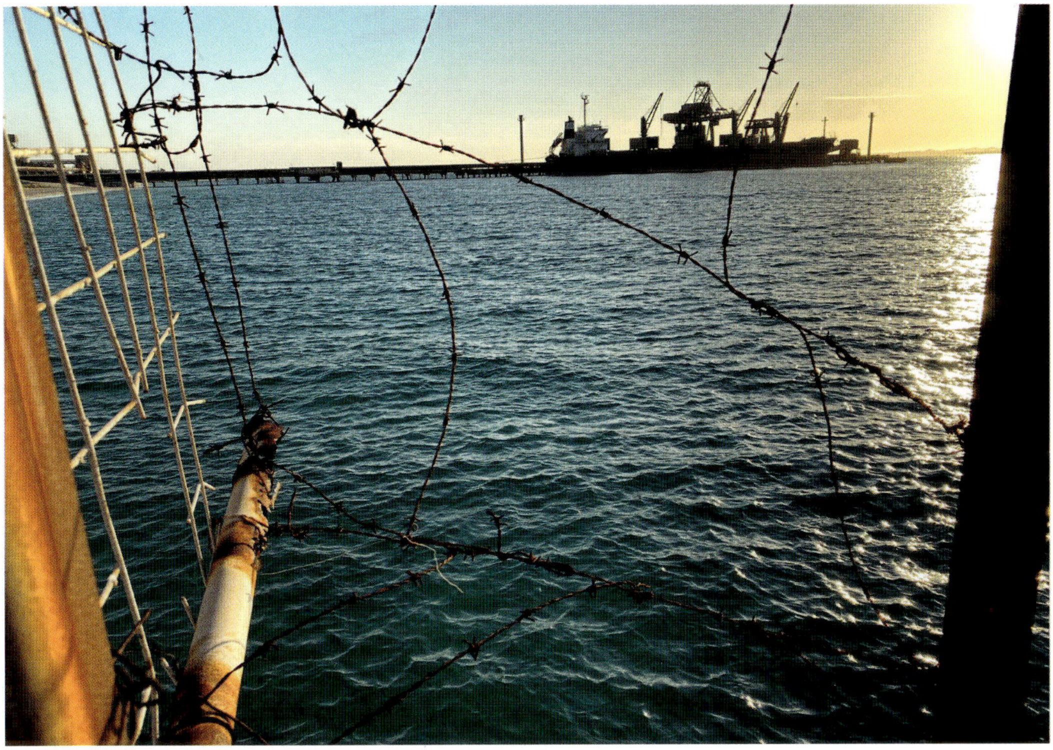

Looking out on to the Kwinana Bulk Terminal where the New General Bulk Carrier is berthed. Barbed-wire attempts to stop people from jumping into the water.

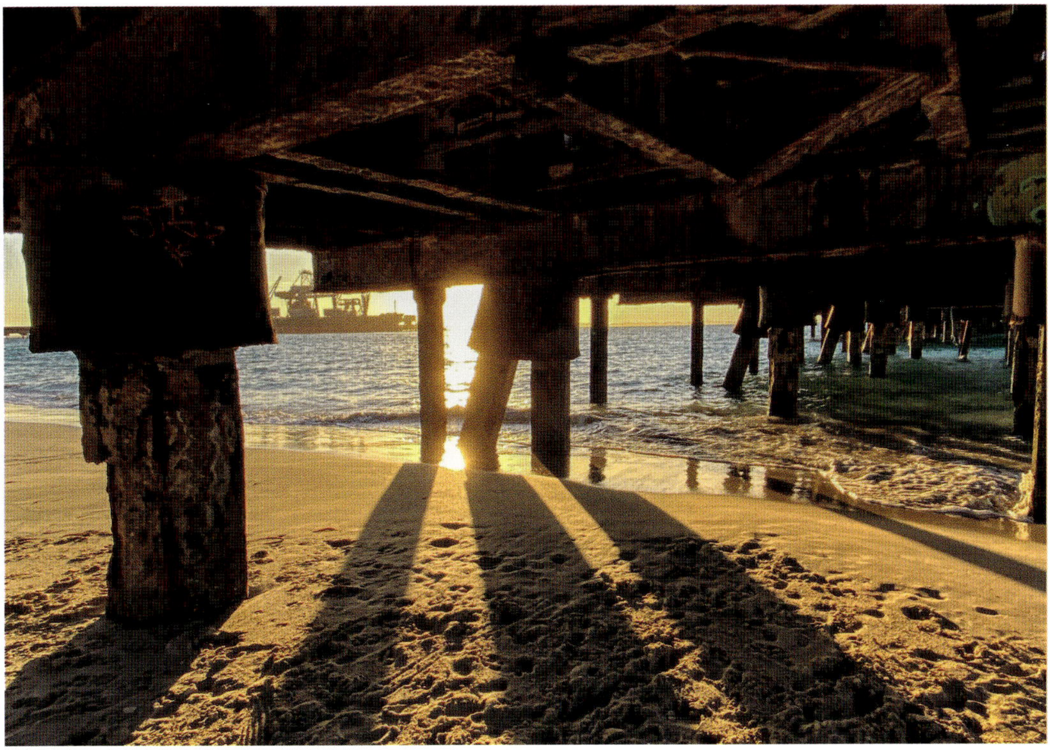

View of the sunset on Kwinana Beach under BHP Jetty Number 1. The dilapidation of the jetty's framework is obvious and, at the same time, contrasts well with the glowing summer colours.

MIDLAND RAILWAY WORKSHOP

A short walk south-east of the Midland train station will magically teleport you to an old England location. The only difference being that we have blue skies and they do not (according to all their TV shows and movies) and we wear warm clothes even on hot days, while they only wear shorts and T-shirts on days as cold as -10°C.

Aside from that (as well as no roads of cobblestone), the scene of what one could imagine some fifty years ago is so accessible. Turning off any technological crap and stopping the pointless yabbering if you are with someone, the silence that flows through the wide streets turns the atmospheric scene into something more vivid.

The occasional breeze or stronger wind taps against vintage window panes and loose bits of tins. Quiet footsteps as you walk, that at times crunches loose debris scattered over the asphalt. The smell of grease penetrates your senses. Staring at the windows, imagining the scene unfolding before your very eyes when the original window panes were first installed as early as 1904.

Can you hear the train whistles, machinery, and perhaps the associated sounds of heavy, hard work? Vibrations of engines and the unknown, can you feel it through your feet?

A vintage car drives past in the distance. The driver nods slightly and it is a wonder his top hat does not fall off his head and out the window. The chugging rumble of his motorcar disappears around the corner, only to be replaced with a horse and a cart. Its wheels crunching through the loose grey stone where cobblestones are yet to be laid.

I enter an open railway workshop. The smell of grease intensifies, as my thoughts begin to visually associate it with old machinery from back in the day. I can feel my intrigue rising like mercury. No longer visible are the hundreds of people who once worked here or in the many other workshops in the area, which all closed in March 1994. Generations after generations. Who knows what dangers they were putting themselves in, in order to bring home a measly packet to feed their families, pay their mortgage, and settle their pub tabs. Who knows what illnesses they would have acquired over the years, without the mandatory, at times, authoritarian workplace safety and personal protection requirements we have now.

The walls are painted a thick lime, many coats over, perhaps with the intention of once hiding the cracks that appeared over time. A Uniform Officer Inwards sign is still attached to the wall and without any idea of what it represents, I look around to see a non-existent Outwards one.

The typical view of pigeon poop covers the concrete floor in corresponding lines from the beams above. Perhaps the sharp nails I often see on the edge of roofs help to plug their pooping orifices but obviously there are none on these beams. Stepping on a pile of dried bird excrement crushes it to dust like a pile of forgotten ashes.

The warm October temperatures, only an hour short of sunset, contributes to the stifling heat I already feel in the workshop. I cannot bear to imagine the extensive heat the workers would have had to endure, despite my own experiences of working in various factories as well as the Mount Whaleback iron ore mine in Newman on a 54°C day.

My imagination goes into overdrive as the place makes me feel like I am the only one left on this earth. No movement to distract the silence. Thick chains with head-sized hooks hang to dry, perhaps never to be used again. The big Avery platform scale is out of touch with reality, showing me I am some 10 kg too heavy. Come to think of it, perhaps I was wearing my backpack.

The fading sun makes the warehouse suddenly colder and darker, yet I am eager to view the remainder of the workshop, despite the dangers of any graveyard shift poltergeists stirring awake. It makes me wonder why my imagination feels the need to run rife to the point of strife when I just want to explore and be left in peace.

Graffiti mars the upstairs rooms, although many pieces are nothing short of thought-provoking. From a well-placed RIP on the window overlooking some nearby workshops to a frequently found devil. My favourite is unquestionably the female wearing a niqab. I cannot help but stop to stare at her eyes, and despite her not looking in my direction, they captivate my thoughts. Wording nearby associates her as a celebration to 'Inter-nat Womans Day'. I cannot help but wonder what struggles this woman has had to endure, what is she thinking, and what dreams and hopes give her strength. She is just a painting.

Before I know it, the sun has dashed my hopes of a longer stay, replacing it with a blanket of night. I walk over to the window, touching the pane which is now slightly cold with lost memories emitting from the workshop. The sounds of crickets rubbing their wings together to mate, or perhaps to warm them up, fills my ears and I know I must leave.

I rush out of the top room and down the big stairs, trying not to sound like a bowling ball, thudding its way down. My imagination is yet to die a horrible death. Visions of souls and entities lurk in the shadows and even a man in hiding has suddenly awaken to my sounds. I run through the workshop, which surely must be at least 100 metres long. Panting, as my appendix appears to signal a tap out, like a combat sport.

I make it outside into the glow of what is left of the sun. Night-time stars faint but ready for a long shift. A breeze sends my fringe flapping like a flag, as my steps crunch through a thick path of gravel.

Long ago history is now fresh in my mind.

From the photos people have been posting on Facebook of the workshop since my visit in October 2020, there appears to be so many more big graffiti pieces. I do not mind seeing them in places like warehouses that are scheduled for demolition, but it is pretty disgusting to see them on the walls of important heritage-listed locations like the railway workshops.

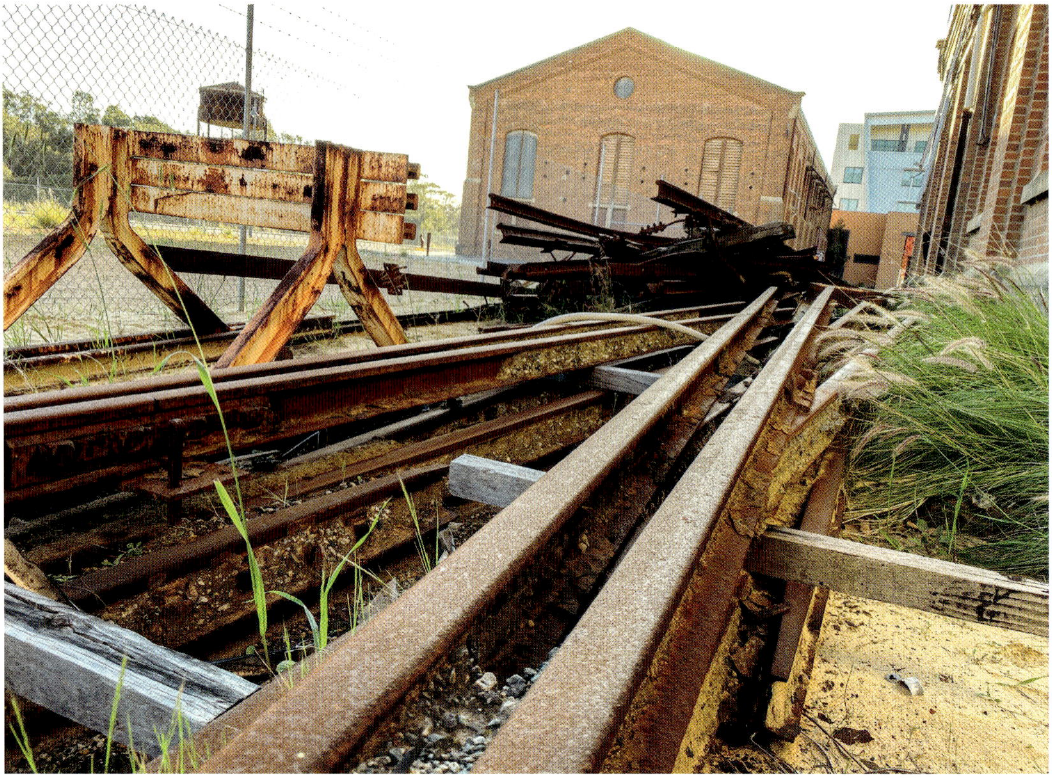

Old track rails and parts lay wasting away. A railway workshop stands the test of time in the near distance, awaiting its restoration day.

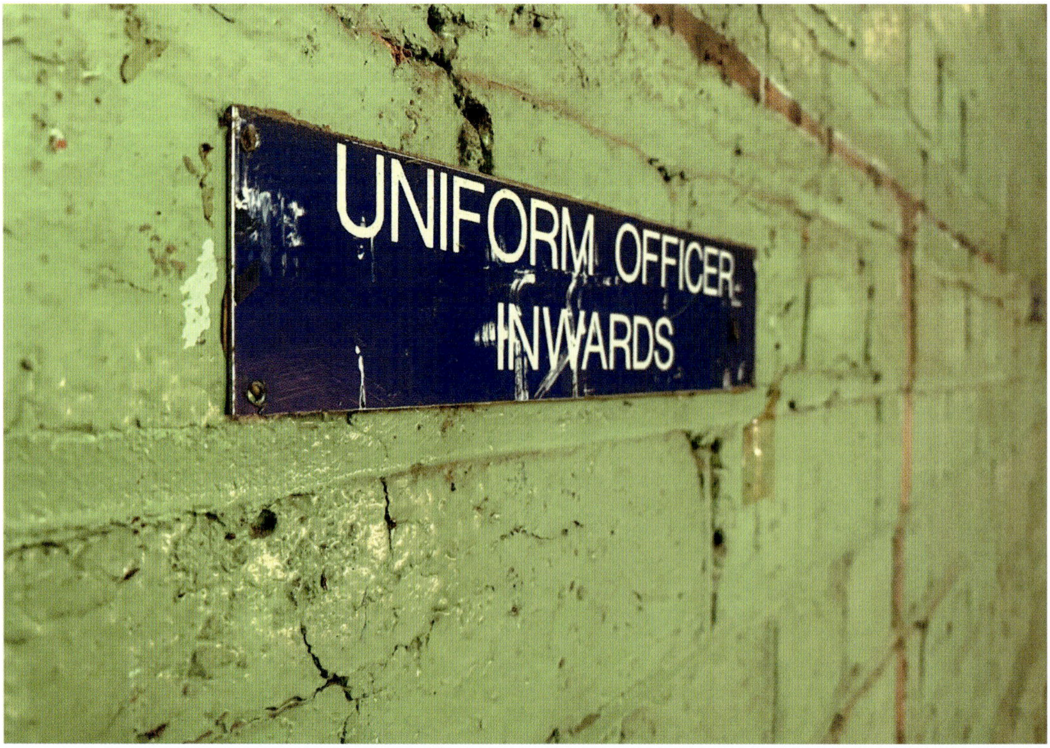

An old sign remains on the lime-painted internal walls of the railway workshop.

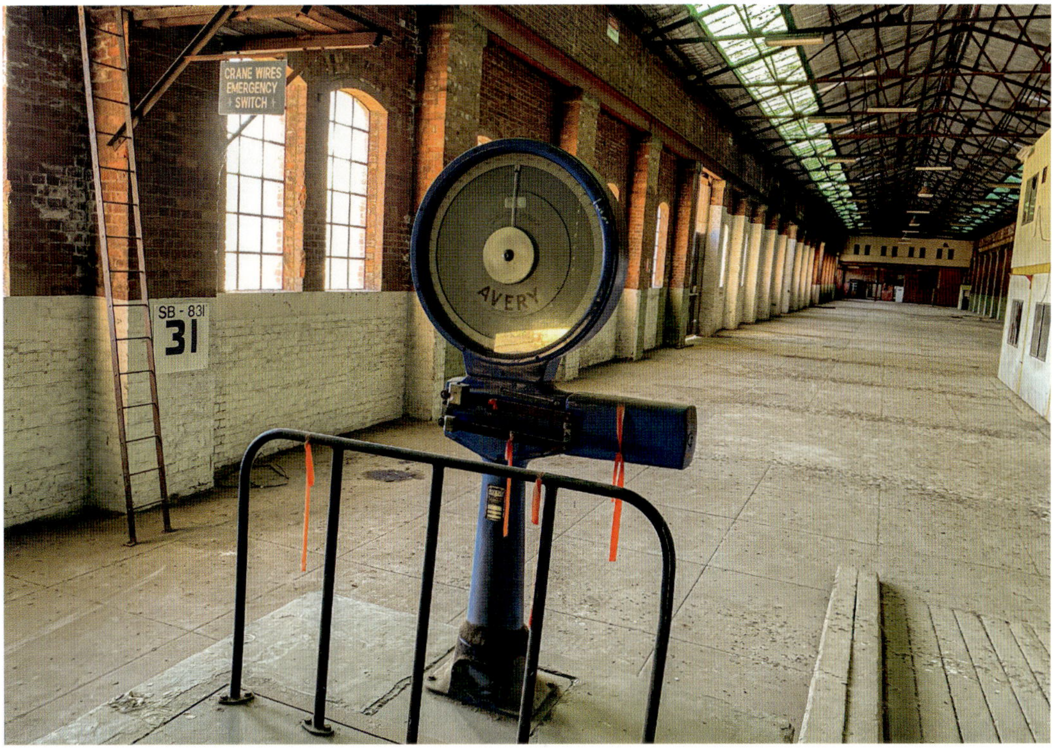

The stripped railway workshop remains silent. It is hard to imagine what it would have looked like back in the day, as well as what the noises, vibrations, and smells were like.

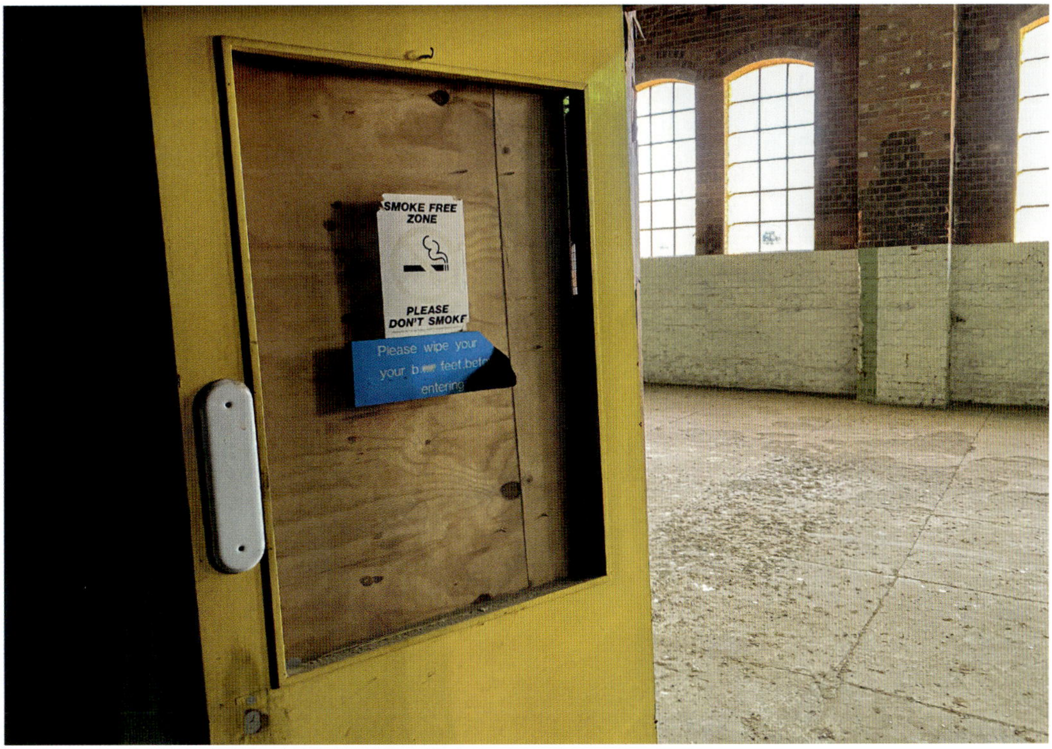

A lovely little sticker on a brightly painted door, reminds people to wipe their feet before entering the lunchroom—assuming there was something to wipe their feet on at all.

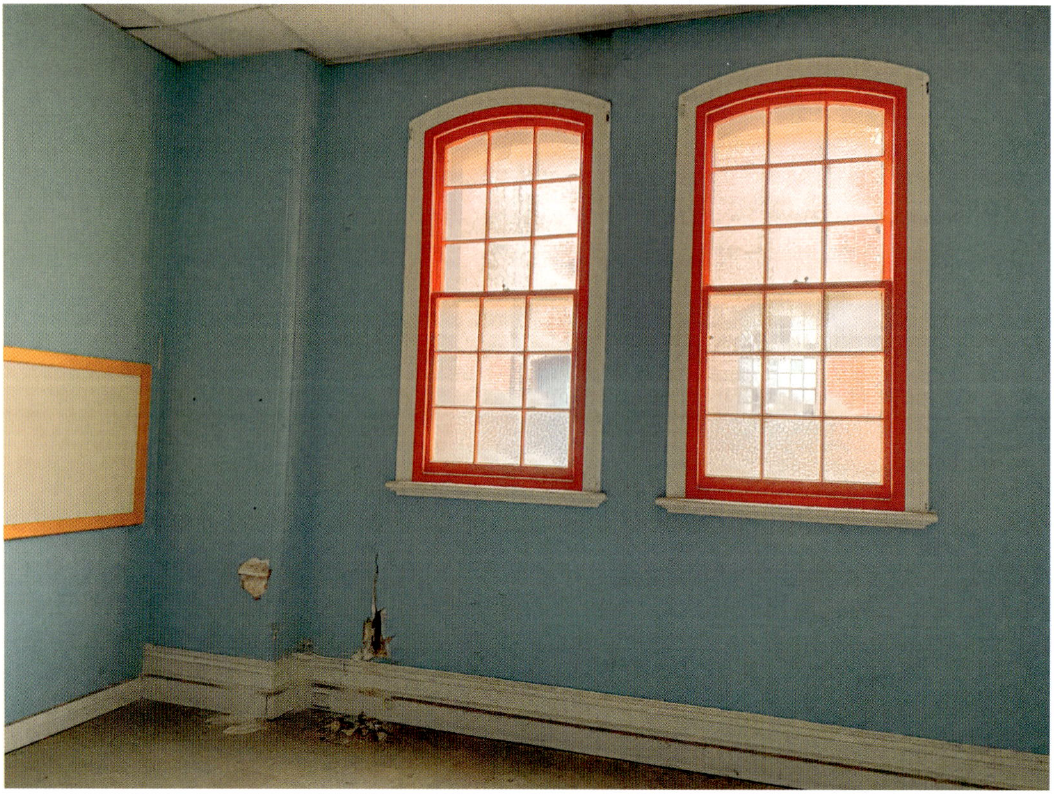

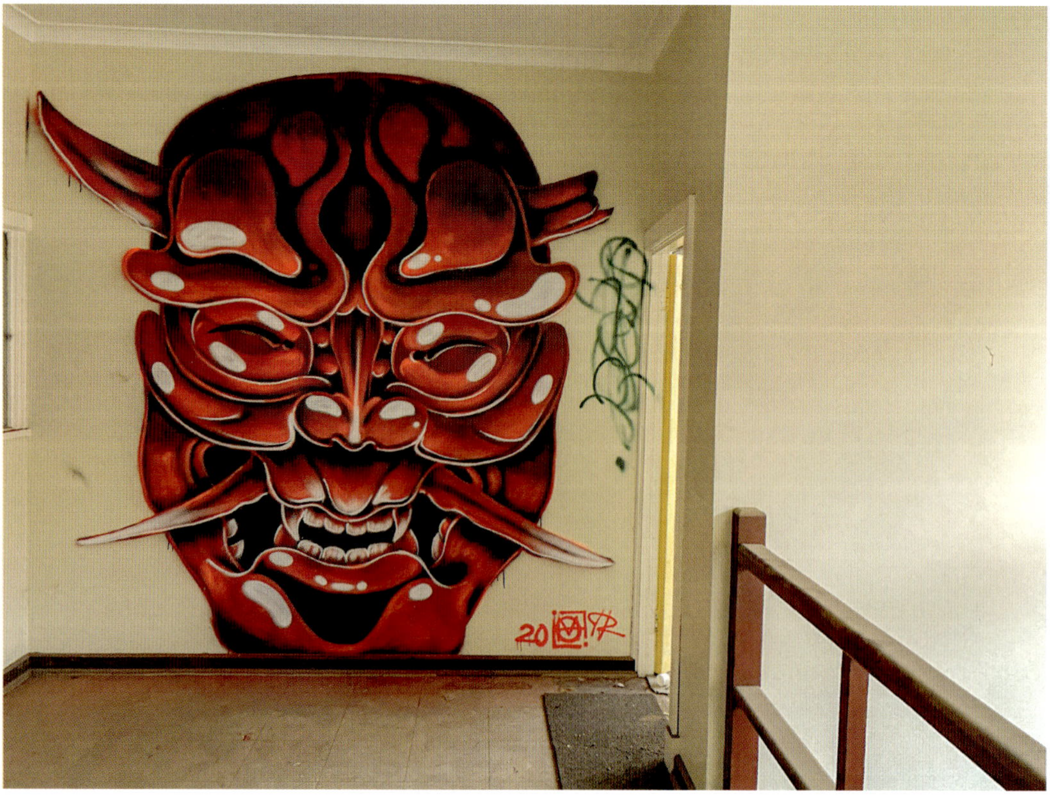

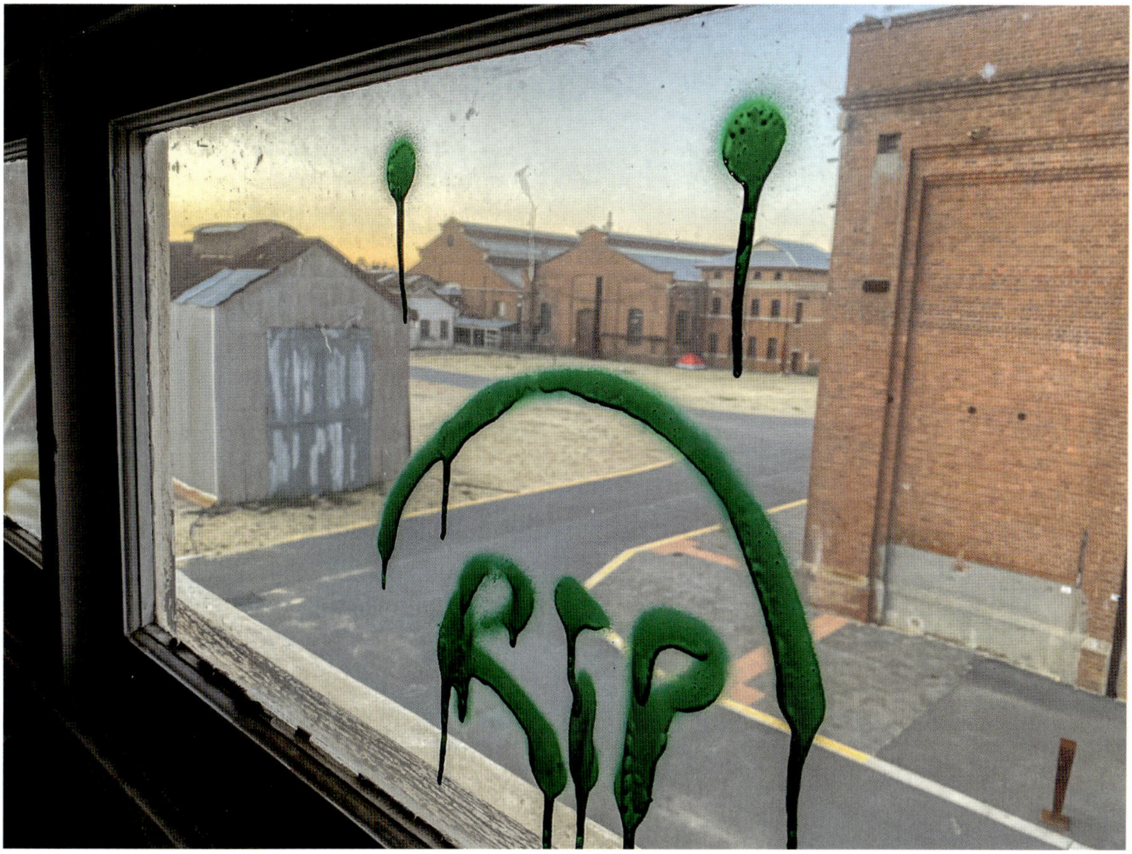

My papa's favourite photo. The words RIP could be interpreted in so many ways such as the death of the railway workshop industrial era. Thousands of its past employees would have since passed on, many taking their valuable memories with them instead of recording it to help preserve history.

OPPOSITE PAGE:

It seems rare for internal walls and window frames of buildings to be painted anything other than white. As if conservatism is a necessary ingredient for customer acceptance and professionalism. *Below:* The red devil returns, seemingly in a more jovial mood that the one painted on the internal wall of the BHP Jetty Number 1.

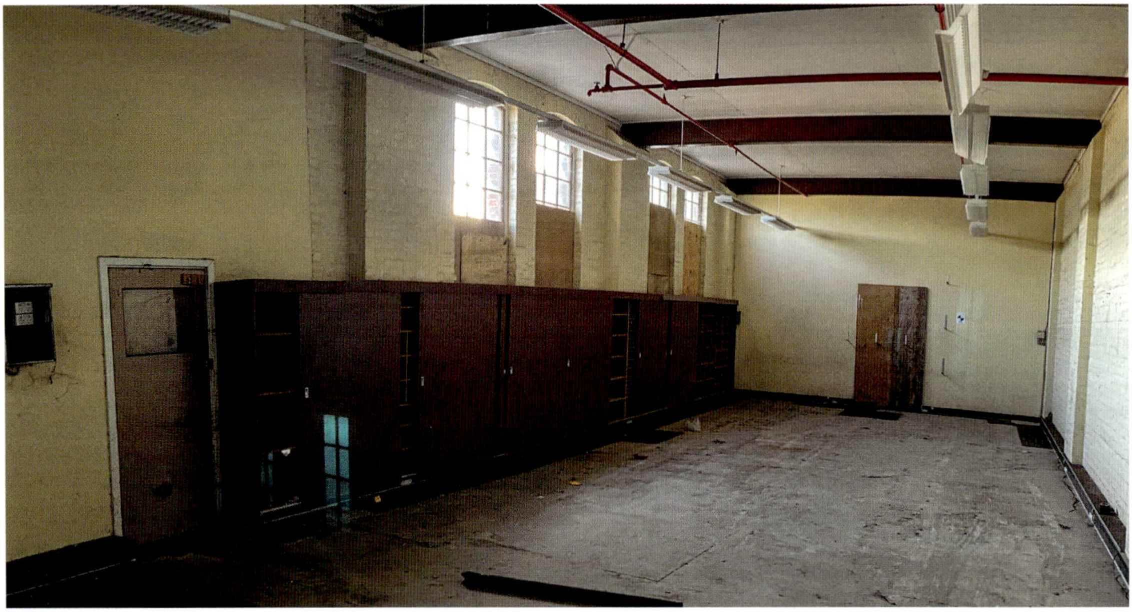

A collection room of some sort, most likely for paperwork and archival systems, located towards the rear of the railway workshop. This room has since been painted with a number of large graffiti tags with no consideration for the important heritage value its canvas holds.

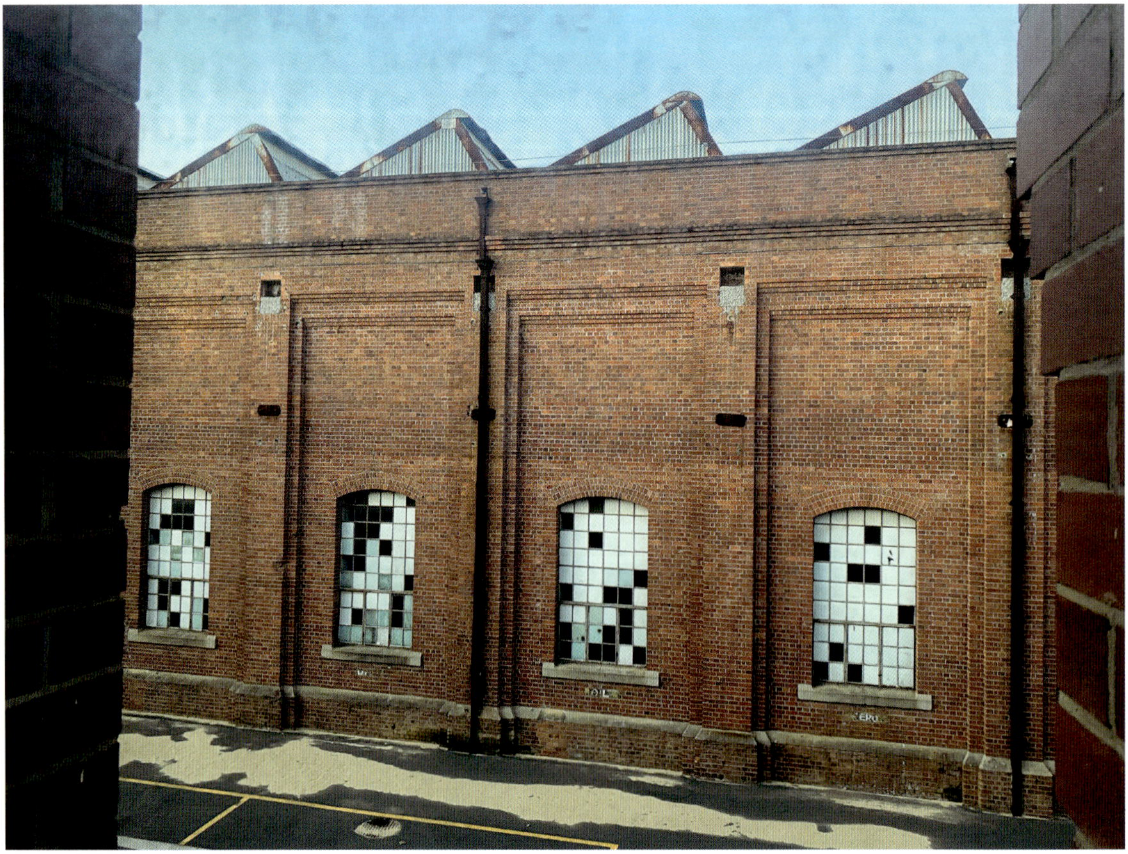

View of an adjacent railway workshop through the window, an image that could easily have been taken from somewhere in England.

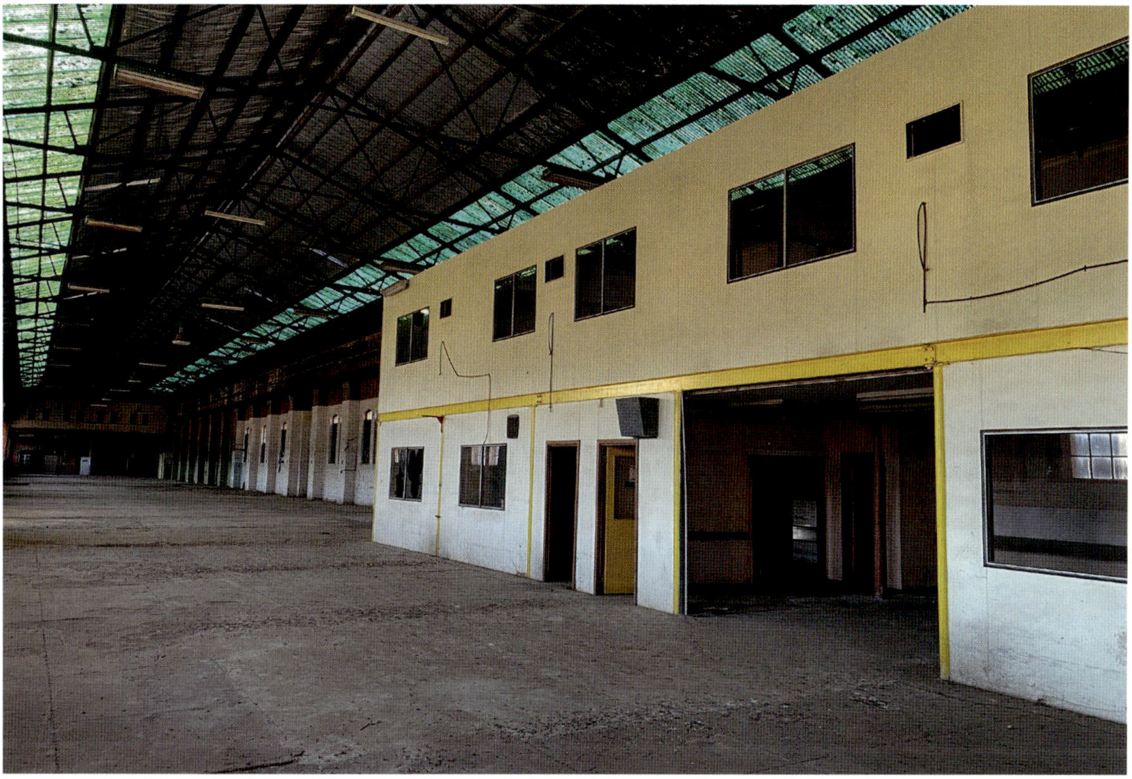

A simple office block overlooks what would have been the hub of the workshop.

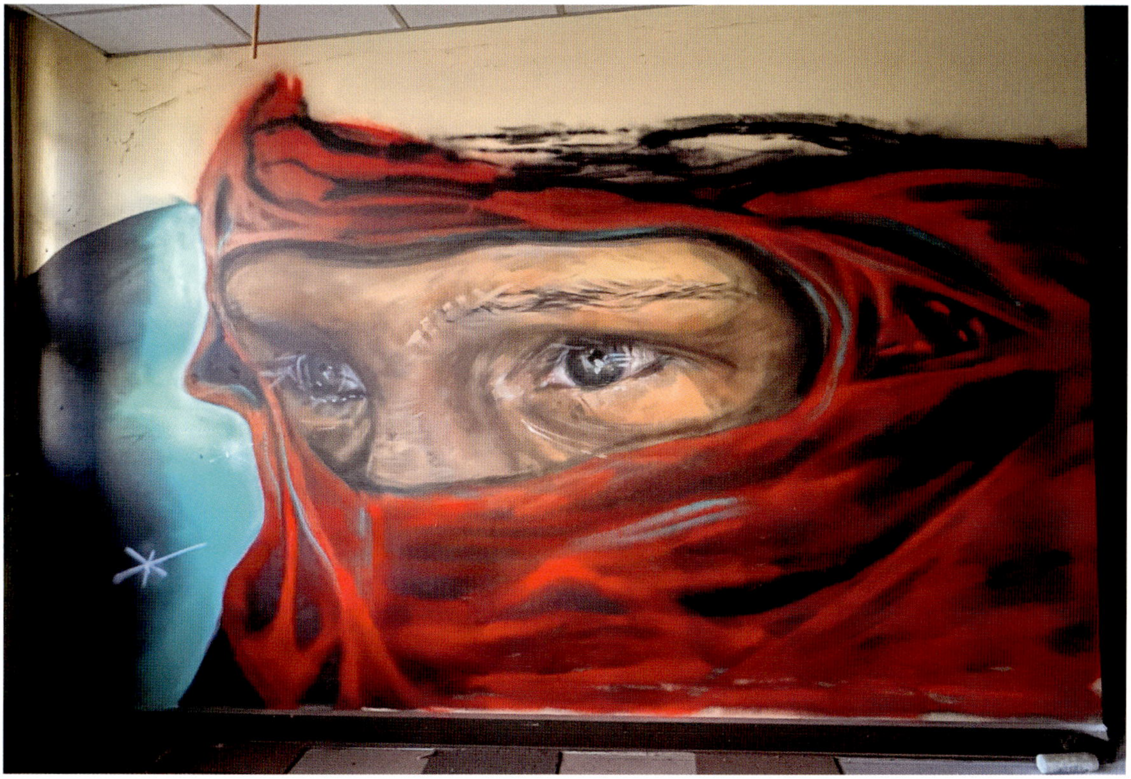

On a wall to the left of this portrait reads the words 'HAPPY INTER-NAT WOMANS DAY!♥'

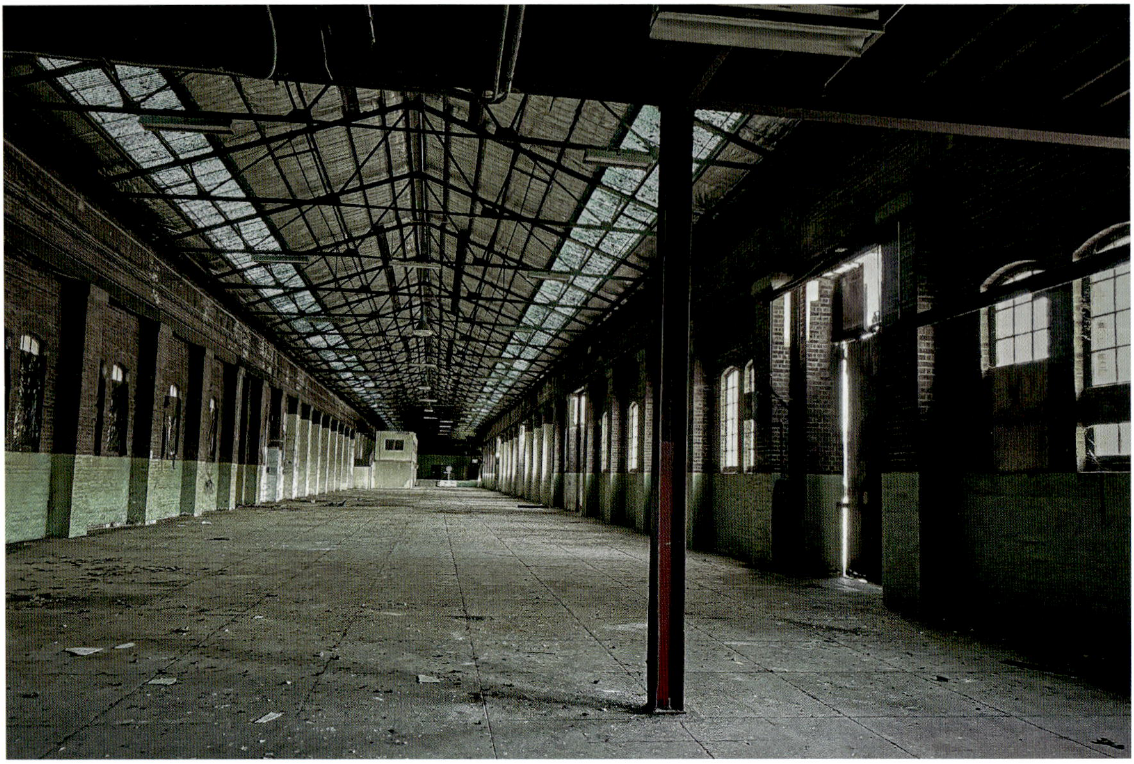

As dusk nears, darkness begins to envelop the workshop with a cold and emotionless vibe.

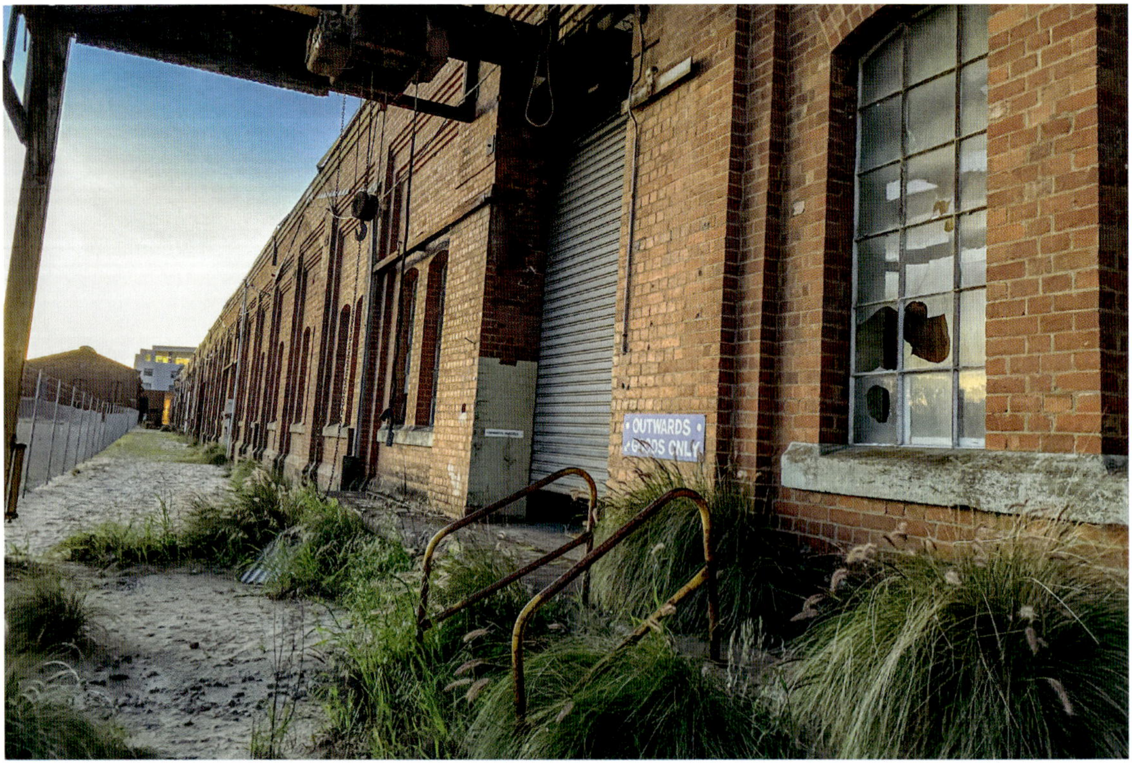

Upon exiting the railway workshop, the sun begins to set for another night. Nothing new for these old buildings that would have lay witness to thousands of sunsets over the past 116 years.

NEDLANDS AGED CARE APARTMENTS

The images I have seen of abandoned buildings in countries like Germany and Russia always feel so imposing, mysterious, and captivating. Not just because many locations were once huge facilities, now forgotten with time. Many of their places, from hospitals to housing estates, tend to be full of possessions as if people had just suddenly walked off, leaving everything behind.

I never imagined I would be lucky enough to explore such a location here in Perth, but I did. Despite being abandoned for as long as ten years, the Nedlands apartment block I was taken to was in fairly good nick and, surprisingly, a very well-kept secret—despite its imposing presence visible from afar.

Of course, nothing could really compare with Germany, Russia, and the like. Perhaps that is a good thing though. I am fairly inexperienced with landmines, booby-traps, guerrillas armed with submachine guns using abandoned buildings as a secretive base for their militant operations, as well as grey wolves who attack in packs.

Perth suddenly appears so much more attractive, despite the limited opportunities for a 'top shelf' explore. So in a nutshell, I certainly found myself with something more valuable than a peanut.

The first room I entered had an old flowery armchair that had clearly seen better days and not just because of some strange bodily fluid markings. I was amazed to see big piles of more than 100 new and almost-new plates piled up on the floor. What a waste!

I have to laugh at that trivial memory. Turns out, it was nothing at all! Photos cannot do justice in capturing the extensive quantity left behind.

Wheelchairs, walkers, gophers, crutches, commode chairs, gurneys, armchairs, tables, a variety of seats, desks, computers, monitors, filing cabinets, storage furniture, TVs, VCRs, a record player, vinyl records, moving boxes filled with VHS tapes, bowling pins, board games, recreation and fitness equipment, crockery, various kitchenware, hundreds of books and magazines, artwork, hobby materials, huge quantities, and varieties of screws, tools, smoke alarms, cleaning products, a lawnmower, etc.

More importantly, and certainly a potential legal issue, aside from what appeared to be complete management records, logbooks, journal, ledgers, invoices, purchase histories, operational procedures, and manuals, a quick glance revealed what appeared to be client and employee records. This included extensive personal and medical histories, as well as case files. They were found in boxes and filing cabinets in at least eight different locations, with one floor of a bedsit's bathroom covered in big piles.

Nobody obviously cared.

The main wing was six storeys high, with another wing equally as high behind. To the left was a third one with three floors. What a horrible place to live the last chapter of your life!

It resembled a jail, and those words have been reiterated by many others I have spoken to, particularly when considering the stereotypical mobility issues an elderly person may be experiencing. A set of stairs are located at the far end of each wing. Each floor has a common room with access to two lifts.

There were many reports and logs of the lifts breaking down and on a few occasions, elderly residents were trapped inside for hours at a time. Some incidents even made the newspaper, particularly when residents were restricted to their floors due to both elevators being out of service and their inability to use the stairs. Now add a fire! Sure, this apartment complex is no longer in use, but I would bet my bottom dollar that there are many replica buildings just like this one with the same legitimate concerns.

From an urbex point of view, it is funny how you start to become attached to a particular place. I have now visited this apartment complex fifty-one times since October 2020, photographing and documenting any changes I saw. Whether it was from dero muppets trashing it or graffiti artists practicing their skills (and the occasional, ill-matured young men secretly obsessed with the penis, despite portraying a false sense of macho heterosexuality, defacing works of art with male genitals).

It was not long before word was starting to get out and an influx of visitors was attracting its demise.

Then everything changed for the worse. It was imminent.

After some ten years of neglect, internal demolition finally began in February 2021. A sad reality I knew I would have to accept sooner or later. My happy place, where I came to cope with this toxic world, was about to fall apart.

An application had been made to demolish the apartment complex and replace it with a new $250,000,000 retirement village, which was approved on 12 December 2018. New plans for the site had been drawn up to build 327 apartments for seniors, between three to five storeys high with a central building of six storeys.

As a result of the demolition taking place, I found myself increasing my visits by going most nights for almost two months, even for just an hour at a time. I no longer had the place to myself. Gone were the long nights of strolling through pitch-black, calmingly silent walkways and lifeless rooms. Gone were beautiful summer days appreciating beauty in decay, with priceless sunset views from the roof. After the National Archives of Australia in East Victoria Park was demolished, I felt so lost. Now I had emotionally attached myself to this apartment complex that, for most, resembled nothing more than an eyesore.

To think I would ever get a site anywhere as good as this again? Yeah, nah!

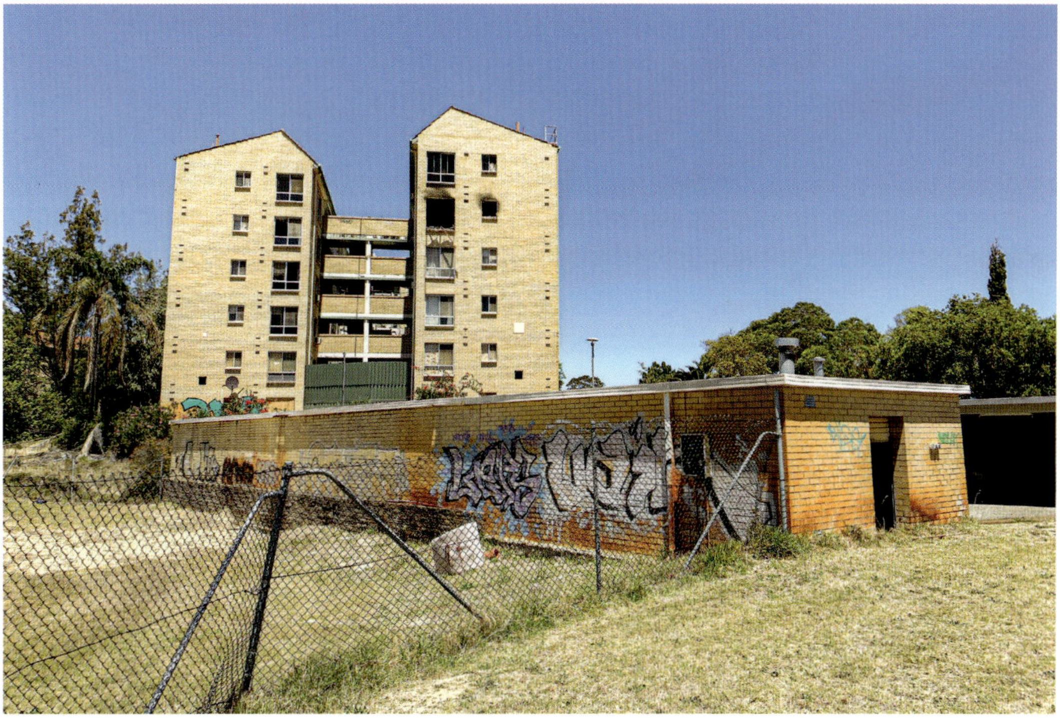

View of the dilapidated main wing of the Nedlands apartment complex. It has since been demolished, just like two other apartment blocks that once existed nearby.

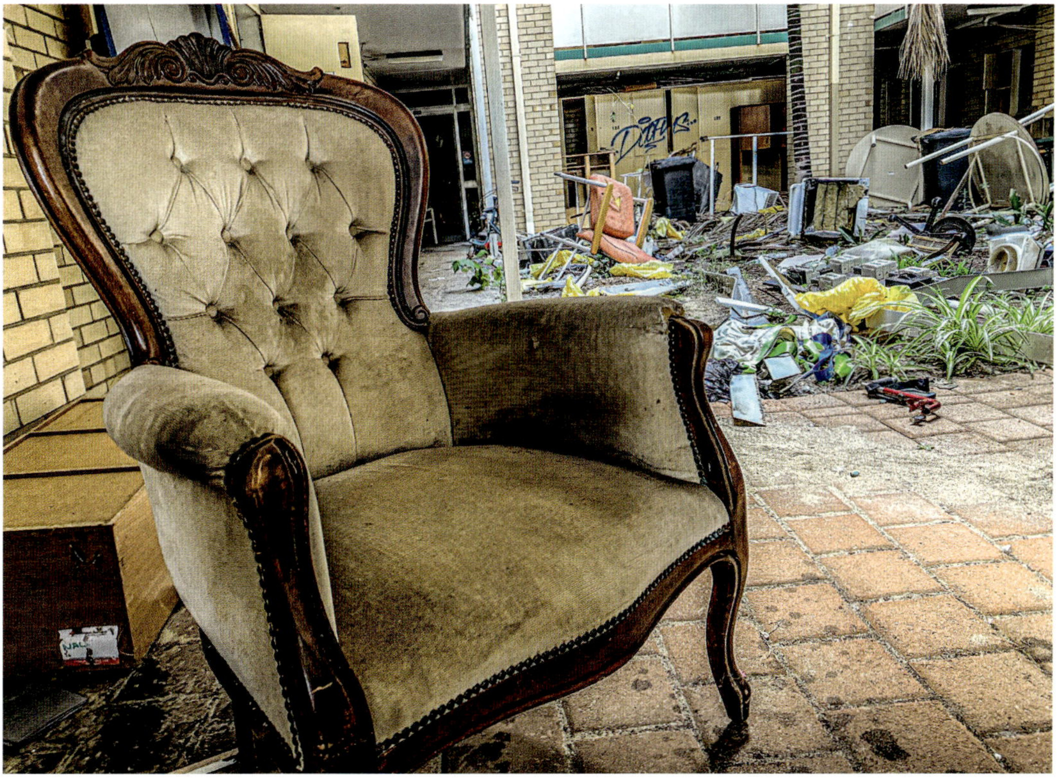

A grand-looking chair on the bottom floor of the main wing, which later surfaced for sale on Facebook Marketplace. Doofus, one of Perth's most famous graffiti artists, has sprayed his tag on the doors of some old lockers.

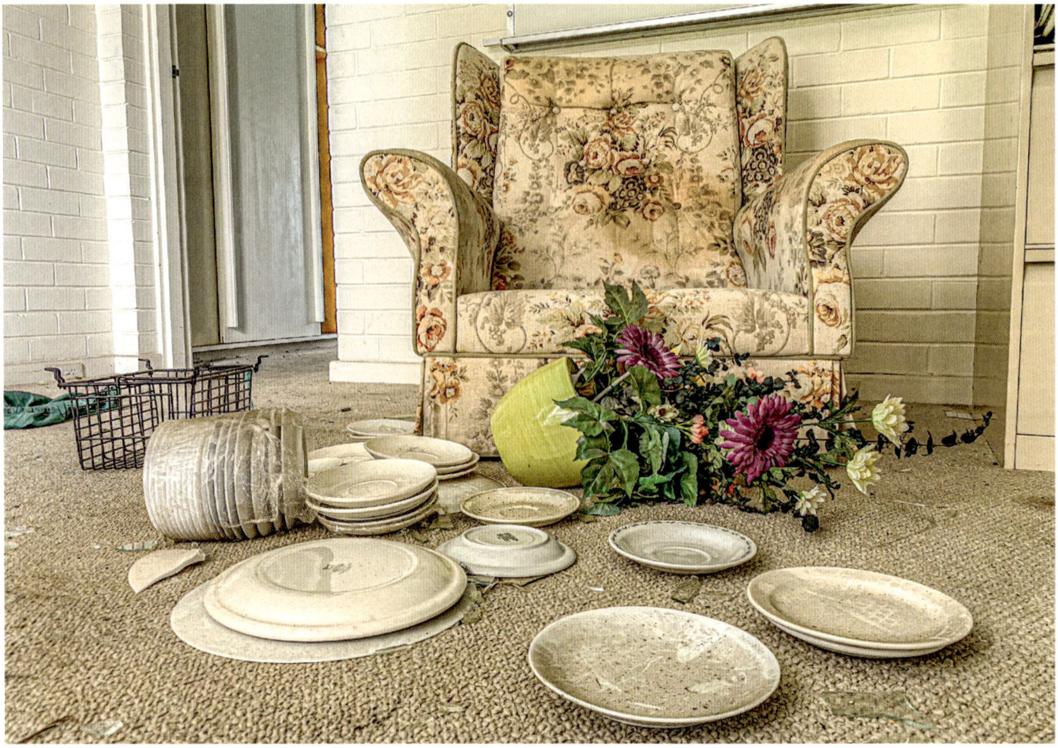

An old sofa chair, one of the many pieces of furniture left behind, sits in a room with more than a hundred new or almost-new plates.

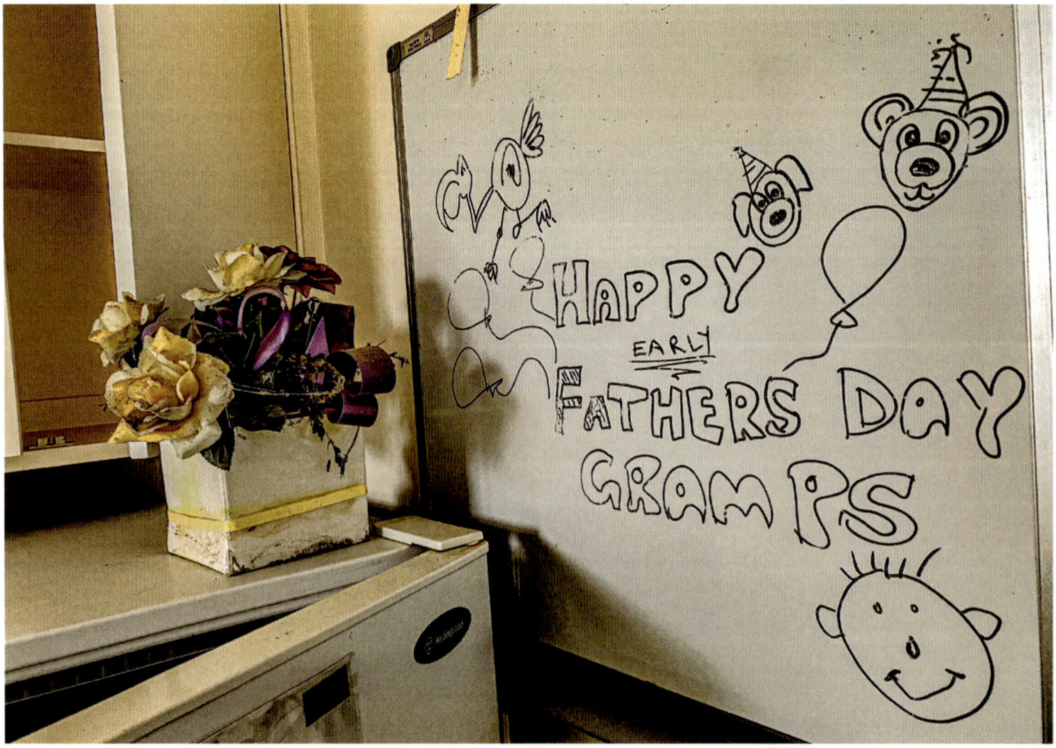

A birthday message remains on the whiteboard of a residents' unit. Perhaps it has outlasted the cherished grandfather, due to the long time that has passed since these apartments were inhabited.

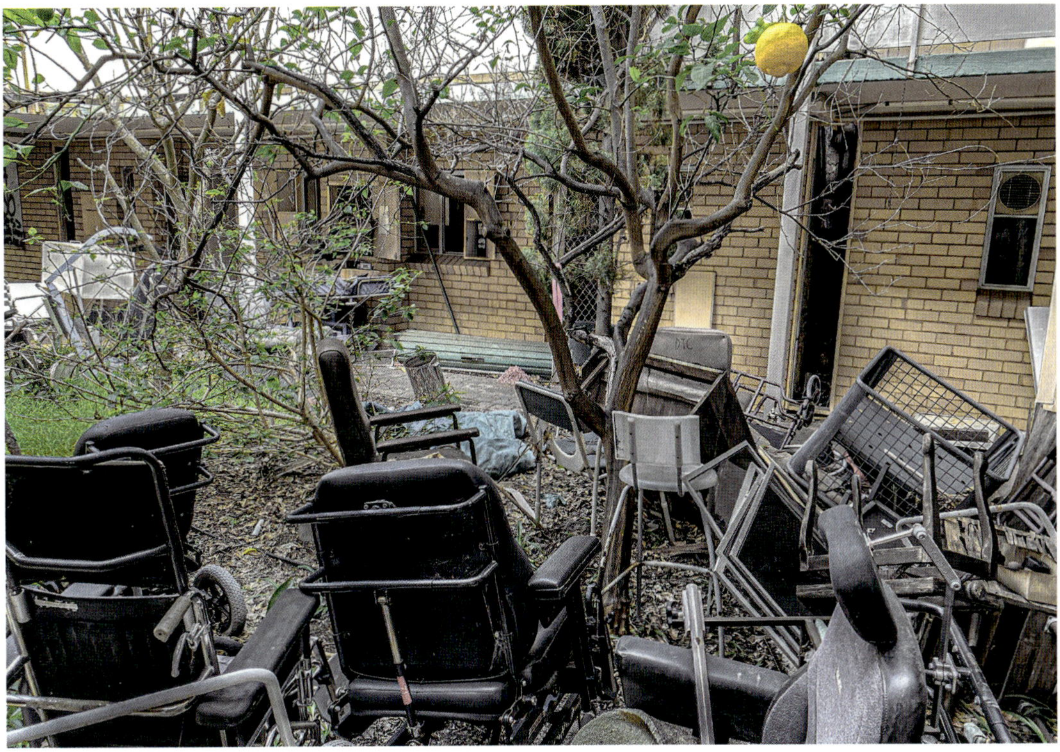

A scene that beings to feel normal after a while. Large quantities of unwanted wheelchairs, scooters, furniture, fridges, tables, beds, mattresses, and possessions are visible everywhere you look.

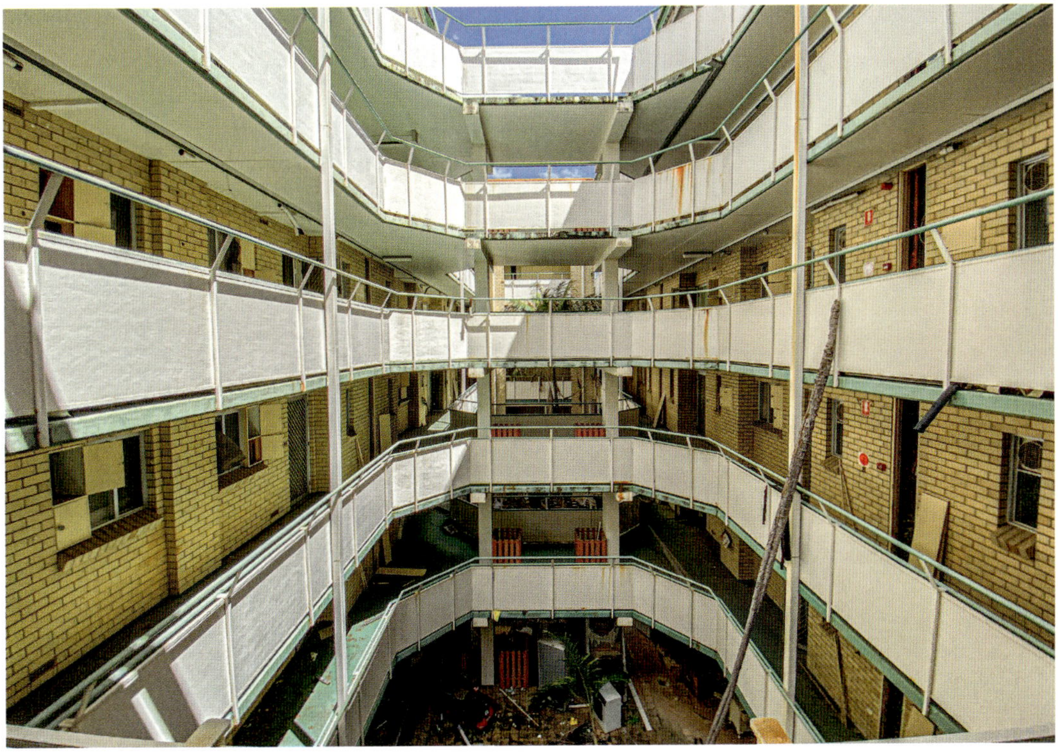

Compact living at its worst. Life on a cruise ship that does not leave the land, which surely could not be an attractive solution for residents struggling with mobility issues, particularly when both lifts are out of service.

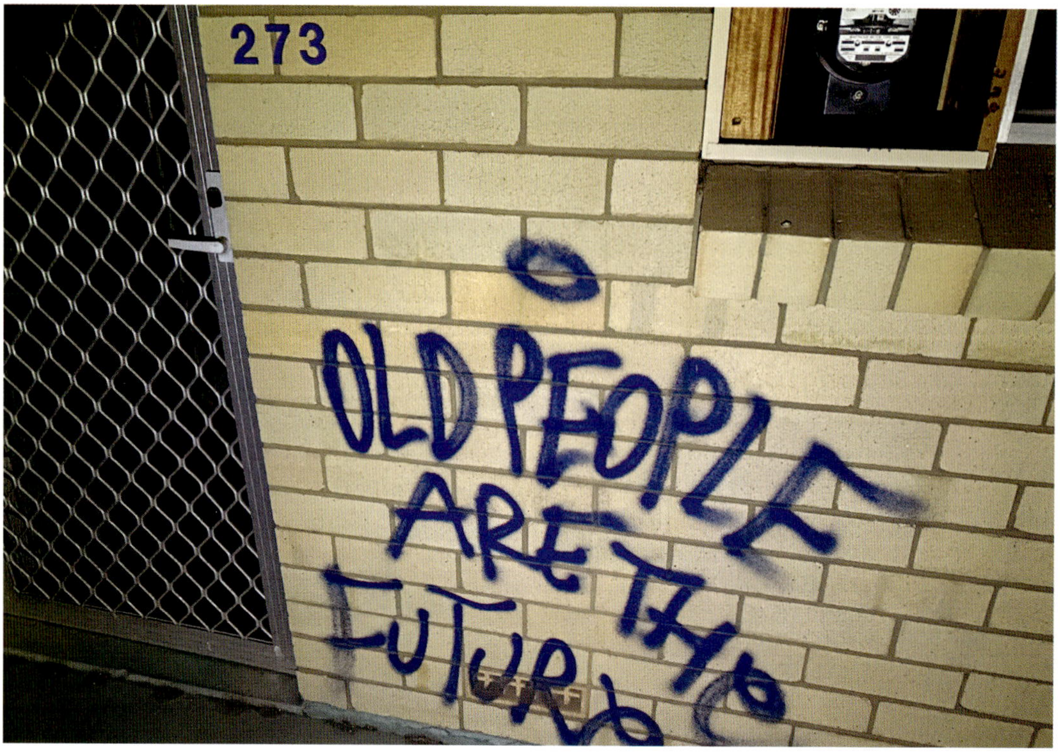

A positive piece of graffiti attributing the value of the older generation. Over the past year, it felt like a lot more positive graffiti messages were appearing in public areas, perhaps more so in abandoned buildings like here.

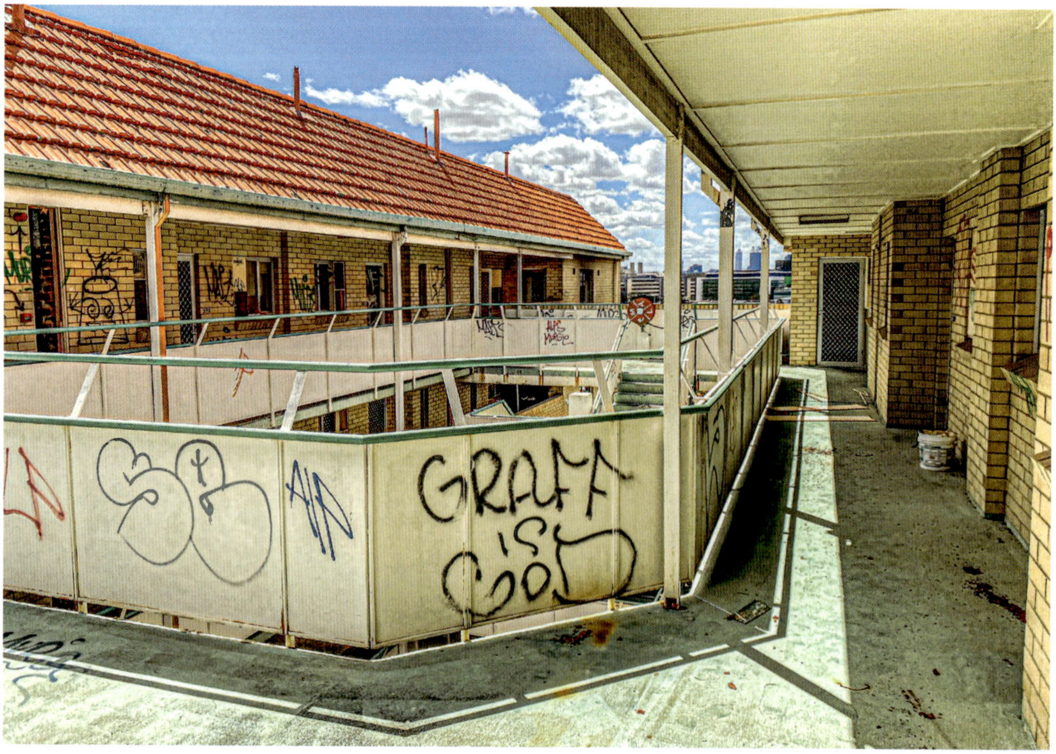

Trashy graffiti mars the walkways of the main wing.

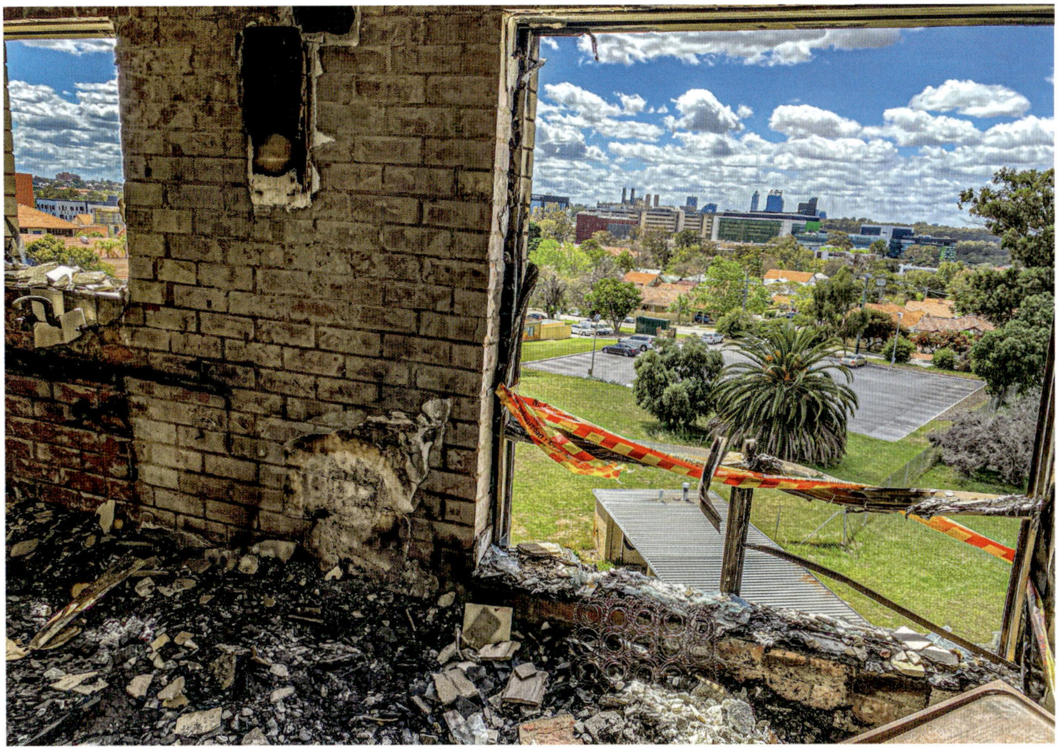

A burnt-out room on the fourth floor of the main wing looks out on to the city. The fire was lit at approximately 10:40 p.m. on 24 October 2019 and was initially thought as suspicious but not investigated due to its impending demolition.

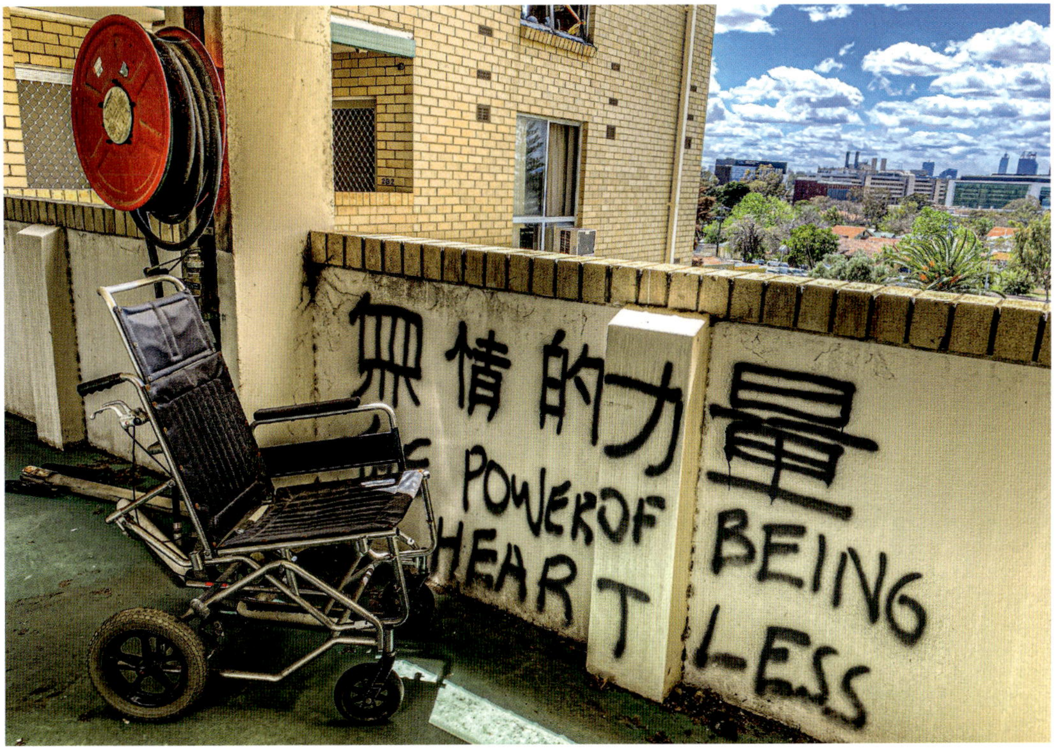

Many people I have spoken to have described this apartment complex as nothing more than a jail for elderly people. It is hard to imagine the joy a place like this would bring to an elderly resident, hence the graffiti.

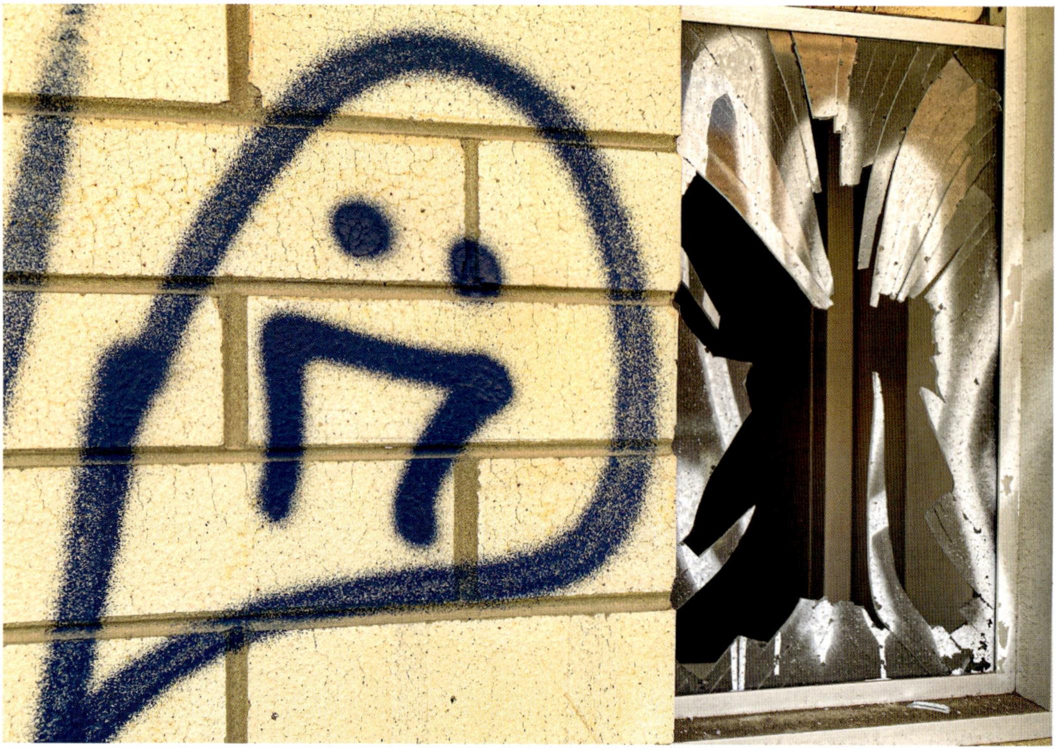

A ghostly expression with a Merv Hughes handlebar moustache next to a window that appears quite artistic, particularly when viewed together.

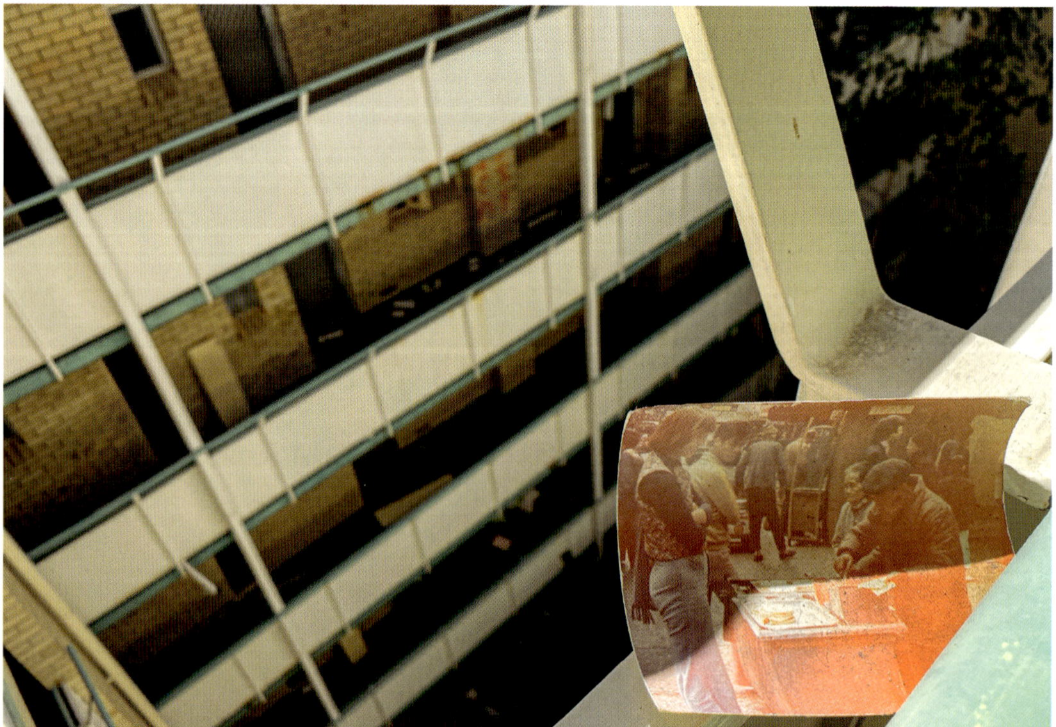

A young lady with a heart-warming expression watches an elderly man serving up food in the markets of an Asian country.

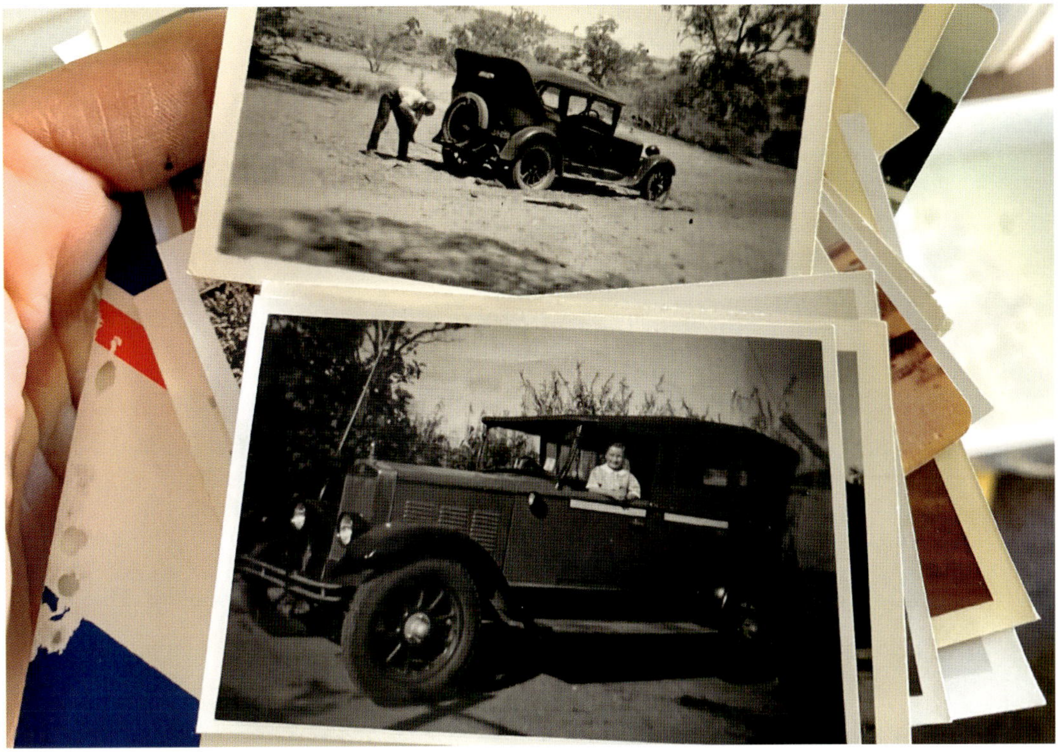

Old photos left behind in one of the apartments, with 'Gun Cars' written on the front of the envelope. The year 1927 appears on the rear of some of the photos.

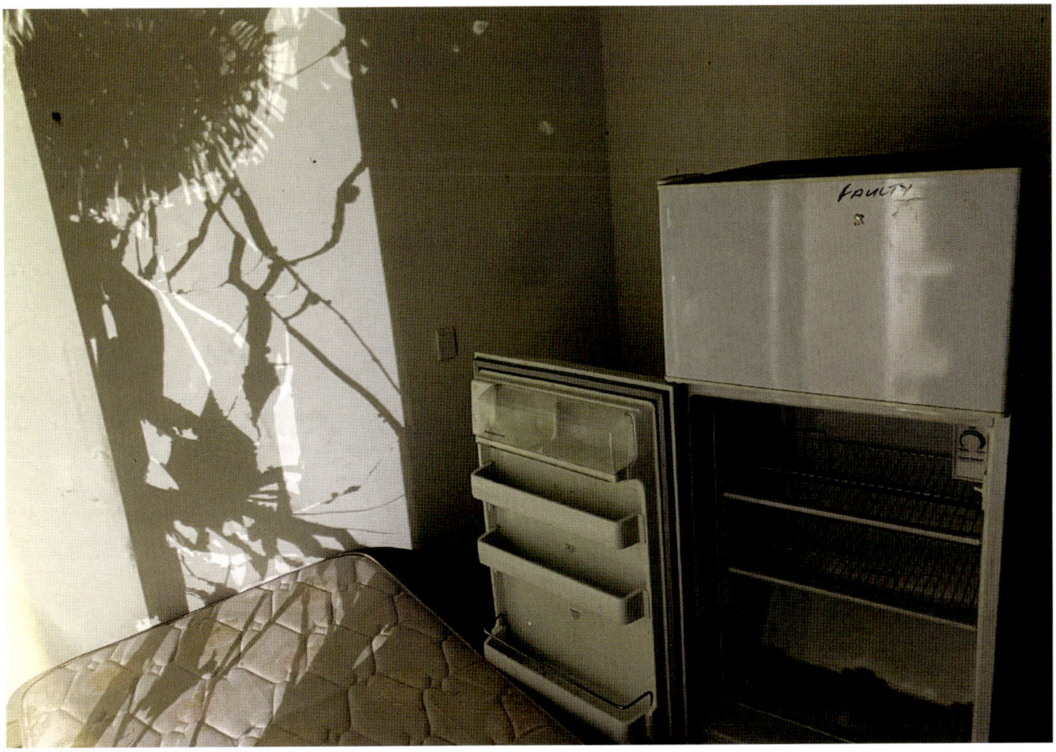

A smashed mirror reflects off the wall like a piece of art. Perhaps resembling a dandelion puffball, waiting for someone to blow its seeds into the wind.

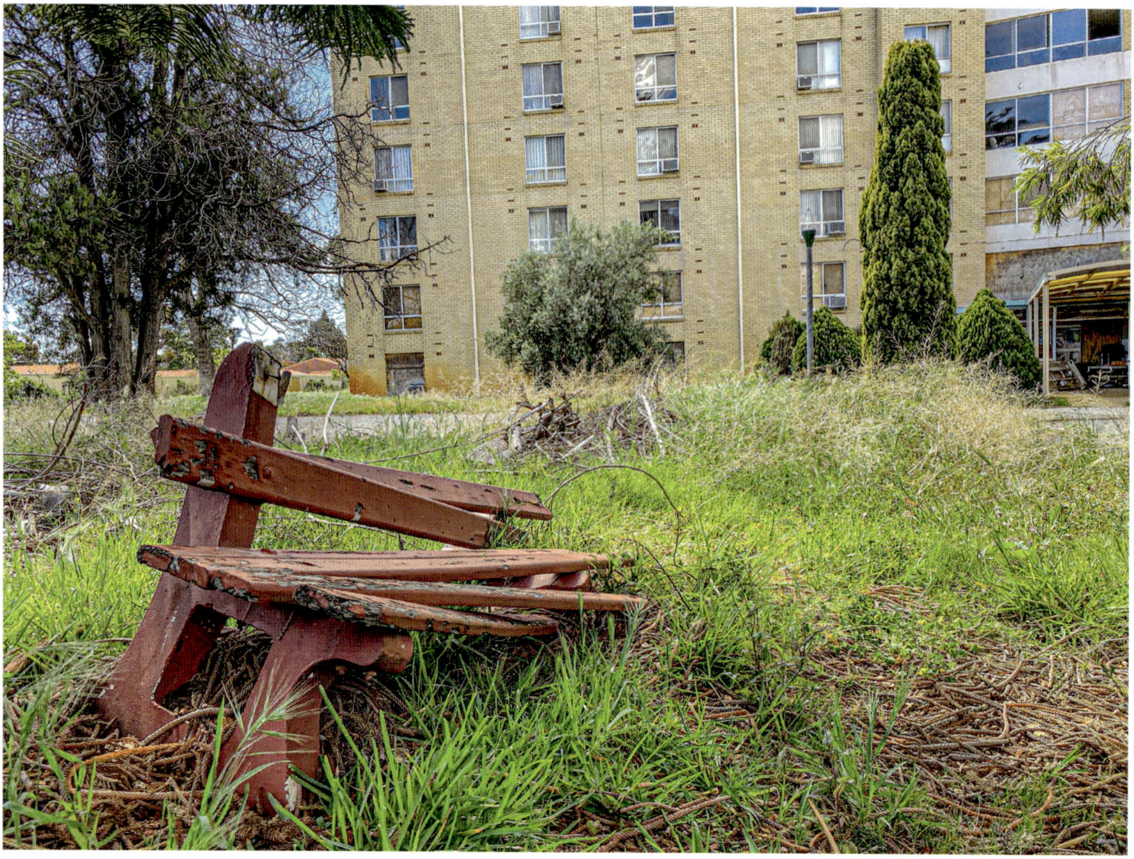

The broken remains of a bench on the grounds of the apartment complex. It is easy to imagine the social scene of elderly people and carers walking about, enjoying the warm sunshine.

OPPOSITE PAGE:
View of the second wing from the far corner of the fence line. To the right behind the tree is the third wing, with units limited to three floors. Common rooms are located on all floors where the wings connect, as shown in the centre of the bottom image. Many of its windows are either boarded up or smashed.

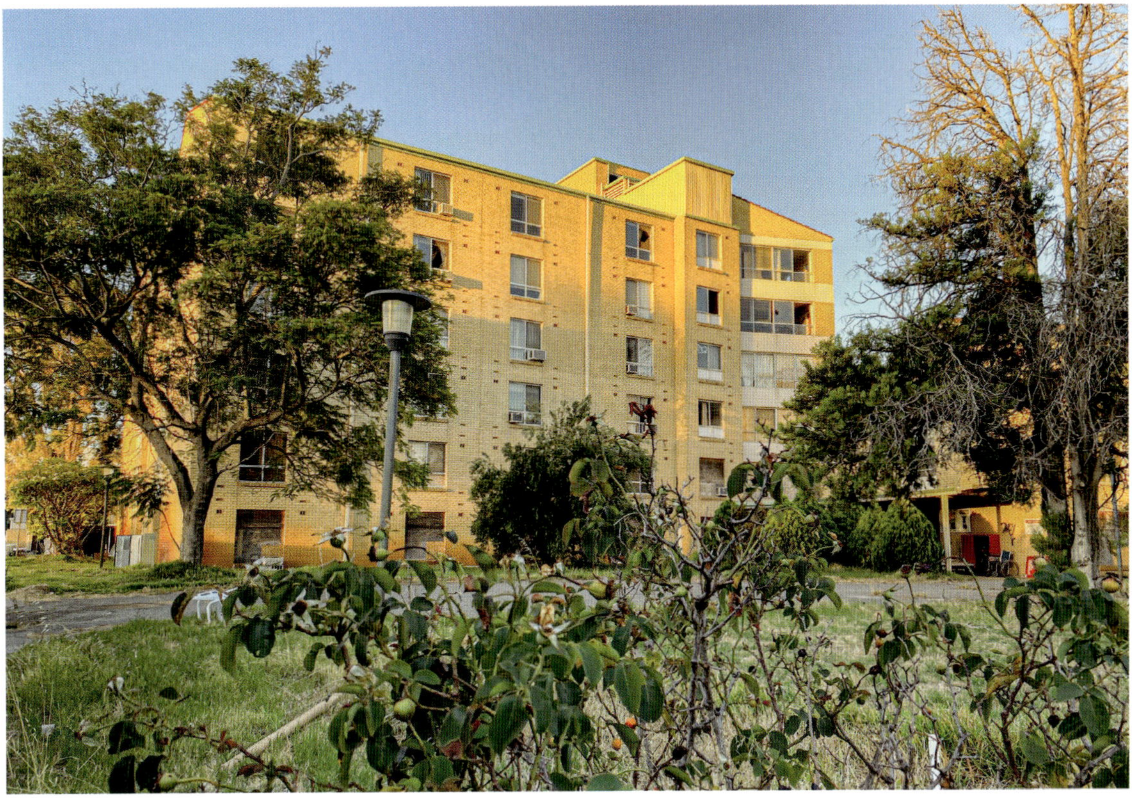

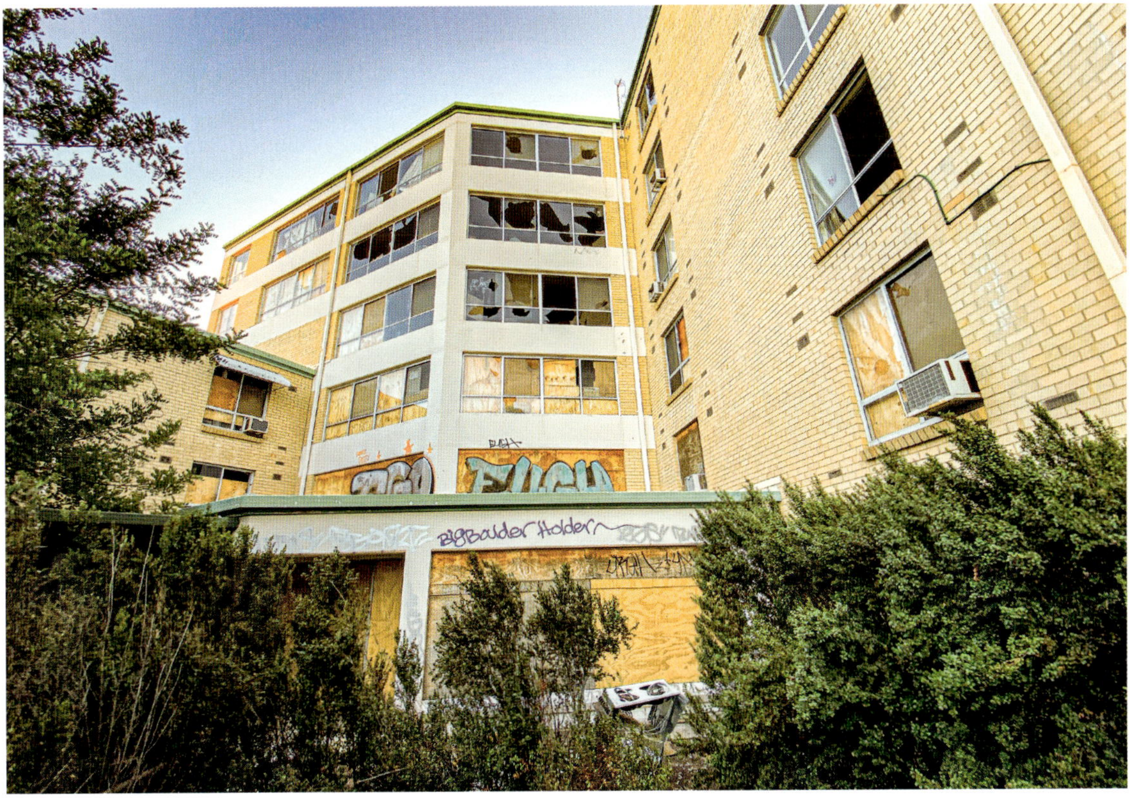
BigBoulder Holder

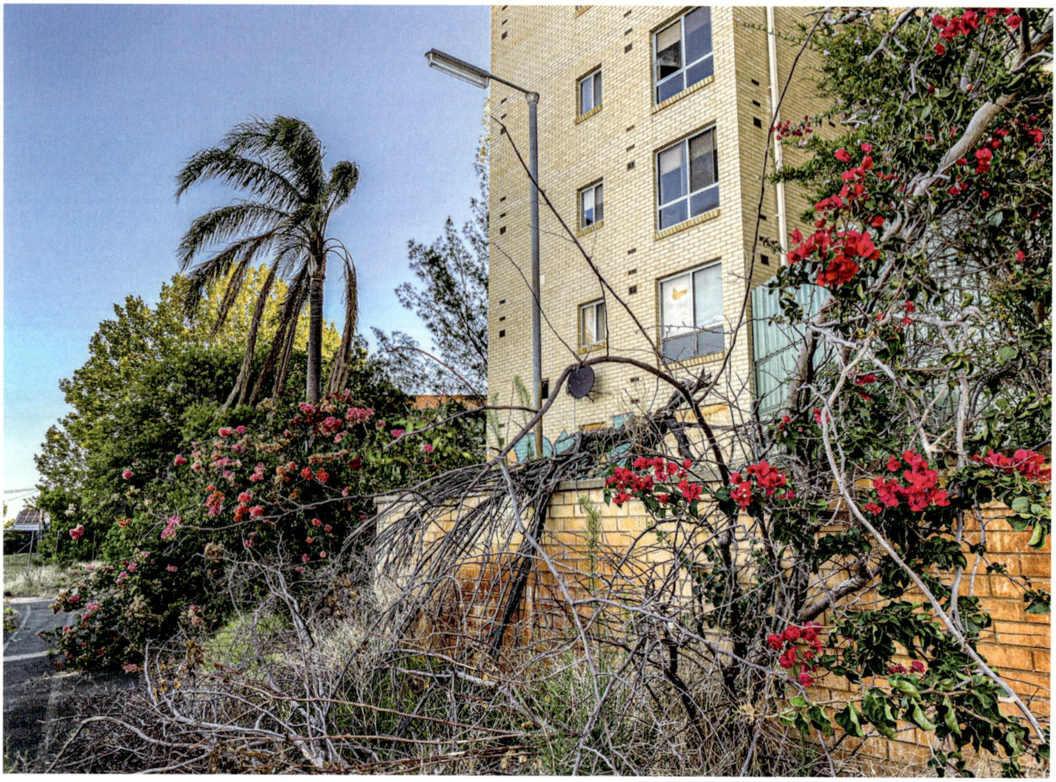

Most of the bushes and trees surrounding the apartment complex continue to thrive, particularly with the warm temperatures of late.

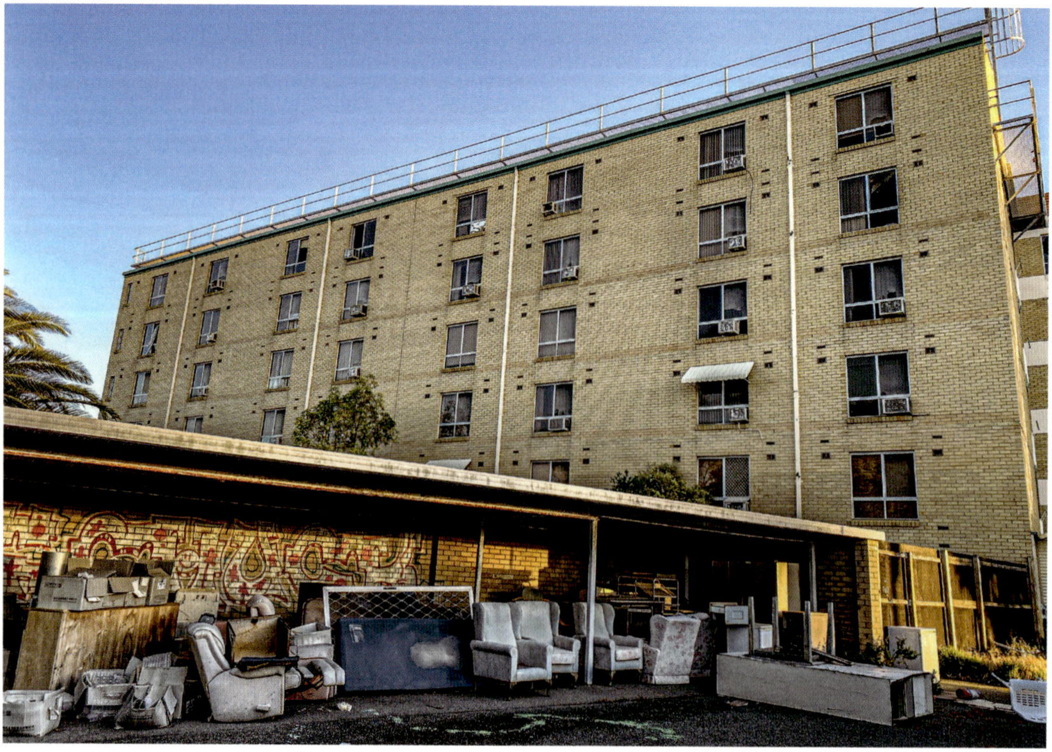

A view from one of the carports at the back of the complex, two mnths before demolition began.

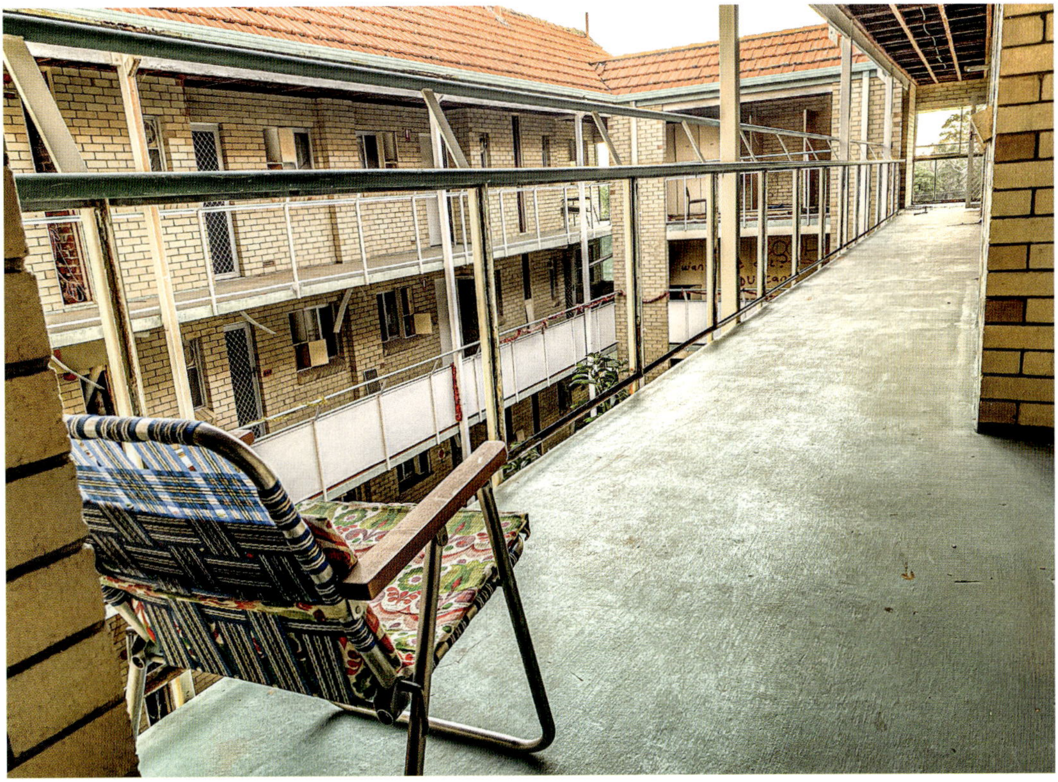

An inviting chair overlooking the simple but quiet second wing.

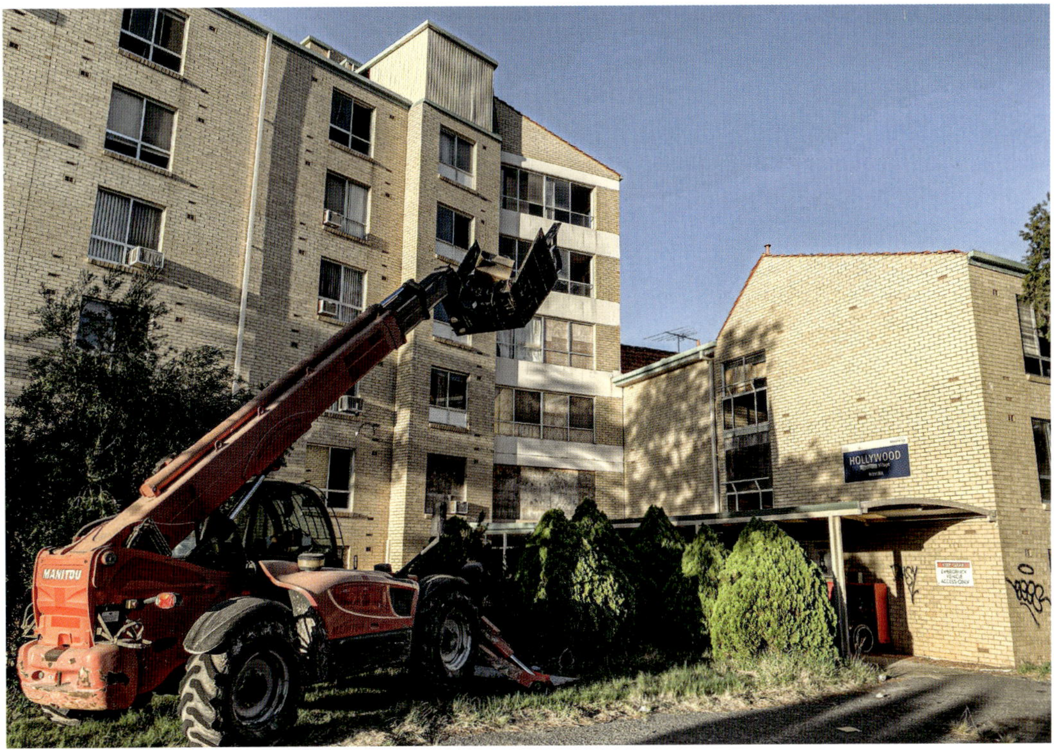

A Manitou telehandler is present on site to assist with the demolition. They are one of the most utilised pieces of hydraulic machinery in the construction, mining and agriculture sectors in Australia.

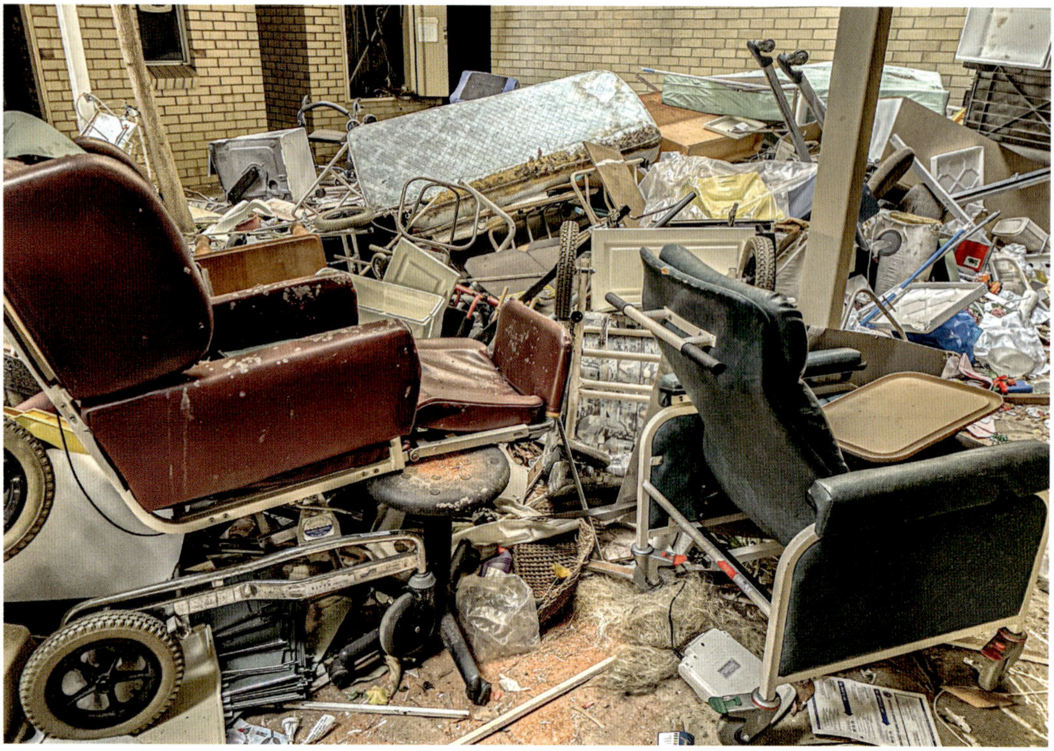

More than a month into internal demolition and the piles continue to grow in the quadrangle on a daily basis, as rooms are completely stripped.

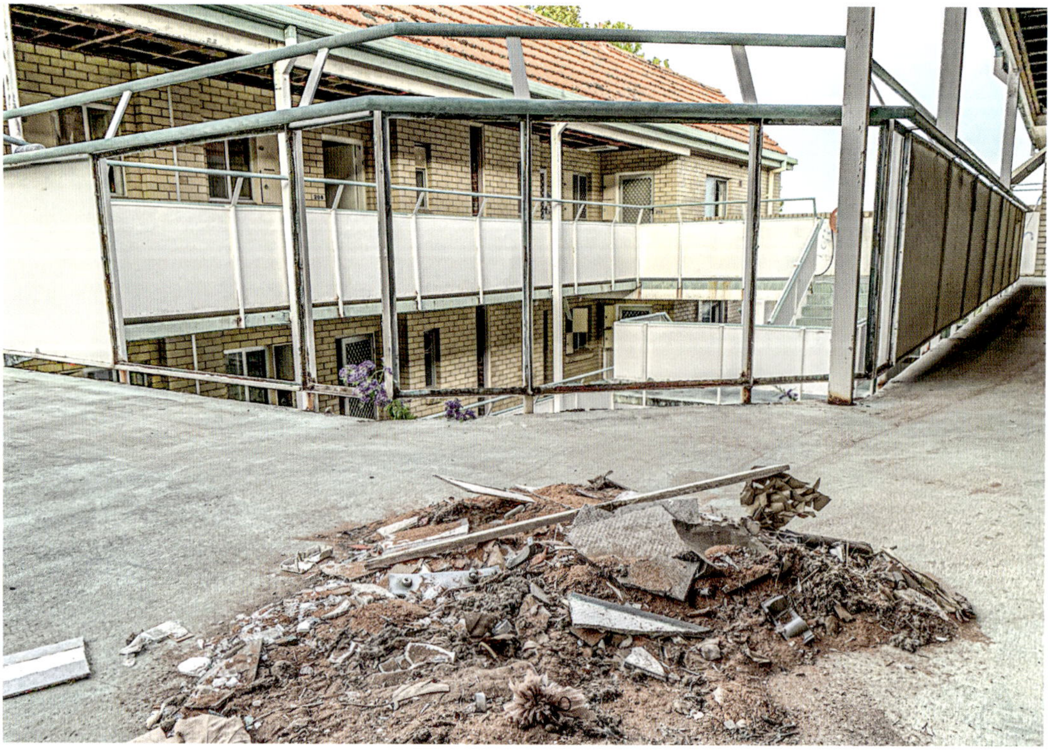

A swept up pile on the top floor of the three-storey block, as infill panels along the walkways are removed. They were made from a fibre cement material identified as Amosite and Crocidolite asbestos, which had a risk rating of Very Low.

PRINCESS MARGARET HOSPITAL

The Princess Margaret Hospital (PMH) was a children's hospital and research centre located on Roberts Road in Subiaco, Western Australia.

It opened in 1909 after twelve years of community fundraising and closed its doors on 10 June 2018.[1] All patients were transferred to the newly built Perth Children's Hospital in Nedlands.

I was lucky enough to find a contractor to help me take some photos of the inside.

Internal demolition had started some time ago, stripping almost everything in sight. As a result, there really was not much to see.

Even though I was not too enthusiastic about urbexing this site, I felt it was important to photograph what remained before it quickly disappeared, in a physical sense. PMH had played a role in the lives of hundreds of thousands of Perth families over the years and throughout many generations. Many foreigners from the Eastern States and tourists alike had also been touched by this place—just like my mate, who was desperate to see the inside, which was made possible with my photos.

I had attended PMH for a number of appointments as a child, as well as at least one emergency department admission for an asthma attack and a one-week stay for tests. I had felt like a lab rat, being prodded and probed, although the results were not drastically going to benefit the human race. Just my health.

It was fairly boring for most of the time, especially when my Game Boy ran out of batteries and I did not dare press the duress button by my bed.

The highlight was definitely the Fun Zone, where they had computer games. I was at the age when that was the only thing that really mattered in life. Unfortunately, it was not the same as home, where I could play for hours on end. The nurses had some fanciful idea of making me accountable, by partaking in education when they could not have possibly known my school curriculum or class level. Still, they tried to ban me from going to the Fun Zone when I failed to complete my school work but their success was rather limited when I took the stairs.

Even if I had been admitted to this hospital recently, very little was recognisable. Apart from the occasional sticker and creative paintwork on the walls, the wards and corridors were so plain. After a while, I felt like I was taking the same photos over and over.

Even the views from the windows started to feel the same, aside from being taken at different angles and from various floors. I had some fanciful idea of photographing the entire main block of the hospital, which was ridiculous. The same intentions had come to mind while first exploring the Swan District Community Hospital, and after some eight hours there and being so close to achieving it, I was ready to pass out. In this case, I certainly did not have the time or energy for such a long stint in PMH and I called it quits after some six hours. I had managed to photograph close to a third of the main building.

The only place that meant more to me than anything was finding the Fun Zone and Radio Lollipop. It was towards the end when I was really starting to feel munted, but I pushed on and it was somewhat worth it. Sadly, a bomb may as well have gone off. Much of it was destroyed or taken down, but still, there was enough to photograph and at least the brightly coloured entry was intact. That was all that really mattered.

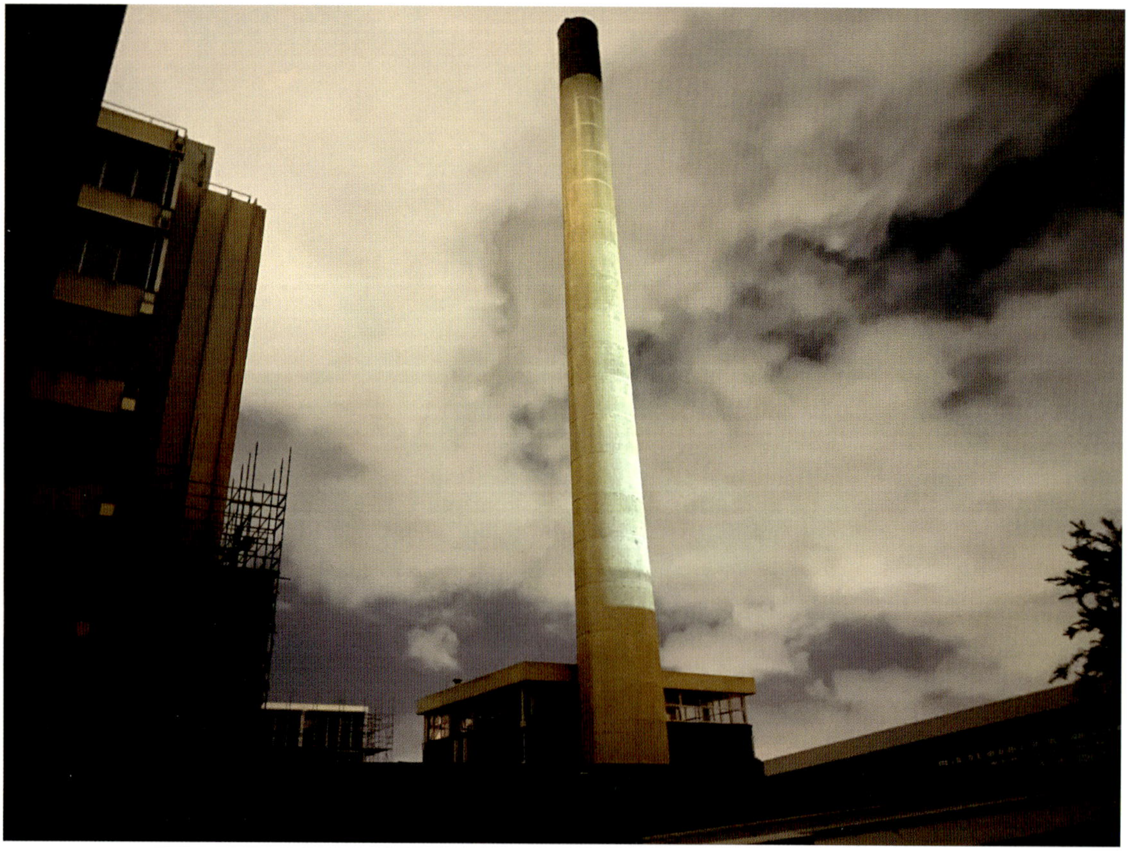

A tall chimney stack attached to the boiler room has become a symbolic landmark. This children's hospital has touched hundreds of thousands of West Australian families. There have been calls to preserve it.

---

1. Perth Children's Hospital, Princess Margaret Hospital (2018).

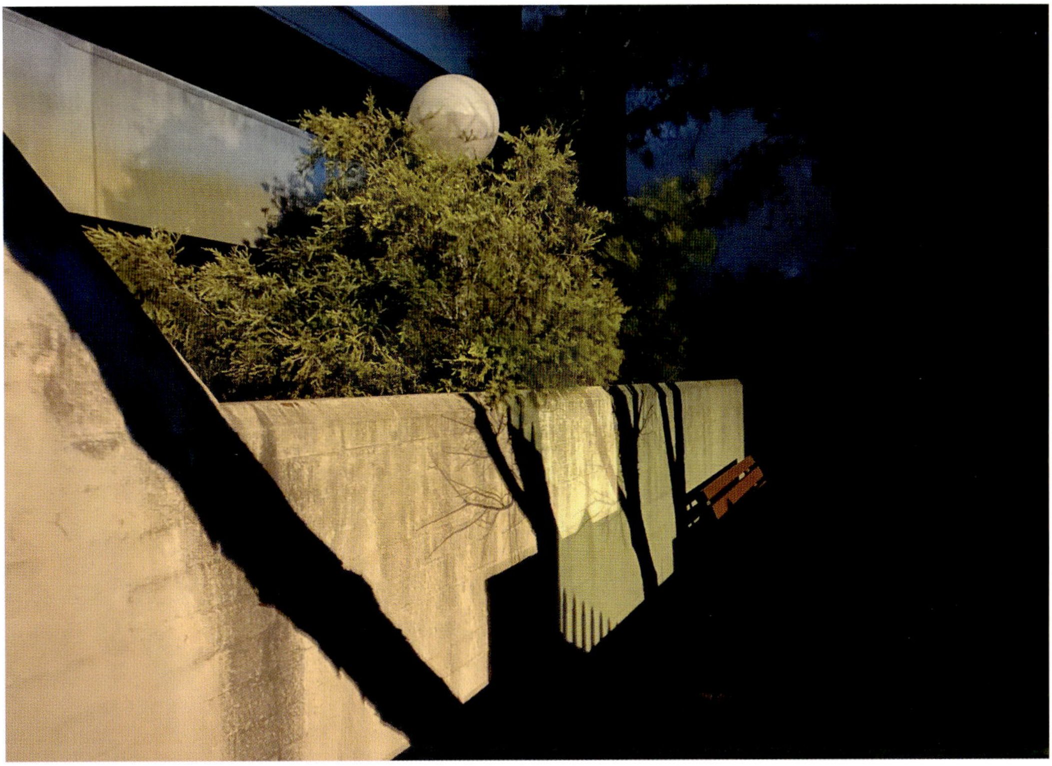

Streetlights reflect silhouettes of the nearby trees on to the wall of the Patient Services Building. An old bulb light looks like a dimly lit moon above an entanglement of green bushes.

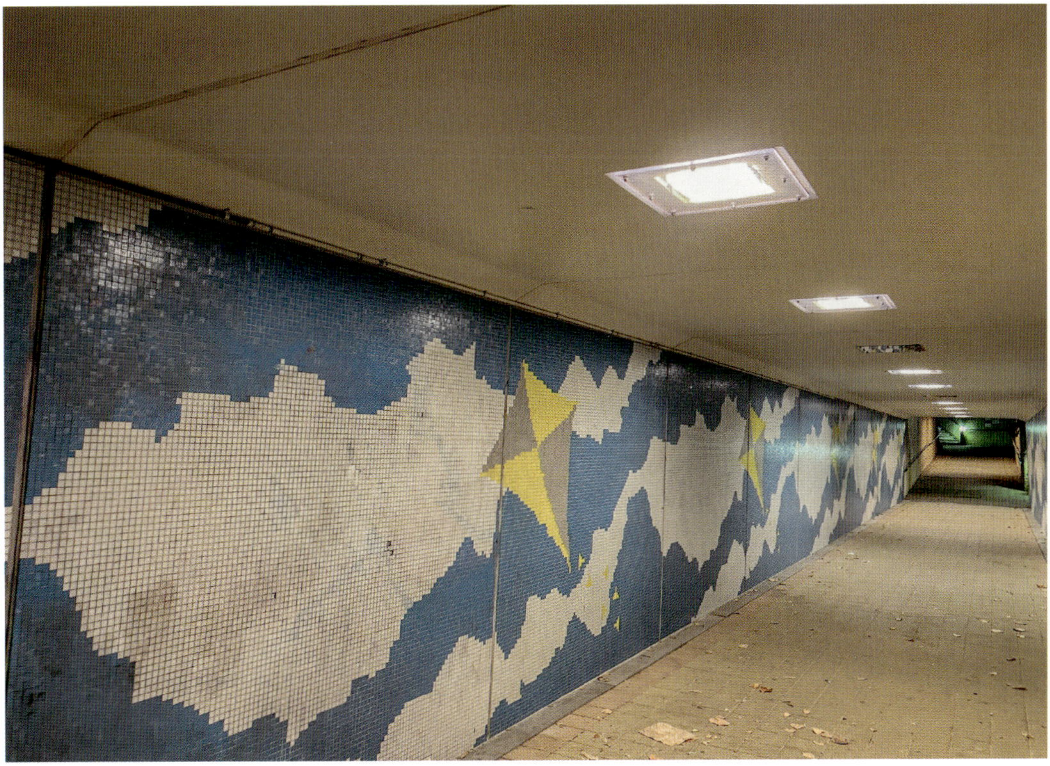

The famous Thomas Road pedestrian underpass that led to the children's hospital.

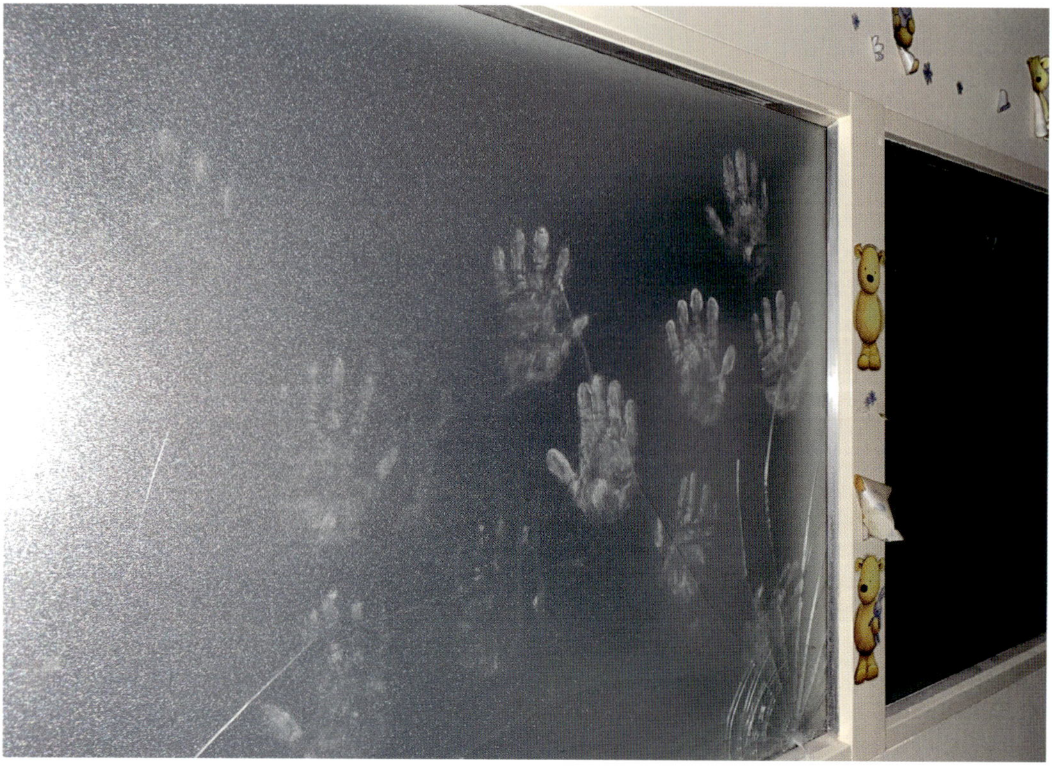

Dusty handprints are left behind on a frosted-glass window, most likely from contractors hired to strip the interior of the hospital before external demolition can take place.

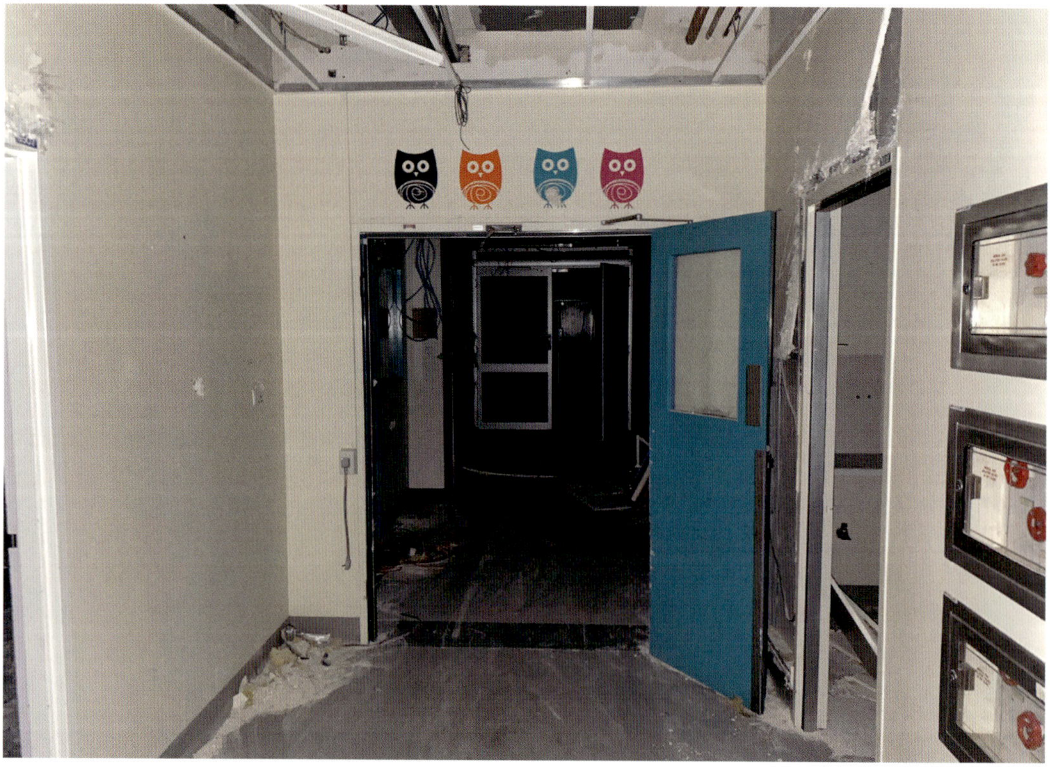

Owls guard a doorway somewhere in the Charles Moore Building.

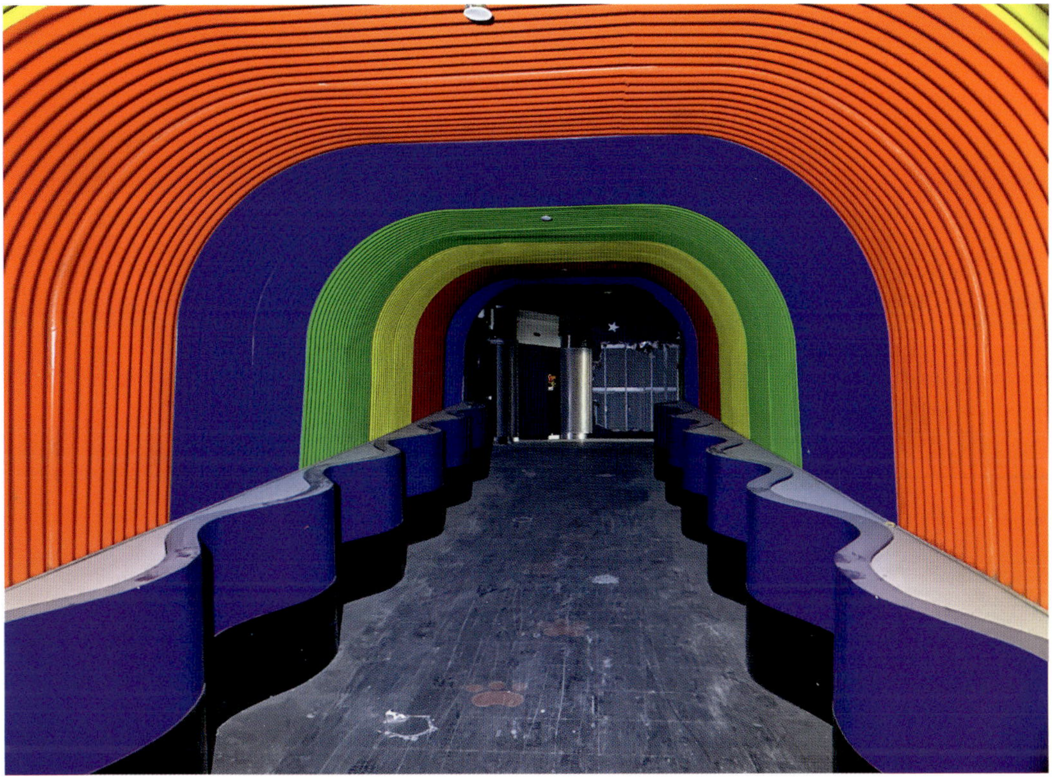

The brightly coloured walkway leading to the Radio Lollipop and Youth Zone, makes it look so much more exciting.

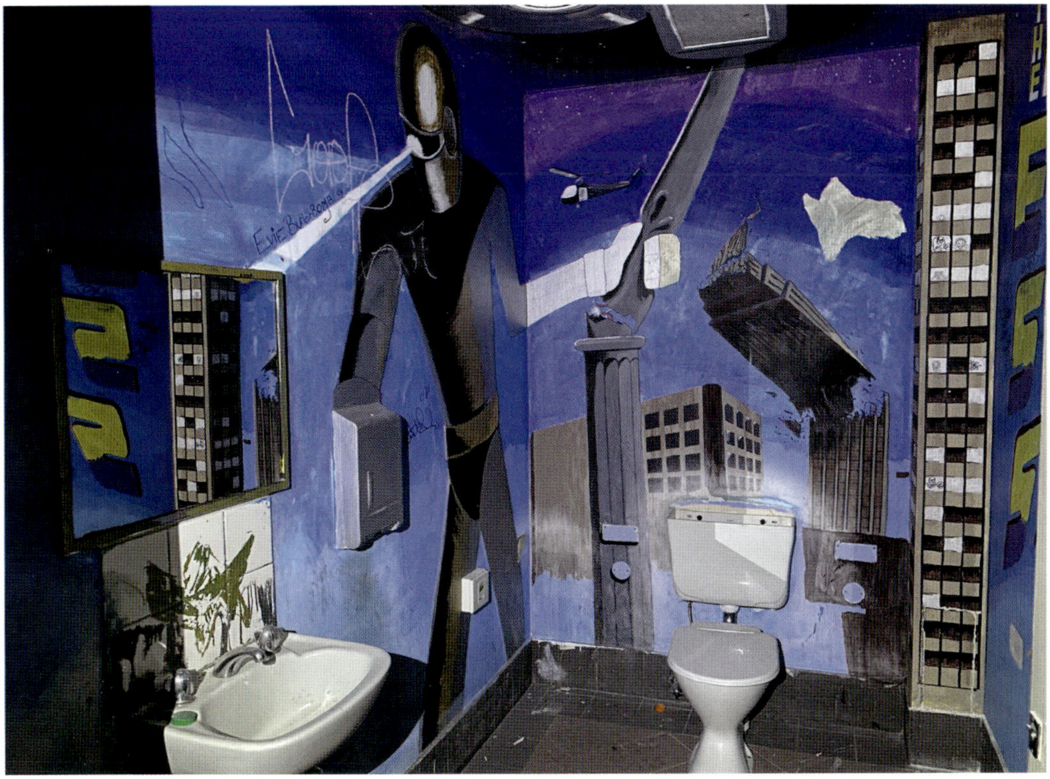

It is not often toilets are worth taking photos of, but in this case, the artwork in this one is quite entertaining.

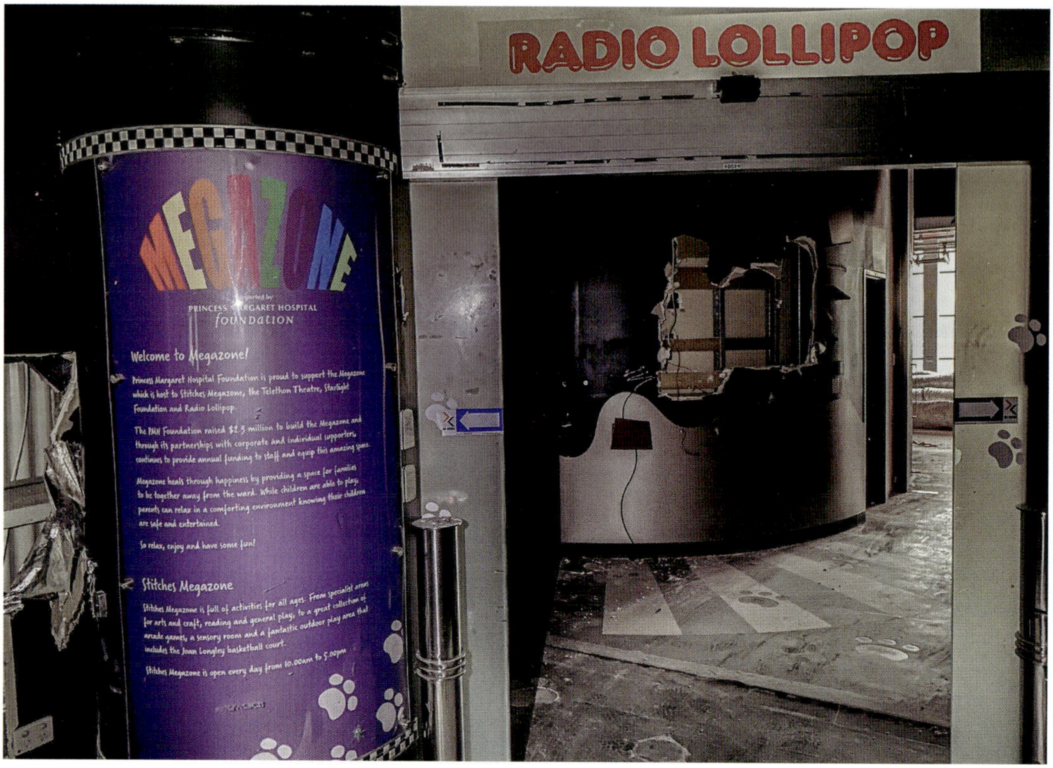

The main entrance to the Radio Lollipop, with demolition visibly in progress.

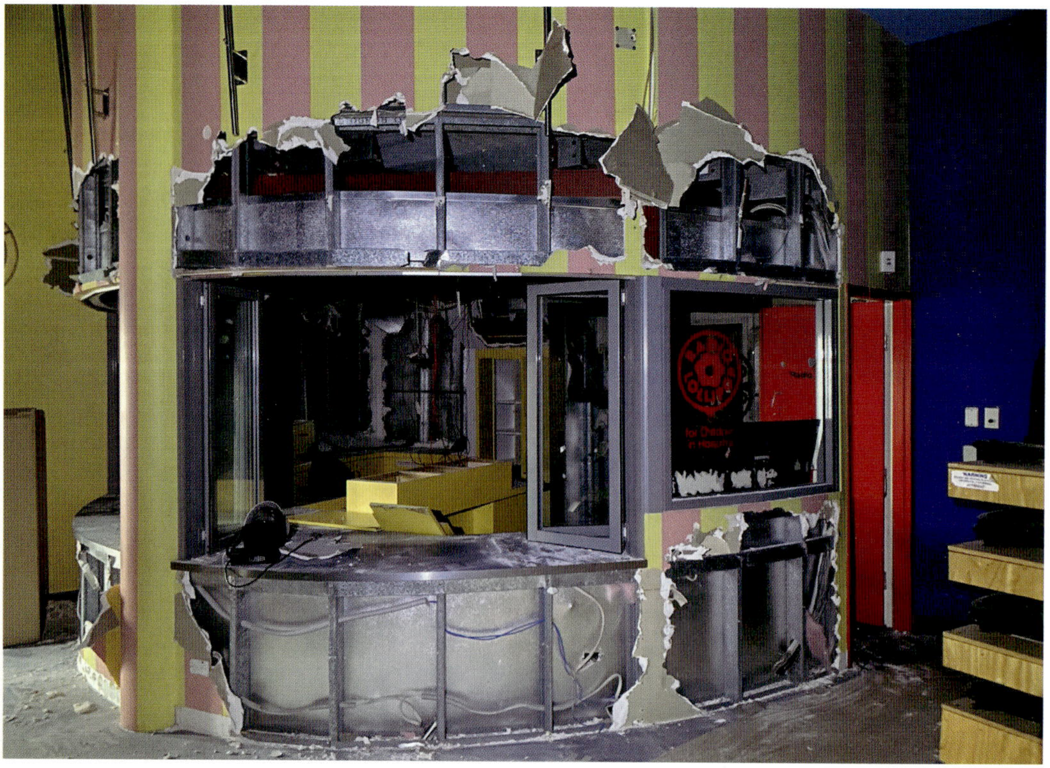

The sad remains of the Radio Lollipop desk, which first started at Princess Margaret Hospital in 1985. Once a place that brought so much joy to children, it is now experiencing the early stages of demolition.

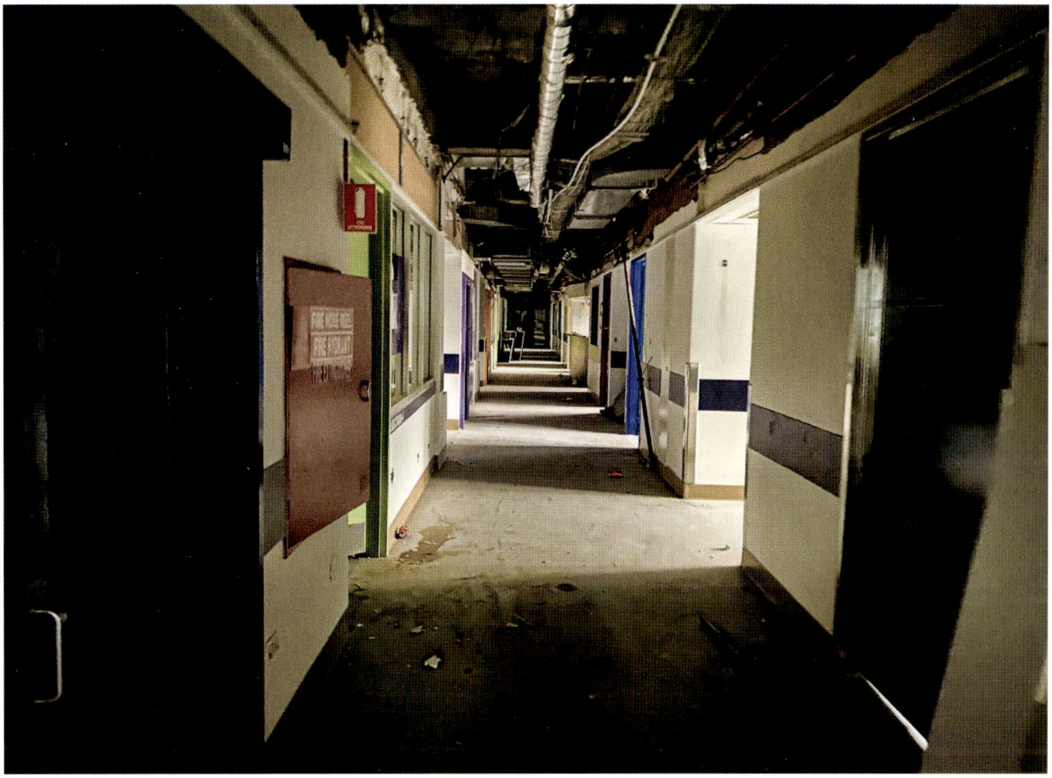

Coloured doorways line the corridor, possibly helping those in the hospital to find where they need to go a little more easily.

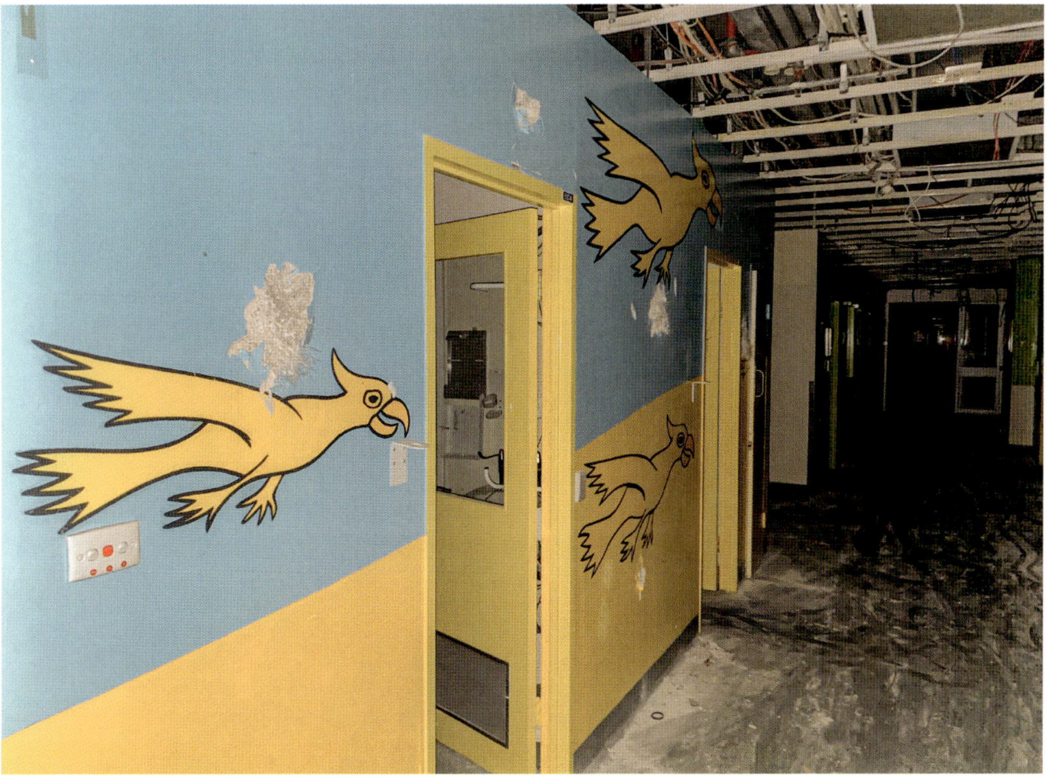

One of the more pleasant hospital corridors, a simple dash of colour makes it so much nicer.

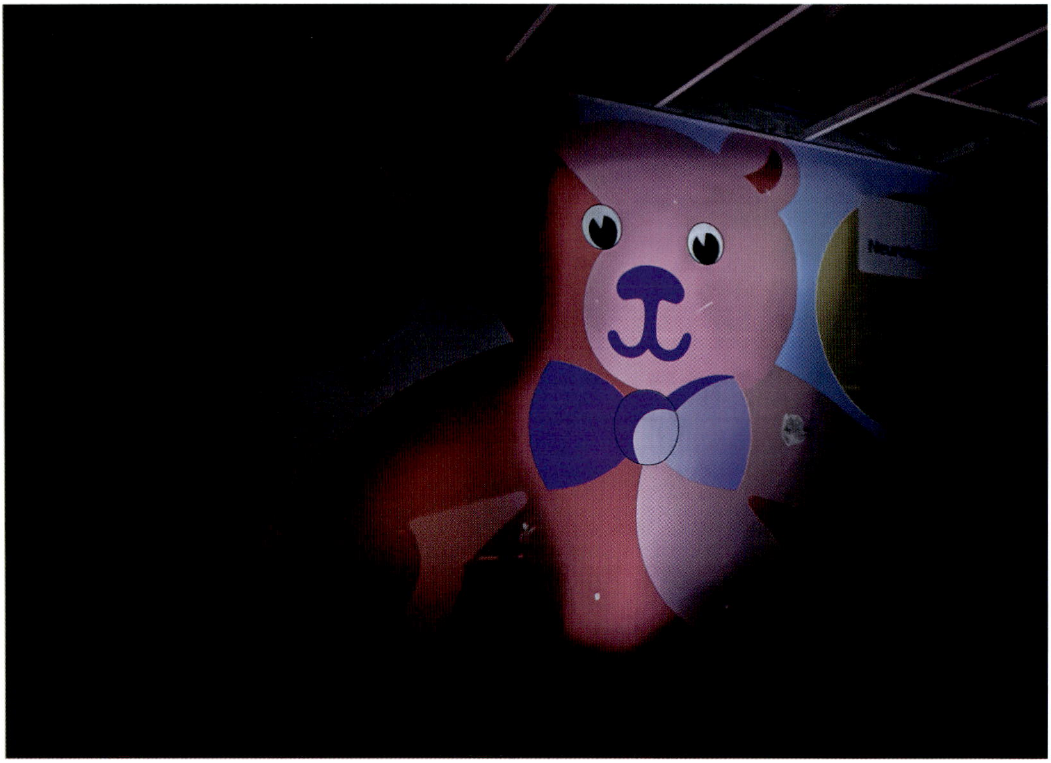

A pink teddy bear looks on with a faint smile, although perhaps with more light, it would look a lot less sinister.

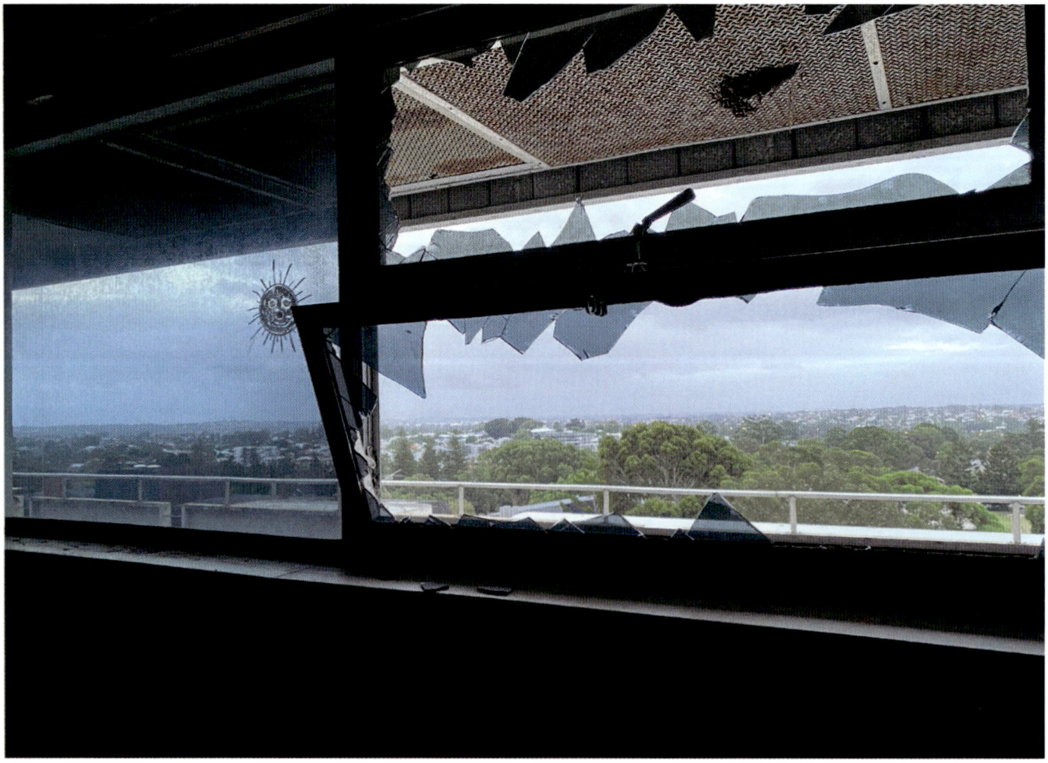

A smashed window looks out into the northerly direction of Perth. Darkening storm clouds roll in, ready to damper the spirits of anyone hoping to wake up to the joys of watching a beautiful sunrise.

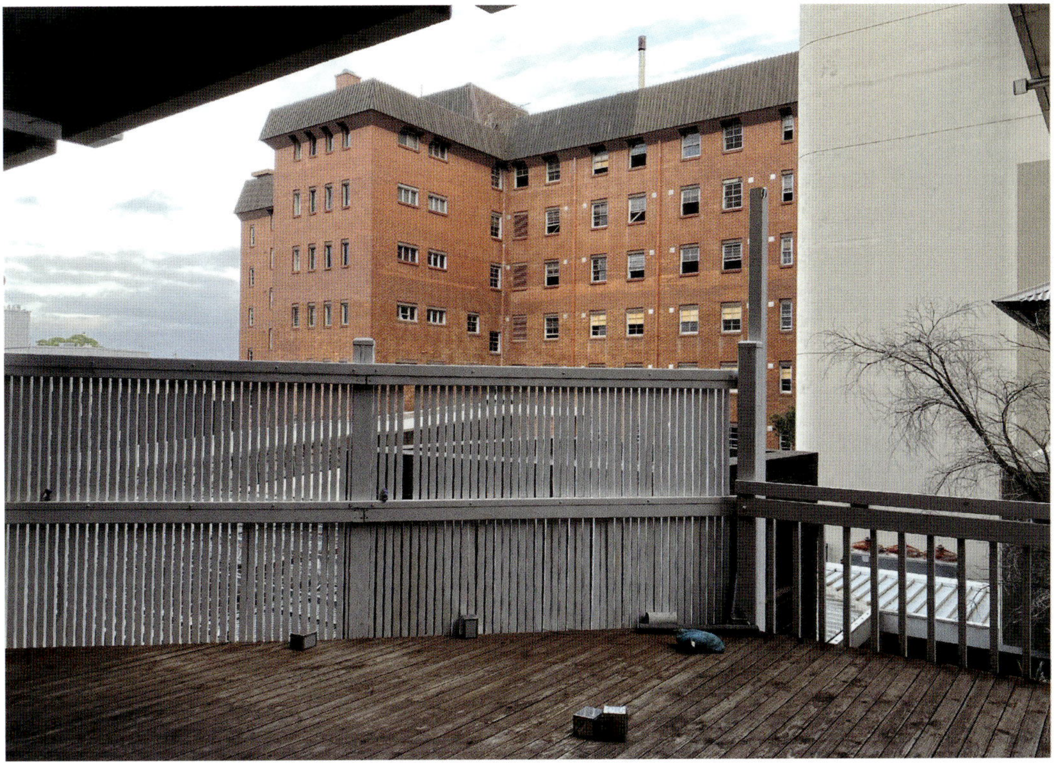

One of the older buildings on the Princess Margaret Hospital site awaiting to be demolished. The sun is starting to rise.

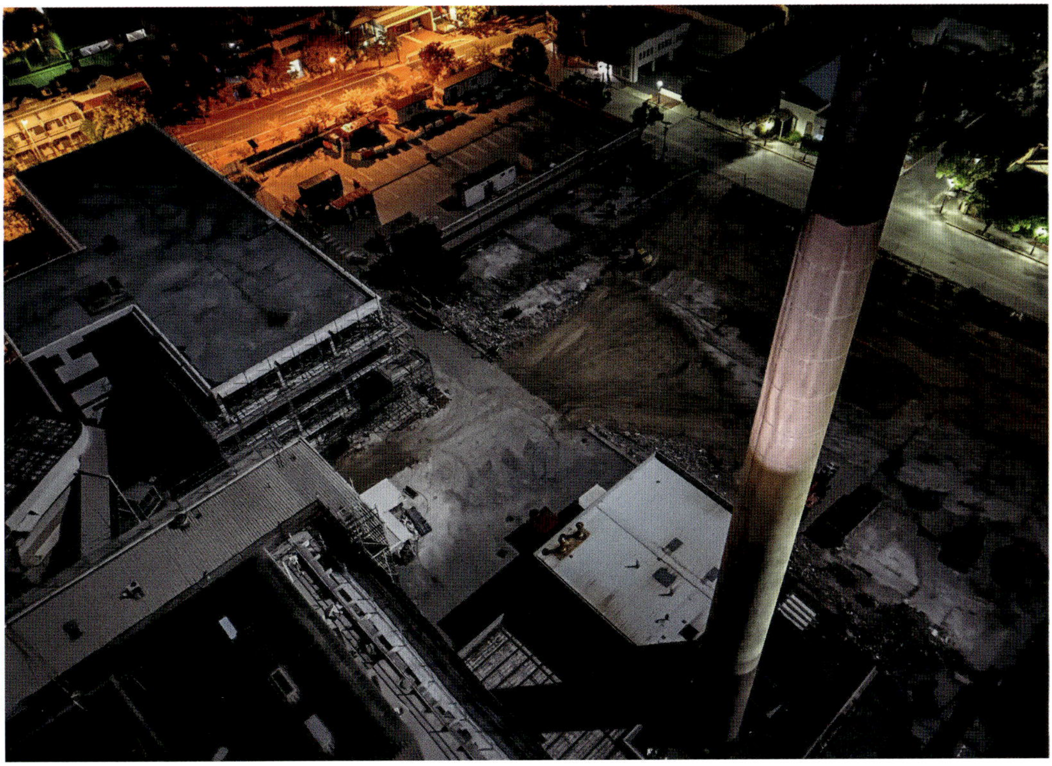

A view from above of the demolition site with a drone.

SWAN DISTRICT COMMUNITY HOSPITAL

Some places seem to evoke a strong sense of awe. Mysteries abound behind wire enclosures. Imagination running wild with the weeds as nature takes back control. Dilapidated building structures start to collapse as they tire with fighting adverse weather conditions, year after year. Vandals, often stereotypically referred to as 'kids', hasten the damage after years of neglect. Maintenance, a thing of the past.

Artists and those who seek respite from their troubled worlds, take to bare walls to practice their murals and graffiti. Messages to the world, limited to the few who come and view them. Witty, strange, and, at times, worthy of a photograph to preserve the memory of it all, once the future finally arrives and demolition takes it away.

People of all ages, including avid urbexers, taking it all in with photos and videos to share with the world, also come here for some downtime. A place of calm and silence, away from the troubles and dramas that surrounds their daily life. Compounded stress, leaving them nothing short of depressed, feeling out of control to the point of suicidal. This place of respite eases the mental wounds, however short it may last.

Many people I know have visited Swan District Community Hospital, but for most, it was more than a year ago. It was only towards the end of 2020 that my fascination for this place began to consume me.

My first visit was solo. A scary, potentially terrifying thought for most. It was around this time, I had lost my fears. Not even the darkest of nights or death-defying heights, once my biggest fears that had been present for most of my life, could scare me.

The rain came in, hard and heavy. Sounds of drips fell from all directions, filling me with a sense of calm and peace, which I had come to seek. Irregular pitter-patters and dings hitting tin, I watched the rings form in puddles around me, ripples circling out and about.

Darkness enveloped my existence in many places, mirroring my moods of late. Occasionally I would use my torch, the brightest light in my life. Shining it in every direction I could to absorb what I had never seen before. From artistic black mould that lined the walls to carpets resembling a map of islands with yellow, orange, and white dots—green algae forming in flooded rooms that had little reason to stir.

Hallways littered with cabling, damaged ceiling panels, pieces of wood, rubber, particles, and hoses. No doubt, all or at least most of the copper pipes had since been nicked.

I ended up coming back a few more times and every visit, I always saw something new, whether it was art, further dilapidation, or the many areas I had somehow missed. I had seen the youth mental health unit the first time I came, but it was not until a few visits later, that I realised there were two replica wings that I had missed. From the basement's crawl space to the ceilings and roof, I never liked to leave anything unexplored. It was fascinating and I wanted to see it all.

Following the opening of the Midland Health Campus in November 2015, the Swan District Community Hospital was subsequently closed.

Located in Middle Swan, north-east of Perth, the hospital was an emergency department with 193 beds and a range of outpatient services.[1] It opened on 22 September 1954 as a twenty-five-bed maternity hospital. In October 1963, an additional forty-bed general wing was opened, with a second wing in August 1971, which included new x-ray facilities and a nursing aide training school.[2] The Swan Valley Centre, a twenty-five-bed mental health unit, opened in early 2001.

During the years since its closure, many plans have been discussed as to what future awaits the ten-hectare site. Proposals have included an aged care facility, a residential estate, recreation area around the nearby Blackadder Creek, as well as an extension of the neighbouring La Salle College.[3, 4]

No ball has yet been rolled. Meanwhile, the site continues to collapse and weaken.

---

1. Department of Health, Swan District Hospital Campus (2001).
2. J. Kelly, 'End of era as Swan District Hospital shuts doors', *The Advocate*, 2015.
3. P. de Kruijff, 'Swan site aged care plan', *The West Australian*, 2019.
4. 'State signals intent for Swan Hospital site', *Echo News* 2020.

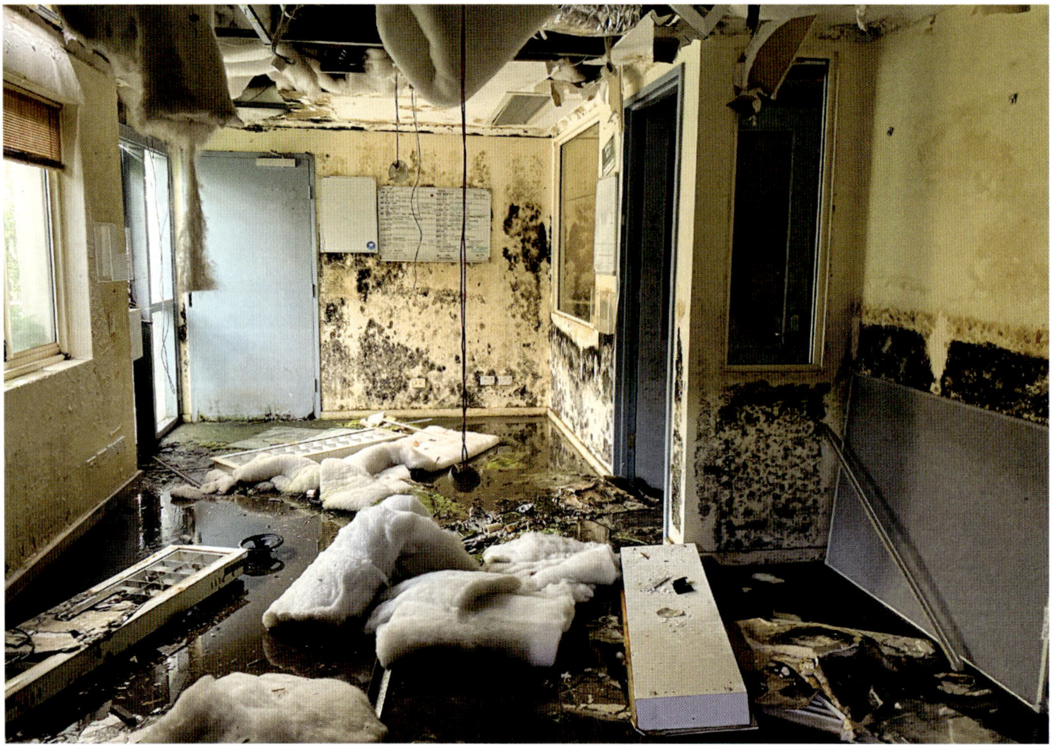

Thick black mould covers the walls of a room in the Nursing Services and Allocations Centre, one of the most dilapidated areas of the hospital.

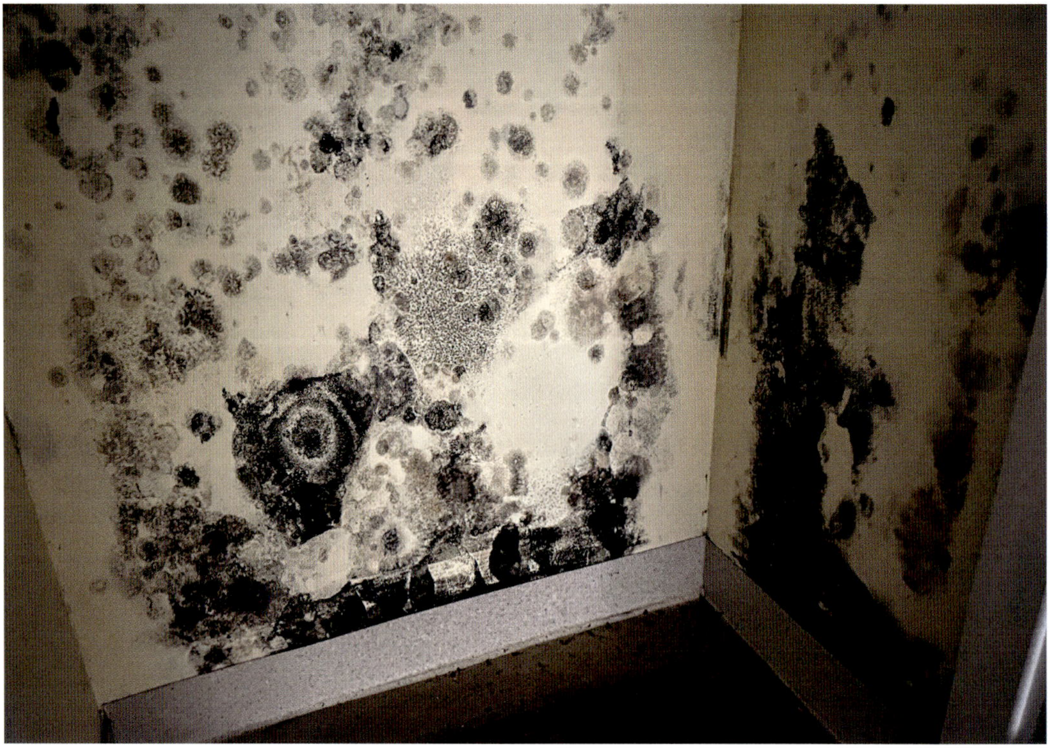

A close-up on the black mould looks more like an intricate painting that could perhaps represent the solar system or even microscopic life in the far depths of the ocean.

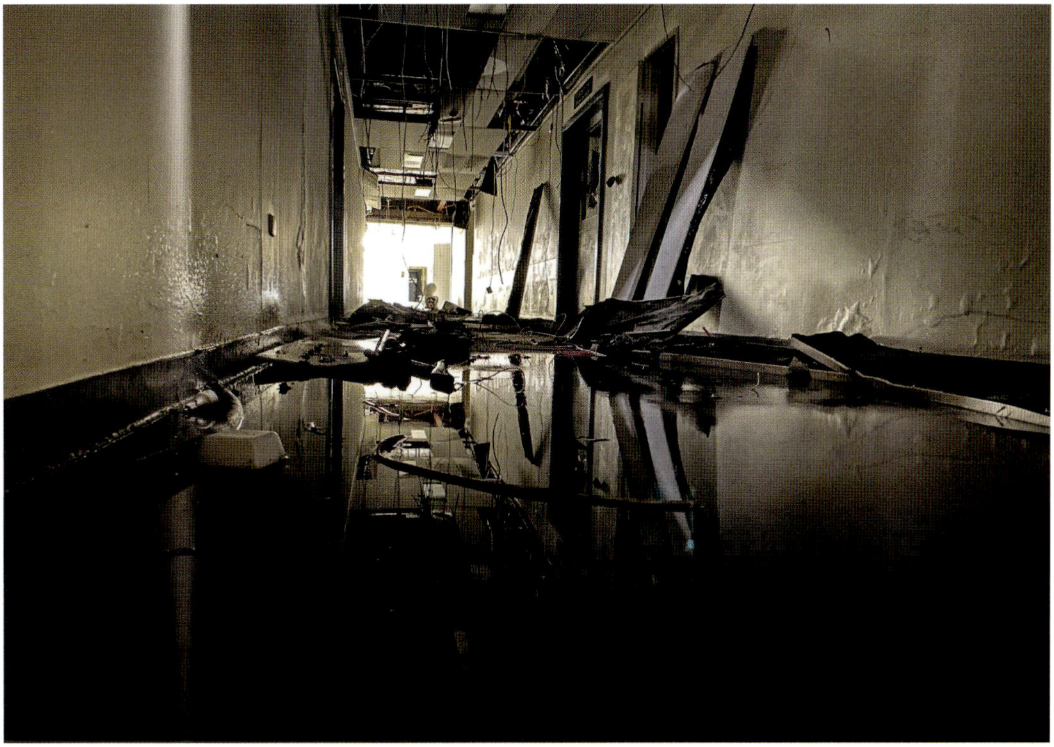

One of many flooded hallways near the emergency department. In some areas such as this one, the water will probably dry up within a week.

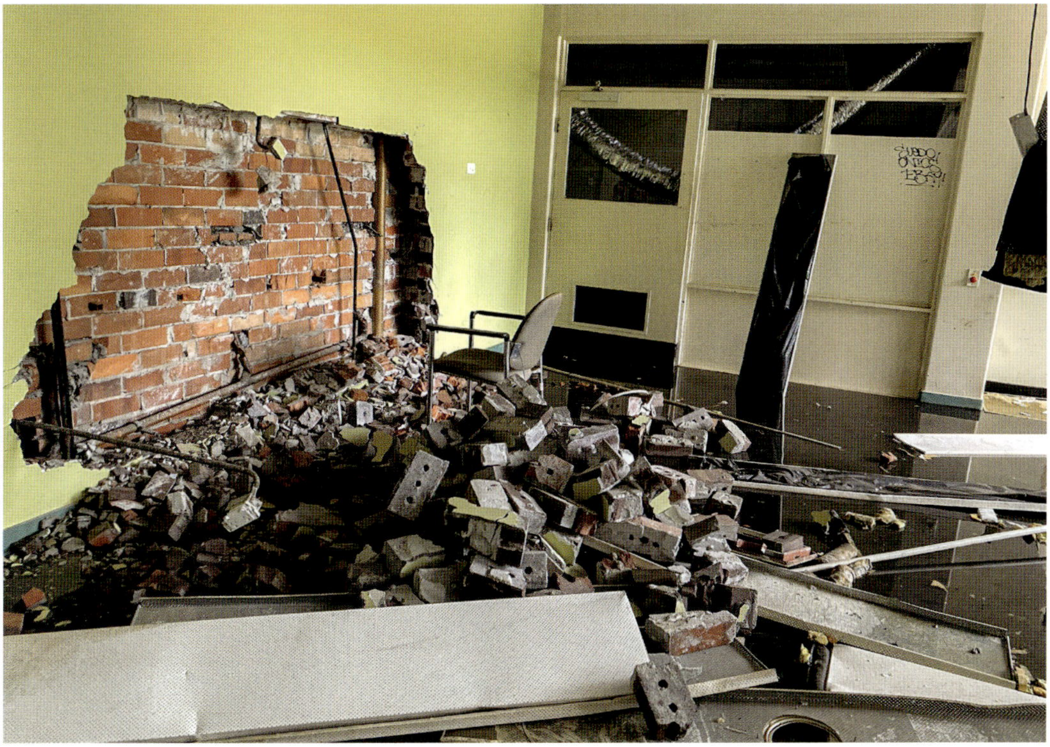

Perhaps the pipes exploded, which somehow left the chair intact and dust free. Or perhaps someone was desperately trying to cash in on the copper pipes.

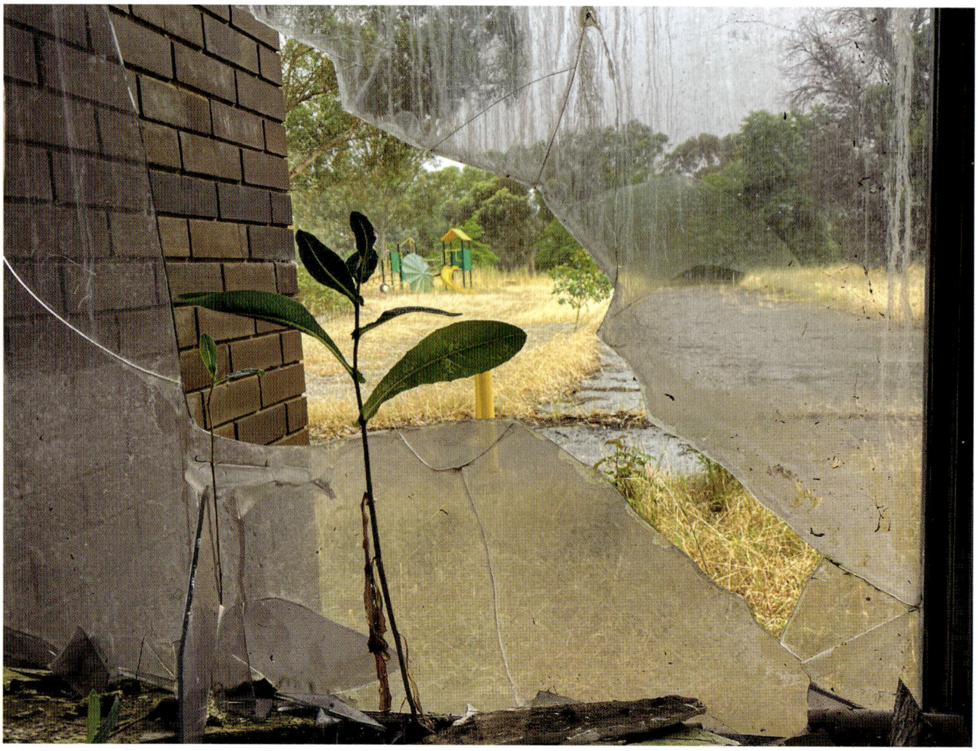

A few small plants have started to grow on the inside of the window. The basic children's playground is visible near the fence line.

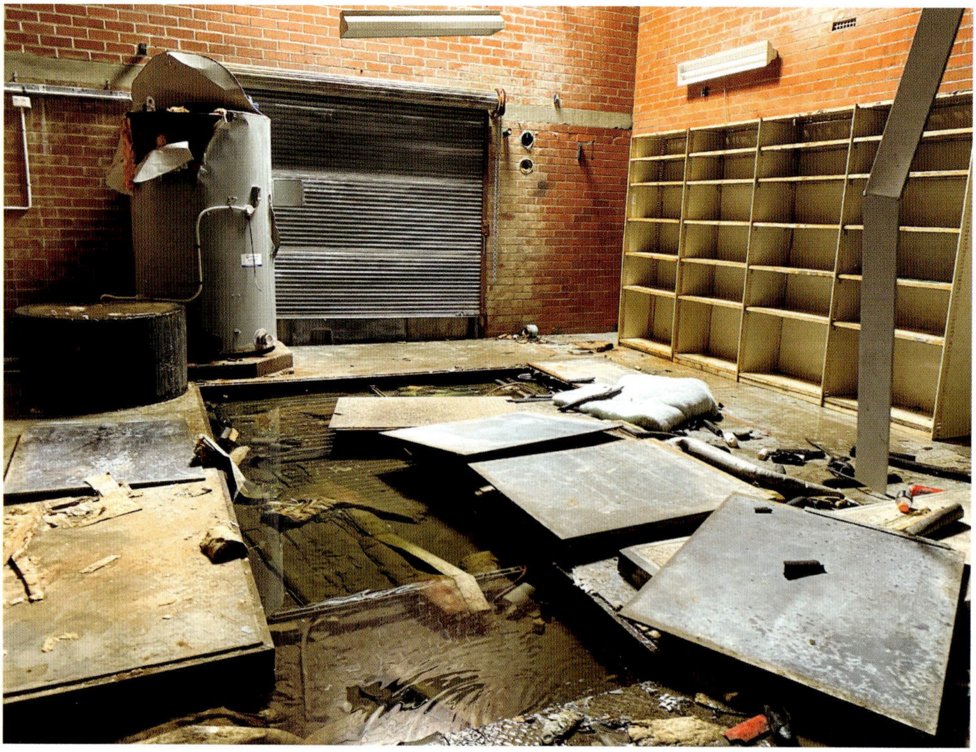

A room that is forever filled with dark, murky water. Slime covering the walkways, makes it easy to slip into the pools, which could be filled with fatal hazards ranging from chemicals, diseases, and even flesh-eating micro-organisms.

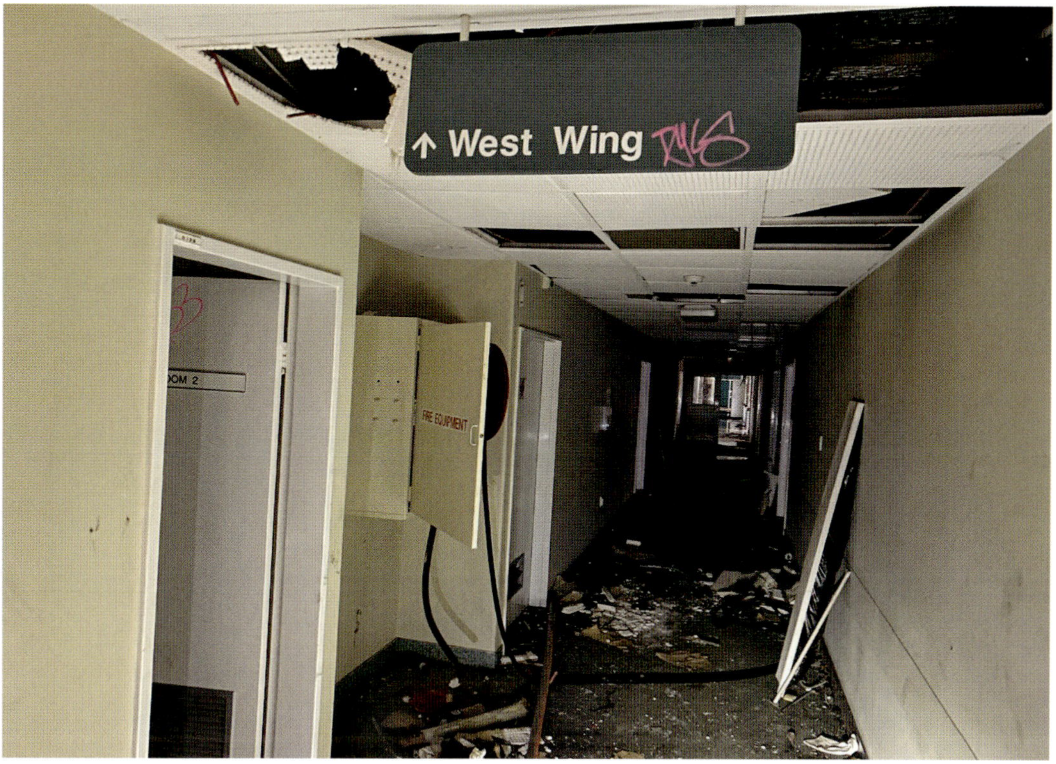

A hallway through to the west wing, one of many that makes this old hospital feel like a labyrinth. Just when you think you have reached the end, the corridor diverts into multiple directions.

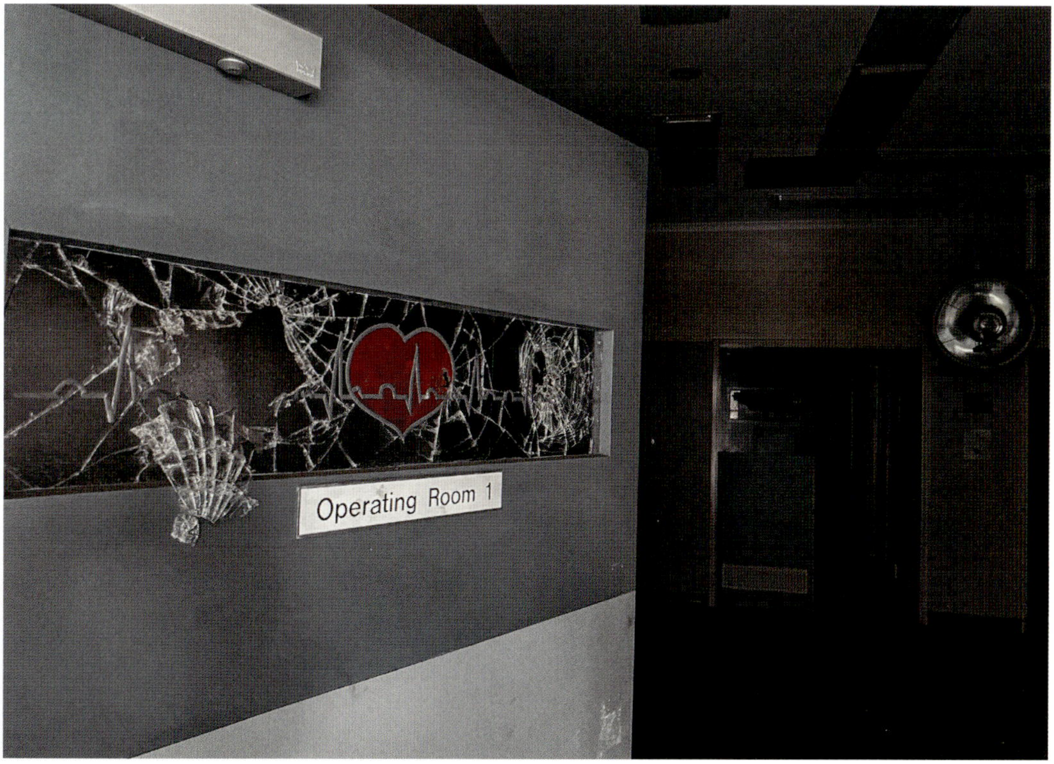

One of four operating theatres in the day surgery unit.

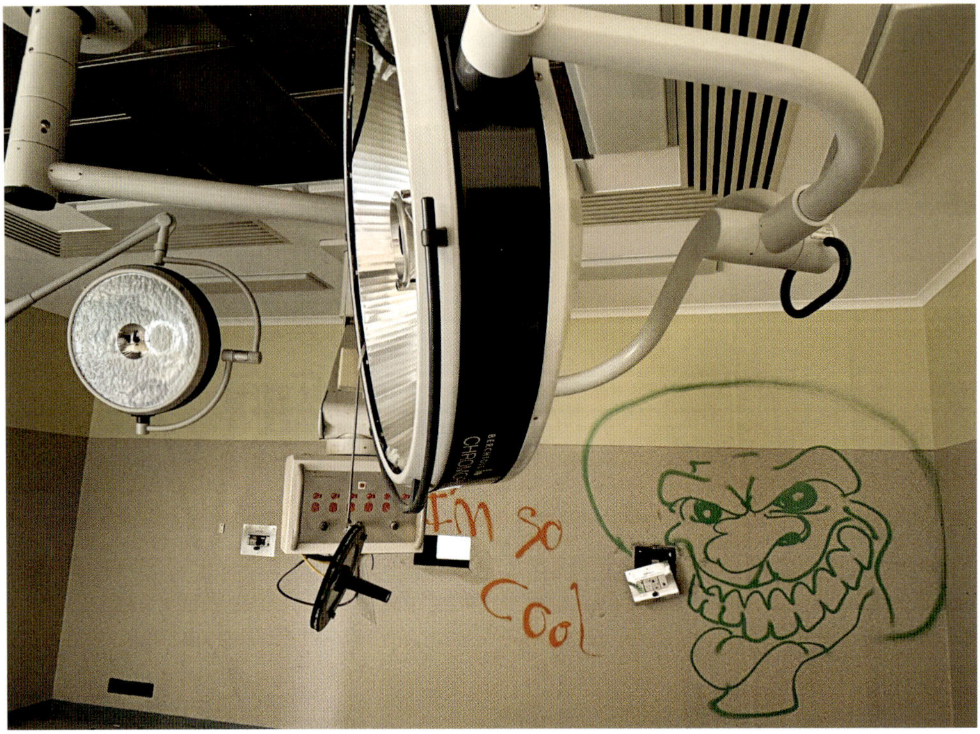

Surprisingly, a few of the operating theatre lights remain intact and not smashed, like many objects and windows in the hospital.

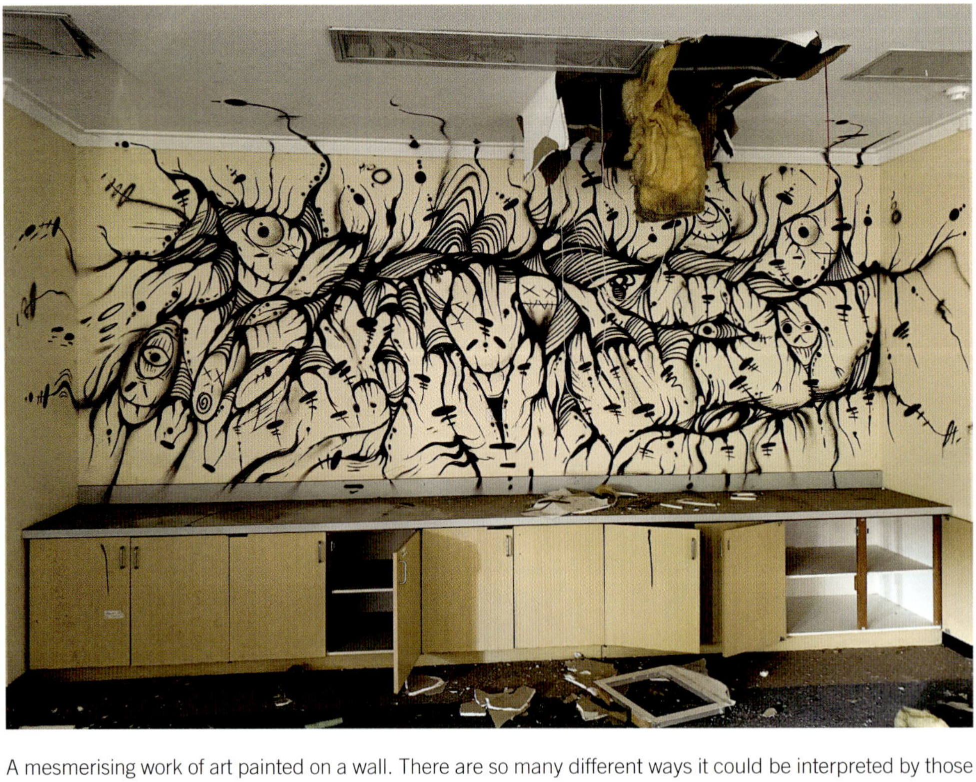

A mesmerising work of art painted on a wall. There are so many different ways it could be interpreted by those who stop to view it. The dark brown solidifies the dark feel and nature of its creation, emphasised by faces with only one eye or none and replaced with stitched marks.

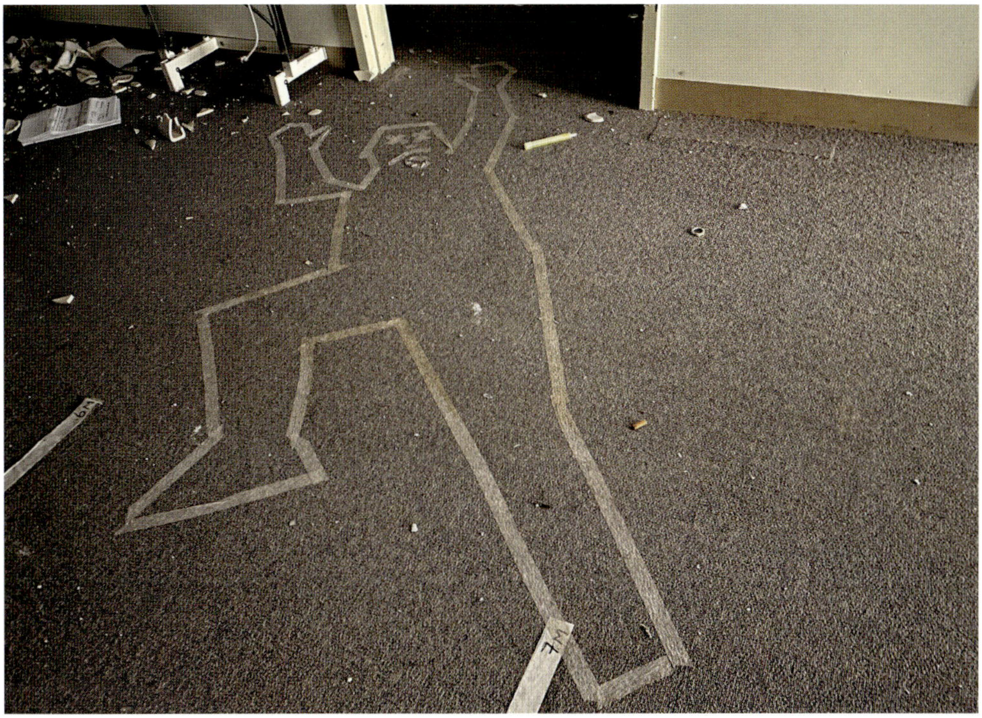

Despite the unlikely chance that someone died on the carpet, there will always be a few with a bigger imagination—although perhaps not as big as the artist with a roll of sticky tape.

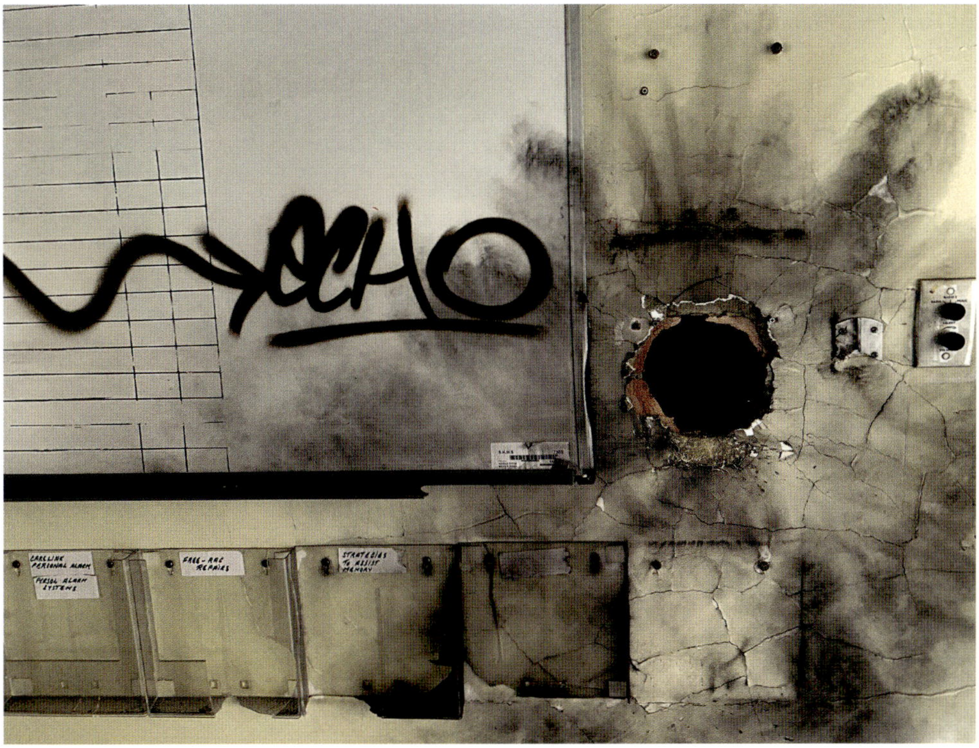

A smoky effect from a can of spray paint makes it look like a cannon ball has been shot through the wall. Reading the tag 'ECHO' feels like it symbolises sarcasm, judging from what kind of sound and how loud you could expect a cannon ball to make.

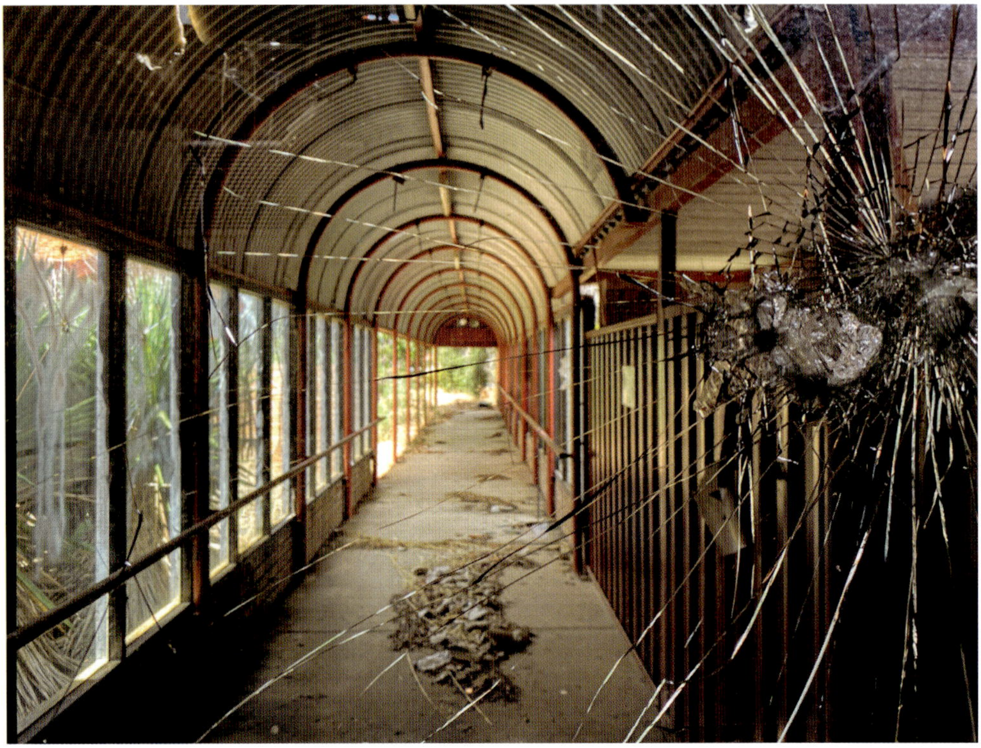

A smashed Perspex window overlooks a walkway. The door is as locked as a door can be, so perhaps the damage was a result of frustration at not being able to exit here.

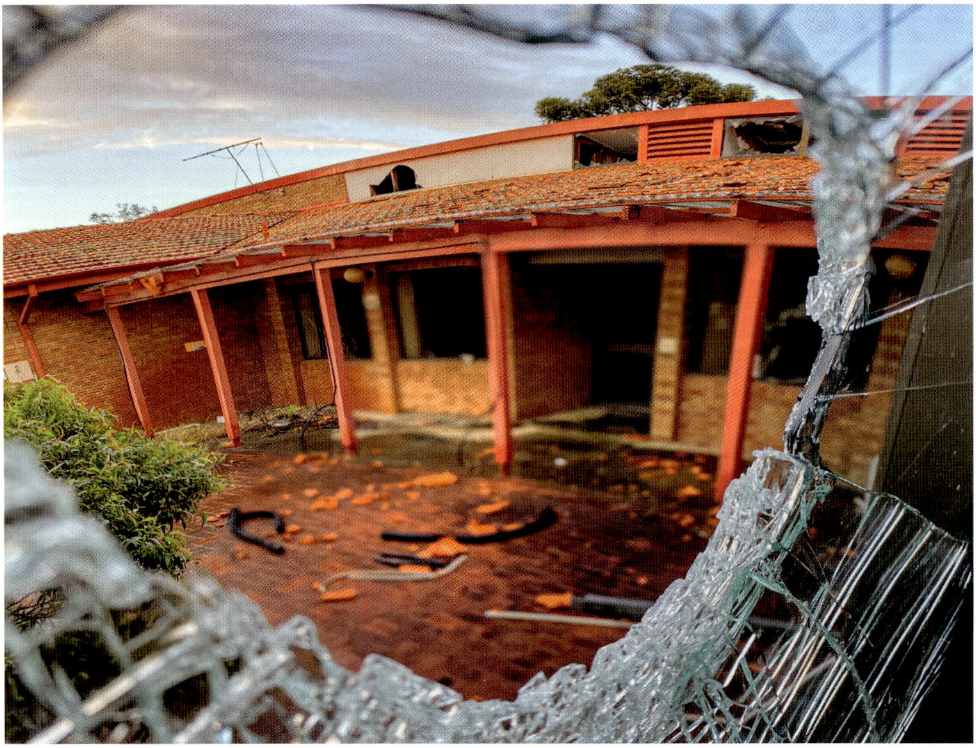

A close-up photo blended with a long shot taken through the hole of a smashed window, some thirty minutes short of a completed sunset.

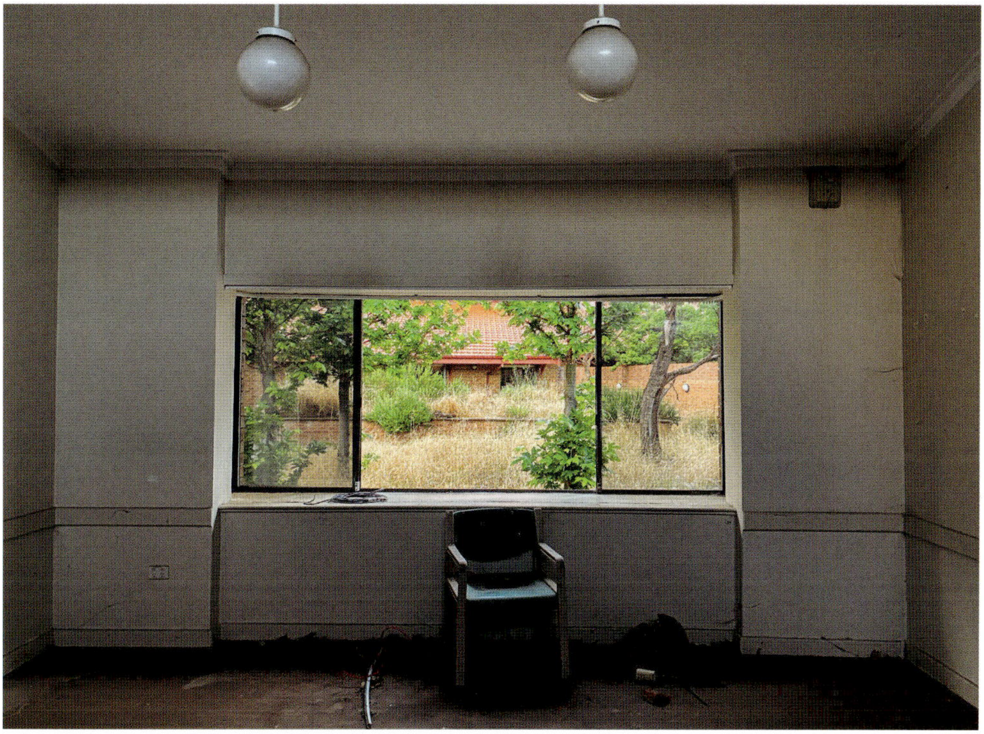

A lonely scene with a single chair. In the meantime, it serves as a safety step leading into the quadrangle of the Adolescent Mental Health Unit.

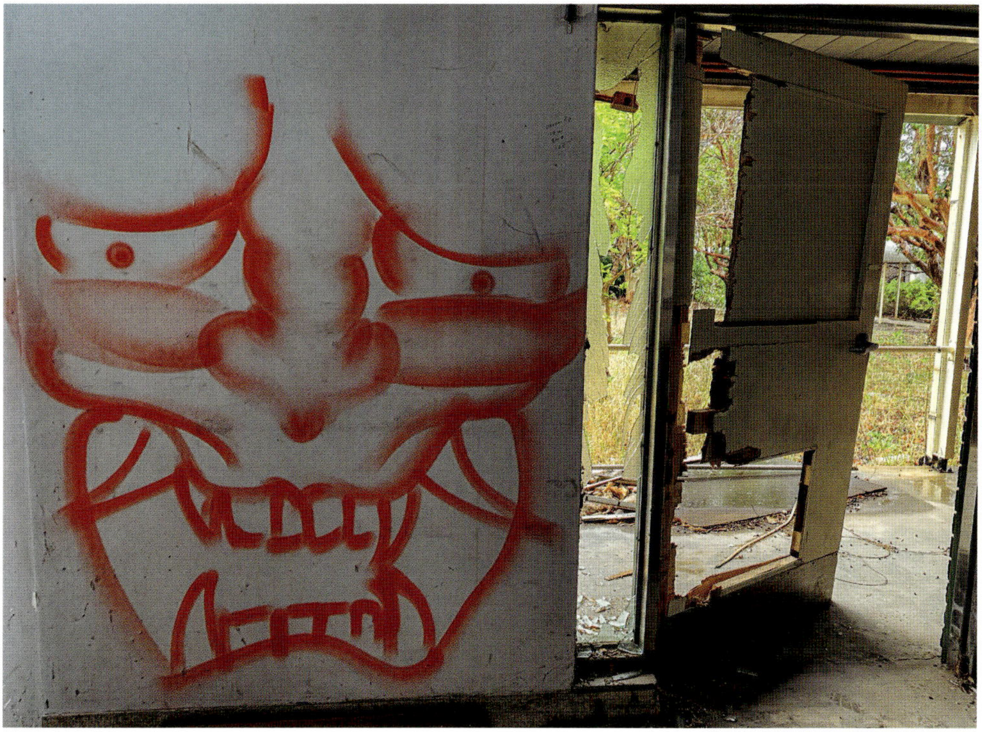

The red devil returns for a third time, after being spotted at the BHP Jetty Number 1 and the Midland Railway Workshop. Sighting known pieces of art or the artist's style, feels like playing a game of *Where's Wally?* and makes exploring abandoned buildings even more fun.

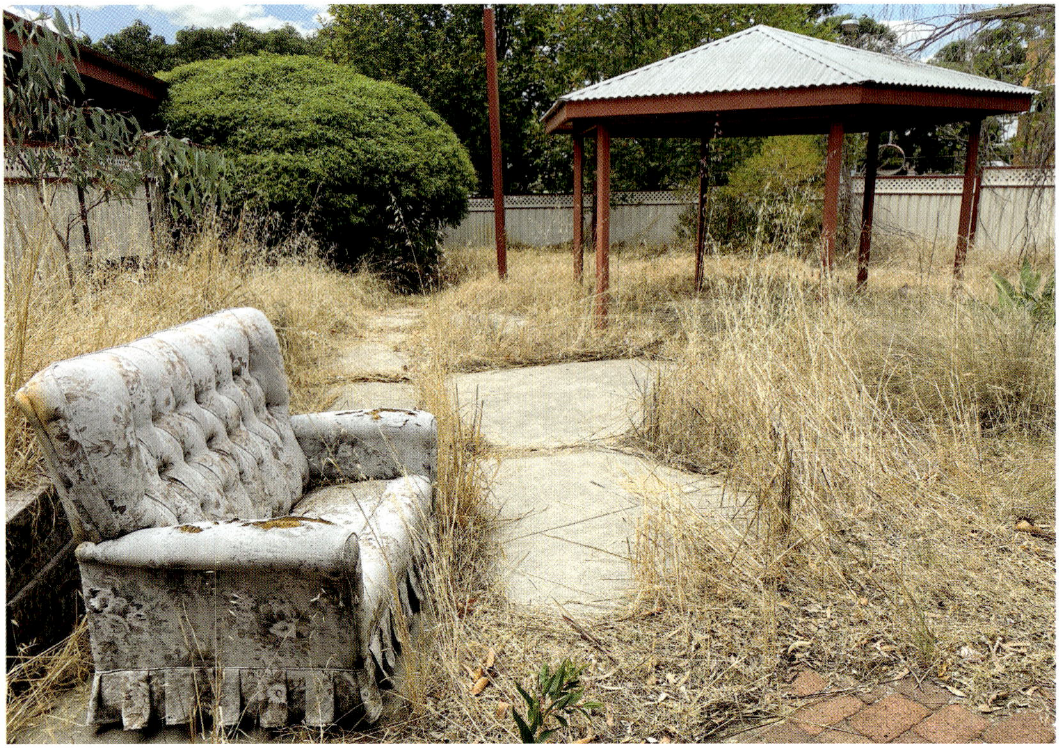

A double-seater couch left exposed to weather conditions, while most likely finding itself a host to many colonies of nasty bugs and spiders.

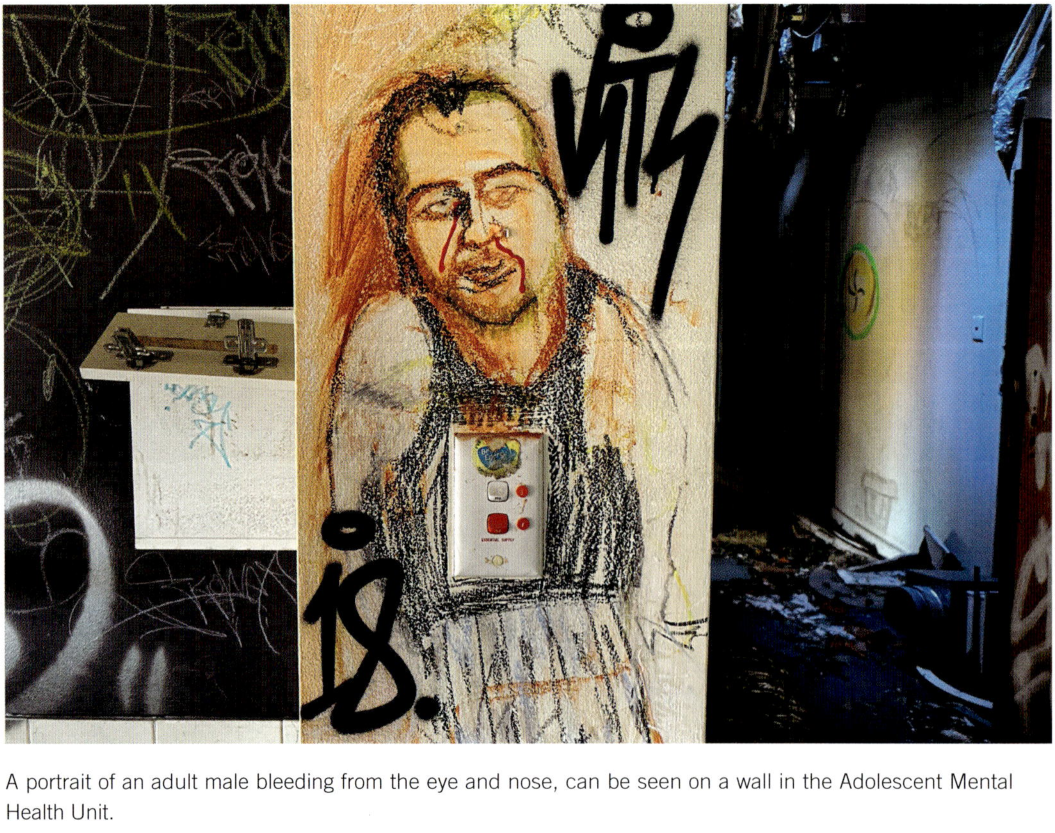

A portrait of an adult male bleeding from the eye and nose, can be seen on a wall in the Adolescent Mental Health Unit.

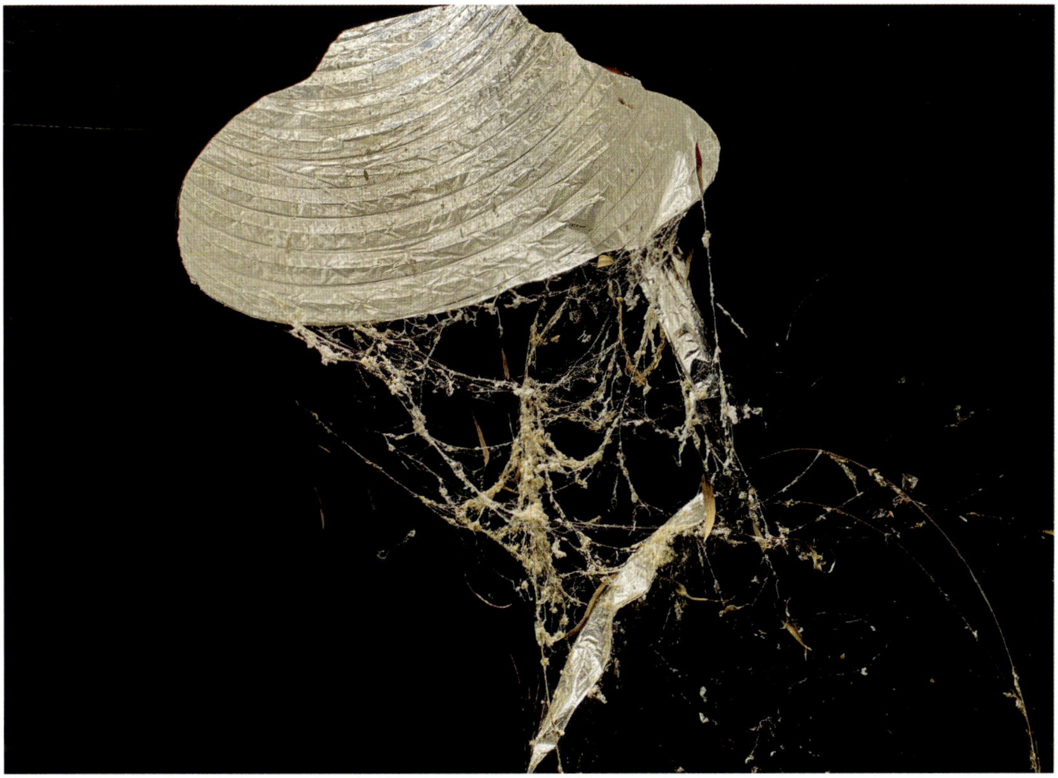

An entanglement of cobwebs hangs from a ceiling duct. No doubt the spider has since chosen to mothball this creation.

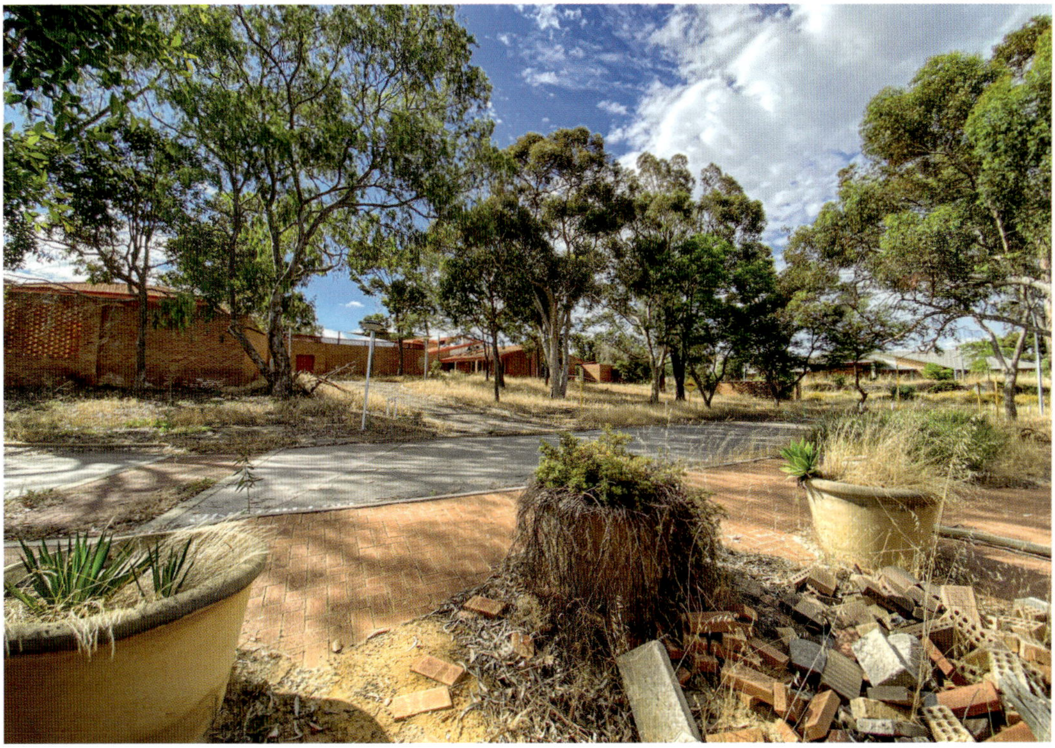

View of the Adolescent Mental Health Unit from the Swan Community Mental Health Centre, both located towards the rear of the hospital site.

BIBLIOGRAPHY

ASIC, 'Notice of meeting of creditors', 2016.

Bell, D., 'Evictions in Beach St', *Fremantle Herald Interactive*, 14 August 2015.

Bell, D., 'Freo moves on skid row', *Fremantle Herald Interactive* 29 June 2015.

Bell, D., '91 and left to sleep in a shed', *The Perth Voice Interactive* 2019.

De Kruijff, P., 'Swan site aged care plan', *The West Australian*, 13 November 2019.

Department of Health, 'Consumer Health Services Directory, Swan District Hospital Campus, 2001.

'State signals intent for Swan Hospital site', *Echo News*, 17 September 2020.

Grant, S., & Bell, D., 'Hidden gem', *The Perth Voice Interactive*, 4 October 2019.

Heritage Council, 'Hostel Milligan, Perth', Government of Western Australia 2013.

Kelly, J., 'End of era as Swan District Hospital shuts doors', *The Advocate*, 4 November 2015.

Lake, B., 'Fragrance Group propose their second Perth City development', *Off The Plan*, 21 June 2016.

Perth Children's Hospital, Princess Margaret Hospital, Government of Western Australia: Child and Adolescent Health Service, 2018.